Palgrave Studies in Cross-disciplinary Business Research, In Association with EuroMed Academy of Business

Series Editors
Demetris Vrontis
School of Business, Department of Management
University of Nicosia
Nicosia, Cyprus

Yaakov Weber
School of Business Administration
College of Management
Rishon LeZion, Israel

Alkis Thrassou
School of Business, Department of Management
University of Nicosia
Nicosia, Cyprus

S. M. Riad Shams
Newcastle Business School
Northumbria University
Newcastle Upon Tyne, UK

Evangelos Tsoukatos
School of Business, Department of Management
University of Nicosia
Nicosia, Cyprus

Reflecting the growing appetite for cross-disciplinary business research, this series aims to explore the prospects of bringing different business disciplines together in order to guide the exploration and exploitation of scholarly and executive knowledge. Each book in the series will examine a current and pressing theme and consist of a range of perspectives such as management, entrepreneurship, strategy and marketing in order to enhance and move our thinking forward on a particular topic.

Contextually the series reflects the increasing need for businesses to move past silo thinking and implement cross-functional and cross-disciplinary strategies. It acts to highlight and utilize the emergence of cross-disciplinary business knowledge and its strategic implications across economic sectors, geographic regions and organizational types.

Published in conjunction with the EuroMed Academy of Business, books will be published annually and incorporate new scientific research works developed specifically for the book or based on the best papers from their conferences. Over the last decade EuroMed have developed a cross- disciplinary academic community which comprises more than 30,000 students and scholars from all over the world.

Each submission is subject to a proposal review and a double blind peer review. For further information on Palgrave's peer review policy please visit this website: https://www.palgrave.com/gp/book-authors/your-career/early-career- researcher-hub/peer-review-process For information on how to submit a proposal for inclusion in this series please contact Liz Barlow: liz.barlow@palgrave.com.

For information on the book proposal process please visit this website: https://www.palgrave.com/gp/book-authors/publishing-guidelines/submit-a-proposal

Alkis Thrassou
Demetris Vrontis
Leonidas Efthymiou • Yaakov Weber
S. M. Riad Shams • Evangelos Tsoukatos
Editors

Business Advancement through Technology Volume II

The Changing Landscape of Industry and Employment

Editors
Alkis Thrassou
School of Business, Department of
Management
University of Nicosia
Nicosia, Cyprus

Leonidas Efthymiou
School of Business, Department of
Management
University of Nicosia
Nicosia, Cyprus

S. M. Riad Shams
Newcastle Business School
Northumbria University
Newcastle Upon Tyne, UK

Demetris Vrontis
School of Business, Department of
Management
University of Nicosia
Nicosia, Cyprus

Yaakov Weber
School of Business Administration
College of Management
Rishon LeZion, Israel

Evangelos Tsoukatos
School of Business, Department of
Management
University of Nicosia
Nicosia, Cyprus

ISSN 2523-8167 ISSN 2523-8175 (electronic)
Palgrave Studies in Cross-disciplinary Business Research, In Association with EuroMed
Academy of Business
ISBN 978-3-031-07764-7 ISBN 978-3-031-07765-4 (eBook)
https://doi.org/10.1007/978-3-031-07765-4

© The Editor(s) (if applicable) and The Author(s), under exclusive licence to Springer Nature
Switzerland AG 2022
This work is subject to copyright. All rights are solely and exclusively licensed by the Publisher, whether
the whole or part of the material is concerned, specifically the rights of translation, reprinting, reuse of
illustrations, recitation, broadcasting, reproduction on microfilms or in any other physical way, and
transmission or information storage and retrieval, electronic adaptation, computer software, or by similar
or dissimilar methodology now known or hereafter developed.
The use of general descriptive names, registered names, trademarks, service marks, etc. in this publication
does not imply, even in the absence of a specific statement, that such names are exempt from the relevant
protective laws and regulations and therefore free for general use.
The publisher, the authors, and the editors are safe to assume that the advice and information in this book
are believed to be true and accurate at the date of publication. Neither the publisher nor the authors or
the editors give a warranty, expressed or implied, with respect to the material contained herein or for any
errors or omissions that may have been made. The publisher remains neutral with regard to jurisdictional
claims in published maps and institutional affiliations.

This Palgrave Macmillan imprint is published by the registered company Springer Nature Switzerland AG.
The registered company address is: Gewerbestrasse 11, 6330 Cham, Switzerland

Contents

1 An Overview of Business Advancement Through Technology: The Changing Landscape of Work and Employment 1
Alkis Thrassou, Demetris Vrontis, Leonidas Efthymiou, and Naziyet Uzunboylu

2 Research on Robotic Process Automation: Structuring the Scholarly Field 19
Dennis Schlegel and Jonathan Wallner

3 The Role of Technology Enabled HRM Systems in Developing Hybrid Workplaces: A Case Study of the Information Technology Sector in India 47
Sandeep Kulshrestha

4 Engineering the Metaverse for Innovating the Electronic Business: A Socio-technological Perspective 65
Giuseppe Festa, Yioula Melanthiou, and Pina Meriano

vi Contents

5 The Changing Technology Use and its Impact on Leadership and Hierarchy Structure in the Virtual Workplace 87
Arkadiusz Mironko, Rosemary M. Muirungi, and Anthony J. Scardino

6 Conceptual Mutations of Change Management and the Strategy–Technology–Management Innovation 109
Charis Vlados

7 The Spread of Artificial Intelligence and Its Impact on Employment: Evidence from the Banking and Accounting Sectors 135
Bernardo Batiz-Lazo, Leonidas Efthymiou, and Kyra Davies

8 Machine Learning, Artificial Intelligence and the Future of Work: Impact on HR, Learning and Development Professionals 157
Niki Kyriakidou, Karen Trem, Joy Ogbemudia, and Nehal Mahtab

9 Technological Innovation and Performance Measurement in the Sport Sector 183
Mario Nicoliello

10 Opening up the Black Box on Digitalisation and Agility: Key Drivers and Main Outcomes 201
Salim Chouaibi, Matteo Rossi, Jamel Chouaibi, and Alkis Thrassou

11 Ecosystem Innovation as the Stepping into Other People's Shoes 227
Gianpaolo Basile, Salvatore Esposito De Falco, Sofia Profita, and Rosario Bianco

Index 247

Notes on Contributors

Gianpaolo Basile got his PhD in Communication Science at the University of Salerno (Italy). He is Professor of Destination Management, Food Marketing and Economy and Management of Innovation in University of Italian Chamber of Commerce, Universitas Mercatorum (Italy). From 2012 is Chair in Business Management PhD course at Vitez University (Bosnia-Herzegovina). He authored numerous published articles and books and he is Kybernetes Associate Editor and Editorial Board Member of the International Journal of Electronic Marketing and Retailing (IJEMR). He is European Parliament Accredited Assistant and Regional Direction (DGRegio) Policy Advisor. His main research interests are Innovation and Competitiveness, Corporate Social Responsibility, Systems Thinking Approach, Place Marketing and Management.

Bernardo Batiz-Lazo is Professor of FinTech History and Global Trade at Northumbria University (Newcastle upon Tyne). He is a Fellow of the Royal Historical Society (2010) and the Academy of Social Sciences (2020). He read economics (at ITAM, Mexico and Autónoma de Barcelona, Spain), history (Oxford) and received a doctorate in business administration (Alliance Manchester Business School). He has been studying financial markets and institutions since 1988. He joined Northumbria after appointments at Bangor, Leicester, Open University and Queen's Belfast.

viii   Notes on Contributors

Rosario Bianco is extraordinary Professor of Economics and Business Management at Università Telematica Pegaso. He is director of two publishing houses, Auditor for private and public companies, Former CNR researcher, Author of numerous contributions on business economics. Member of several scientific and editorial committees for publishing series and scientific journals in the field of economics and law.

Jamel Chouaibi holds a PhD degree from the University of Sfax in Tunisia. He is now associate professor of Accounting at the Faculty of Economic Sciences and Management of Sfax (Tunisia) and a Researcher at laboratory of research in information technology, governance and entrepreneurship "LARTIGE". His research works focus on financial and accounting information, corporate governance, standards and accounting principles and corporate social responsibility. He has published several papers in various refereed journals such as International Journal of Law and Management, Journal of the Knowledge Economy, Journal of Economics Finance and Administrative Science, International Journal of Managerial and Financial Accounting, Accounting & Management Information Systems, EuroMed Journal of Business.

Salim Chouaibi is a Doctor in Accounting Methods at the Faculty of Economic Sciences and Management of Sfax, University of Sfax, Tunisia.

Kyra Davies attended Bangor University between 2016 and 2019 gaining a Bachelor of Science degree in Accounting & Finance. This led her to a role as a graduate accountant where she gained experience in Taxation. Kyra is currently studying towards a Masters degree in Data Science and Artificial Intelligence at the University of Liverpool. At present, Kyra is working on a Natural language processing model to classify Reddit commentary as either left-wing or right-wing with a particular interest in the hazards of social media echo chambers.

Salvatore Esposito De Falco is Full Professor of Economics and Business Management, in the University of Rome "Sapienza". He teaches Corporate Governance and Corporate Governance in Family Business (in English). In his scientific and academic career he has published over 110 papers in national and international journals of which 11 with impact factor, 8 indexed by ISI-WOS and 7 in band A, 7 monographic works. He was also guest editor of four Special issues on international journals and was the winner of 3 Best Paper Awards. He is Co-Editors-in-Chief of the journals Corporate Governance and Research & Development Studies and Corporate Governance and Organizational Behavior Review. He has been project manager of more than 30 ministerial research programs. Finally, he is a PhD, Chartered Accountant and Statutory Auditor. He is also Grant Office Manager of some important business groups. His main research interests are: Corporate Governance, Executive Compensation, Family Business, Shareholder right e Shareholder Engagement, Strategic Management, Sustainable Development e Environmental Social Governance (ESG).

Leonidas Efthymiou is Assistant Professor in Organisation, Tourism and Hospitality Studies at the University of Nicosia, and adjunct faculty at Unicaf University. He previously worked Intercollege, Pearson Education and the University of Leicester. He has also taught online for Universities in Europe, Africa and the United States. He also travels frequently to Africa, in his capacity as Instructional Designer. He has co-edited and published several books, articles, media reports, policy papers and encyclopedia articles. His research output lies at the intersection of employment, digitisation and education. He has received a number of awards, including the best PhD Thesis award, by the Academy of Management in 2011, Boston Massachusetts. Prior to this, he trained at the universities of Leicester (PhD, MSc), Derby (BA) and the Higher Hotel Institute Cyprus (Dip. Hons).

Giuseppe Festa is an Associate Professor of Management at the Department of Economics and Statistics of the University of Salerno (Italy). He holds a PhD in Economics and Management of Public Organizations from the University of Salerno, where he is the Scientific Director of the Postgraduate course in Wine Business. He is also the Chairman of the Euromed Research Interest Committee on Wine Business. His research interests mainly focus on wine business, corporate venture capital, information systems, and healthcare management.

Sandeep Kulshrestha is a People, Culture and Strategy consultant, a former corporate executive and an academic based out of Hyderabad, India. His academic work includes visiting and adjunct professorships at

x   Notes on Contributors

Institutions like ICFAI University, Indian Institute of Management Indore, DoinGlobal Argentina, Holy Mary Business School etc. As far as educational background is concerned, Sandeep has Master's degrees in Financial Management, Political Science and Psychology from India and has also completed his International MBA studies at the United Business Institutes, Belgium. His corporate experience was in Finance and Human Resources job roles with organisations like the Royal Commonwealth Society for the Blind, Dr. Reddy's Foundation, Lepra, Holiday Inn Hotels and others. Sandeep's research areas include Human Resources Management, Positive psychology, and Business transformations. He has presented papers at the International conferences organised by International Stress Management Association (India). Sandeep is the author of the book, Positive Psychology – A handbook (ISBN 978-87-403-2892-9). Sandeep is the founder and chief Consultant at Rectangle Consulting, a business consulting firm based at Hyderabad, India.

Niki Kyriakidou is a Senior Lecturer in HRM at Leeds Beckett University, UK. Niki has more than 17 years of academic experience, having developed and delivered a wide range of undergraduate, postgraduate and professional courses in CCHRM, Leadership Development and Talent Management. She holds a BA Hons in Political Sciences and Public Administration from the University of Athens and has obtained a Masters (MA HRM) and PhD from the University of Leeds. She holds various memberships (Senior Fellowship in the UK Higher Education Academy (SFHEA), Academic Membership in the British Academy of Management (AMBAM) and the Chartered Institute of Personnel and Development (AFCIPD) and Psychometrics Accreditation (EQi-360; TMPSE and Coaching). Niki has extensive experience in European funded research programmes, collaborating effectively with academic, professional and government institutions at an international level. She is an experienced external examiner with strong expertise in Business and Management courses in the UK HE institutions (in the UK) and an External Reviewer of Academic Programs in Greece's Higher Education Quality Assurance and Accreditation Agency (HQAA). Niki is a reviewer in many international journals in HRM and Organisational Behaviour and guest editor of the International Journal of Organisational Analysis,

International Journal of Business and Globalisation, and Global Economic and Business Review.

Nehal Mahtab is an Assistant Head of Department of Management at Nottingham Business School, Nottingham Trent University. He received his PhD from the Leeds Beckett University in Strategic Decision Making and HRM. He did his Bachelor's and Master's in the area of Finance and Banking and did his second Master's as a Fulbright Scholar in Management Information Systems from USA. He is a Senior Fellow of the HEA. His teaching and research expertise include Strategic Decision Making, Strategic and Responsible Leadership and Business Strategy. His research work has been published in Journal of Business and Management and Research Journal of Social Science and Management. His work has also been disseminated at various conferences including British Academy of Management, Euromed Academy of Business and University Forum for Human Resource Development. He is the immediate the Past Chair of the Practitioner and Organisational Activities Committee, The University Forum for HRD (UFHRD). Nehal is a manuscript Reviewer for Journal of Global Responsibility.

Yioula Melanthiou is an Assistant Professor of Marketing at the Cyprus University of Technology. She holds a PhD in Marketing (University of Manchester, UK) and has been in academia since 2004 where she served as Head of the Department and Director of Doctoral Studies at the University of Nicosia. Her academic experience involves teaching Marketing at all levels and supervising doctoral students. Her primary research interests are in the areas of Social Media Marketing and Consumer Behaviour, presenting and publishing extensively on related topics. She has also served as Research Director and Marketing Consultant at a Multinational Company.

Pina Meriano is the Editor-in-Chief of the online magazine "Inside Marketing" (www.insidemarketing.it). M.A. in Business Communication at the University of Salerno (Italy), she is a freelance journalist specialized in marketing and communication, a strategic marketing consultant, a trainer in the writing and copywriting fields, and collaborates with many editorial projects. Her research interests mainly regard digital culture, consumer behavior, and brand management.

xii   Notes on Contributors

Arkadiusz Mironko is an assistant professor of management at Indiana University East, School of Business and Economics. Previously, he worked at the Rotterdam School of Management Erasmus University in the Netherlands, and the Anderson Graduate School of Management at the University of California, Riverside. Most recently, he is engaged in research on dynamics in global virtual teams, global leadership, and innovation. His core research interests are in the area of global business strategy, global competition, and knowledge creation and transfer through R&D between multinational corporations entering developing economies and collaboration with indigenous firms. Mironko is the author of the book Determinants of FDI Flows within Emerging Economies: A Case Study of Poland, published by Palgrave Macmillan, a number of journal articles and chapters. He teaches courses in global competition, business strategy, entrepreneurship, and leadership. He received his Ph.D. in International Business Strategy from Rutgers University.

Rosemary Muriungi holds a Ph.D. in Leadership Studies and a Master's in Business Administration (MBA). She has been an educator in institutions of higher learning both in Africa and the United States. Her broad and rich experience includes working as an administrator and human resources practitioner for international organizations advocating for children, human rights, and sustainable human development, such as the United Nations (UN). Her most recent roles include being a professor of Leadership Studies at Gonzaga University and a Business Advisor at the Washington Small Business Development Center (WSBDC)—both in the United States—and as an entrepreneur in her home country Kenya. In addition to her professional life, Rosemary has served on several Boards in Kenya and the United States where she had the opportunity to serve as the Board President to Partnering for Progress (P4P). Dr. Muriungi's research interests touch on leadership of women, youth, organizations, and doing international leadership research; small business development; higher education of under-served and marginalized populations; humanitarianism; forced displacement and migration. She is passionate about talent and leadership development of women and youth and has mentored and coached many in organizational and communal settings.

Notes on Contributors   xiii

Mario Nicoliello is a researcher in Business Administration at University of Genoa, Italy, where he teaches Management Accounting and Business Administration. His research interests are in Accounting Education, Accounting History, Sport Management and Performance Measurement in Public Sector. In particular, in Sport Sector his research regards the Management of Big Sport Events.

Joy Ogbemudia is a Lecturer and a researcher at Leeds Beckett University. She specialises in Human Resource Management, Gender and Migration studies, and Equality & Diversity Management. A prolific academic with a BA in English Language, MSc in Human Resource Management, and a PhD in Women's Studies. Joy started her career as an English teacher in Nigeria before migrating to the UK. She worked as a HR Consultant after completing her MSc in Human Resource Management, and during her PhD studies, she worked as a Graduate Assistant at the University of York in the Department of Sociology and the Department of Social Works and Social Policy. Upon completing her PhD, Joy continued her teaching career as a lecturer at Leeds Beckett University, where she teaches mainly HR and leadership courses to both undergraduate and post-graduate students. Joy's research interest includes gender and skilled work, Work/Life Balance, Intersectionality and Futures, Ecofeminism and migration. She is presently a member of the Chartered Institute of Personnel Management (CIPD), a member of the British Sociological Association (BSA), and the British Academy of Management (BAM). She has recent publications in the Journal of International Women's Studies, writes review papers, and presently working on a book project which is close to completion with Taylor and Francis.

Sofia Profita graduated in 2019 in Economics (concentration in Psychology) at Columbia University in New York (US). She is board member of Columbia Women's Business Society. She is Senior CFO Advisor in UniCamillus, a private medical university in Rome that mainly caters to international students from developing countries. She is also board member of Virgil Academy, cultural organisation aiming at enhancing and promoting Italian Archaeological and artistic heritage. She was financial analyst at Santander Bank, N.A. New York, US. from August 2019 to December 2021, working in a team servicing the principal investing arms of leading institutional investors across the US, Europe and LatAm, gaining significant experience on Real Estate, Infrastructure, Commodities and Conventional & Renewable Power sectors as well as a broad understanding of the Private Equity industry. During 2018 she was summer analyst at Credit Suisse, New York, US, focusing on analyses and marketing materials in successful pitches for IPOs of prominent companies in fashion retail and digital banking.

S. M. Riad Shams is a senior lecturer at the Newcastle Business School, Northumbria University, UK. He has published eleven books, contributed articles to top-tier international journals, and guest-edited for various reputable journals, including the Journal of Business Research, Journal of International Management, International Marketing Review, and Technological Forecasting and Social Change. He is the founder and co-editor of the Annals of Business Research and the Palgrave Studies in Cross-Disciplinary Business Research. His research interests are in the areas of organizational identity, brand and reputation management; strategic management and sustainable development; and stakeholder relationship management focusing on people, planet and profit, strategic agility in international business, and pedagogic management. He obtained a second place in the Cambridge-Kent-Czinkota Competition for Excellence in International Business Research – 2019 and is entered into the Kent Business School's Book of Honour. He received the Emerald Literati Award (Outstanding Paper) in 2019, the Emerald Literati Award (Outstanding Reviewer) in 2018, and the EuroMed Research Award in 2014.

Matteo Rossi received the Ph.D. degree in Management from the University of Sannio, Benevento (Italy). He is currently an Associate Professor of Corporate Finance at the University of Sannio, an Adjunct Professor of Advanced Corporate Finance at LUISS, Rome (Italy), and a Research Assistant Professor at WSB University, Poznan (Poland). Dr. Rossi is the Editor-in-Chief for the International Journal of Managerial and Financial Accounting and the International Journal of Behavioural Accounting and Finance.

Anthony J. Scardino has a BA in Political Science focused on International Relations, a Master of Public Policy in Economics, and a Ph.D. in Leadership and Organizational Change. His research is deeply embedded in Servant Leadership and Organizational Change focused on higher education, community engagement, and ethical business practices. Anthony is the author of several academic articles on leadership and economics. After many years in the traditional business world in various management positions and as a consultant, Anthony desired an opportunity to take his experience and share it within the classroom. Anthony's focus on quality leadership and change, he championed organizational change within the institution to create new pathways of success for the adult learner. Anthony is currently Interim Dean of the School of Business and Information Sciences, Associate Professor and President of the Faculty Senate at Felician University in NJ. He teaches Economics, International Business, Business Ethics and Leadership, and Entrepreneurship.

Dennis Schlegel is a Professor of Business Informatics (Information Systems) at Reutlingen University, Germany. He teaches various Business-related courses on undergraduate and postgraduate level. His current research interest lies in the business and societal implications of emerging information technologies. Originally coming from a Business Administration background, his earlier research focused on the field of Finance & Accounting. After graduating with a PhD from Leeds Beckett University in 2013, Dennis has gained many years of practical experience at a Big Four consultancy firm, most recently at Senior Manager level, before finally returning to academia.

Alkis Thrassou is a Professor at the University of Nicosia (Cyprus, EU). He holds a Ph.D. from the University of Leeds (UK), and is a Chartered Marketer (FCIM), a Chartered Construction Manager (FCIOB), a Chartered Management Consultancy Surveyor (MRICS), and a Senior Research Fellow of the EuroMed Academy of Business. He is the Director of Gnosis Mediterranean Institute for Management Science, the Associate Editor of EuroMed Journal of Business, and the Managing Editor of the Palgrave Studies in Cross-disciplinary Business Research. He has edited and published in numerous internationally esteemed scientific journals and books, and he retains strong ties with industry, acting also as a consultant.

xvi   Notes on Contributors

Karen Trem is a Senior lecturer at Leeds Business School, specialising in employability skills and HRM. A firm belief that education should be a mix of academic and personal development underpins Karen's approach to teaching, emphasising the practical application of knowledge and encouraging students to think independently. A child of expatriate parents, Karen grew up in Southern Africa. A degree in Mechanical Engineering from the University of Bristol led to 10 years working in manufacturing industry. Self-employment as a consultant followed, working full-time and completing an MBA with three children under five. Karen was also a parish councillor and a school governor. She has been a member of the CIPD since 1987 and is also a member of the CMI and a Chartered Manager. Karen has worked in Higher Education since 2005 and at Leeds Beckett University since 2011, teaching on a range of different Undergraduate and Postgraduate courses, particularly enjoying time spent teaching in Southern Africa. Karen's background of rich experiences is incorporated in her teaching; passionate about working towards a more inclusive society. Key learnings from her doctoral study on values emphasise the value of experience, education, travel and collaboration in the development of open mindedness and tolerance.

Evangelos Tsoukatos is associate professor of Management at the Hellenic Mediterranean University and adjunct faculty at: the University of Nicosia, Cyprus and the Hellenic Open University. He holds a Ph.D in Management Science from the Lancaster University Management School (LUMS), UK, a B.Sc. in Mathematics from the "Aristotelion" University of Thessaloniki, Greece, a Postgraduate Diploma and M.Sc. in Operational Research from LUMS, UK. Dr Tsoukatos holds the position of Vice President – Operations and Development at the EuroMed Research Business Institute. He authored and edited books and journal special issues and has heavily published internationally in scholarly journals and presented in academic conferences. For his published research, he has gained wide recognition from his peers. He is Associate Editor of the EuroMed Journal of Business (EMJB) and editorial board member in a number of international scholarly journals.

Naziyet Uzunboylu received her BA in Events Management from Manchester Metropolitan University and a MBA in Marketing from University of Nicosia (Cyprus). She worked as a senior event manager in The Academic Events Group (TAEG) and Social Activities Coordinator in Cyprus International University. She is a Doctoral student of School of Business at University of Nicosia. Her research area covers social media marketing, user-generated content and branding. She presented her work in EMAC 2018. Recently, her paper is published in Qualitative Market Research: An International Journal.

Charis Vlados obtained his Ph.D. ("Very Honorable Distinction") for his thesis on the types/forms of evolutionary integration of the firms operating in Greece into globalization that took place within the framework of the Research and Studies Center on Multinational Enterprises (C.E.R.E.M) of the University of Paris "Paris X-Nanterre." Charis Vlados' primary research focus is on the scientific fields of business strategy, competitiveness, entrepreneurship, economic policy, and globalization, having also founded and established the "Stra.Tech.Man approach" in the field of business dynamics. Charis Vlados has worked with various research centers and as a business consultant, both domestically and abroad, for approximately twenty years. He is Assistant Professor in "International Economics and Entrepreneurship" in the Department of Economics of the Democritus University of Thrace, having taught in the past in the University of the Aegean and the University of Peloponnese, and in various public and private educational institutions. Charis Vlados is the author of thirteen scientific textbooks, having more than one hundred contributions in peer-reviewed international journals and conference proceedings.

Demetris Vrontis is a Professor and Vice Rector for Faculty and Research and a Professor of Strategic Marketing Management at the University of Nicosia, Cyprus. He is the Founder and Editor in Chief of the EuroMed Journal of Business, an Associate Editor of the International Marketing Review, an Associate Editor of the Journal of Business Research and a Consulting Editor of the Journal of International Management. He has wide editorial experience and has successfully edited over 60 guest edi-

xviii   Notes on Contributors

tions in top tier journals. He is the President of the EuroMed Academy of Business, which serves as an important and influential regional academy in the area of Business and Management and the Managing Director of Gnosis: Mediterranean Institute for Management Science. He has widely published in about 300 refereed journal articles, 45 books and 60 chapters in books, and has presented papers to over 80 conferences around the globe. He is a fellow member and certified Chartered Marketer of the Chartered Institute of Marketing and a Chartered Business Consultant. He is also currently serving as a consultant and is a member of the board of directors to several international companies.

Jonathan Wallner is a final year master's student in Business Informatics (Information Systems) at Reutlingen University, Germany where he also received his bachelor's degree within the same course of studies. Being well acquainted with a variety of technologies due to his field of studies as well as personal enthusiasm, his research attentions concentrate on state-of-the-art and emerging technology trends along with their significance and implications on commerce and businesses.

Yaakov Weber is a Professor and teaches courses on Strategic Management, Mergers and Acquisitions Management, Strategic Alliances, Corporate Strategy, Cross Cultural Management, and Global Strategic Management. He lectured in various universities in United States (for example NYU), Western and Eastern Europe and China, in graduate schools of business administration as well as Executive programs, in private and public organizations as well as Industrial Associations for CEOs and Directors He also participating and conducting international Ph.D. seminars, in PhD committees as well as referee in international PhD exams. Prof. Weber's studies were published in top leading international academic journals, such as Strategic Management Journal. Journal of Management, Management Science, Journal of Business Research, California Management Review, and Human Relations, among others. His papers received more than 7000 citations in leading journals and books. Several papers were selected by various academic collections and were described as represent "the most significant new material" and, "most important works published in Sociology" (in 1996). Other papers are "2nd most cited in last 5 years" (2010-2015) and "most read" (2011-2015), or "most download" in 2017, in leading journals. He served as associate editor and in editorial boards of several journals and act as a referee for numerous leading journals. He is Guest Editor for special issues in leading journals, such as California Management Review, Human Resource Management, Journal of World Business, and more. Recently Prof. Weber is the winner of the Outstanding Author Contribution Award. His recent book that was invited by Financial Times, A Comprehensive Guide for Mergers and Acquisitions, was published in 2014. This and his other books, can be seen in AMAZON. Also, currently, coeditor of 3 book series at EMERALD, Rutledge, and Palgrave Macmillan. Prof. Weber is Co-Founder and Co-President (for the last 10 years) of the EuroMed Business Research Institute (www.emrbi.org), the EuroMed Academy of Business and the EuroMed Research Centre. Prof. Weber has been senior consultant to CEOs, top executives and directors in leading domestic and international companies such as Coca-Cola, Dead-Sea Works, Society of Israel Plastics & Rubber Manufacturers, largest International Engineering company in Israel, Health-care Organizations, The USA-Israel Chamber of Commerce, large and small organizations in Chemical industry, High-Tech industry and many others in various industries as well as to the largest international consulting firm in Israel. His recent large project of international consulting was to an international merger in Moscow, Russia. Prof. Weber conducted numerous workshops to top executives in many countries. Recently he conducted workshop to the senior executives of one of the 4 largest investment companies in China.

List of Figures

Fig. 2.1	Classification framework	22
Fig. 2.2	Final framework	32
Fig. 4.1	A trans-conceptual vision of the metaverse (Author's elaboration)	73
Fig. 6.1	Strategic behaviour, technological and managerial potential within the chaos of contemporary global dynamics, based on Kotler and Caslione (2009)	120
Fig. 6.2	Stra.Tech.Man innovation at the various organisational levels and correlative-evolutionary SWOT analysis	124
Fig. 6.3	The five steps of innovation and change management in the Stra.Tech.Man approach	125
Fig. 11.1	The ecosystem: structure and results	234

List of Tables

Table 2.1	Details on classification of papers	33
Table 3.1	Survey/Interview participants' overview	60
Table 4.1	Some business experiences in the metaverse (Authors' elaboration)	77
Table 4.2	Tentative SWOT analysis about metaverse as business opportunity (Authors' elaboration)	79
Table 5.1	Top challenges of virtual teams	97
Table 5.2	Strategies employed in leading virtual teams with actions and outcomes	99
Table 8.1	Common themes in the case studies	172
Table 9.1	The innovations of Omega at Tokyo 2020 Olympic Games	196
Table 10.1	Sample selection	211
Table 10.2	Measures and items	214
Table 10.3	Regression results	217
Table 11.1	Main differences between ecosystems and networks	232

xxiii

1

An Overview of Business Advancement Through Technology: The Changing Landscape of Work and Employment

Alkis Thrassou, Demetris Vrontis, Leonidas Efthymiou, and Naziyet Uzunboylu

1.1 Introduction

The ever increasing diffusion of technology among the society, is also visible at the workplace. Automation and digitization have engendered a wide array of transformations (Ferreira et al., 2019; Vardarlier, 2020), in several industries and sectors. Technology has become a great (Chatterjee et al., 2022a) and integral aspect of corporate life (Damianidou et al., 2018), with a wide range of factors driving and enabling it (Ferreira & Franco, 2019), including socio-economic structures, ecosystems, lobbying, organizational cultures, and wider corporate phenomena

---

A. Thrassou • D. Vrontis • L. Efthymiou (✉) • N. Uzunboylu
School of Business, Department of Management, University of Nicosia, Nicosia, Cyprus
e-mail: thrassou.a@unic.ac.cy; vrontis.d@unic.ac.cy; efthymiou.l@unic.ac.cy; uzunboylu.n@unic.ac.cy

© The Author(s), under exclusive license to Springer Nature Switzerland AG 2022
A. Thrassou et al. (eds.), *Business Advancement through Technology Volume II*, Palgrave Studies in Cross-disciplinary Business Research, In Association with EuroMed Academy of Business, https://doi.org/10.1007/978-3-031-07765-4_1

(Leonidou et al., 2020). However, other than enhancing business performance, technology-led transformation is also associated with workplace controversies and challenges. Some examples, include employment-related tensions due to worker-monitoring and loss of privacy (Efthymiou, 2018; Efthymiou et al., 2020), loss of interpersonal communication, fewer employment opportunities, and a negative impact on broader society (Efthymiou & Michael, 2016). Within this framework, the current chapter discusses the contextual and theoretical grounds of business advancement through technology, along with the impact of technology on work and employment.

1.2 Contextual and Theoretical Foundations

New work arrangements, which are becoming increasingly commonplace (Naim & Lenka, 2018), have an impact not only on the structure of labor markets (Ogbeibu et al., 2021) but also on how work activities are carried out and spatially organized (Sardi et al., 2021). As today's consumers become increasingly tech-savvy (Mele et al., 2019) and aware of what they can do with technology (Kumar et al., 2021), they demand fast (Hoffman et al., 2022) and seamless digital experiences (Ferreira et al., 2019). They also expect instant responses to their needs (Thrassou et al., 2020). Firms are altering the way work is managed and performed in response (Wisetsri et al., 2021), by accelerating the application of technology (digital transformation) (Favoretto et al., 2022; Ferreira et al., 2019) and reinventing business processes (Verhoef et al., 2021; Vial, 2019), organizational structures (Hahn, 2020), and business models (Haaker et al., 2021; Venkatesh et al., 2019). In addition, businesses utilize technology as a response to different critical events and crises (Thrassou et al., 2022a, 2022b; Vrontis et al., 2022). Within such contexts, work practices are represented as becoming more flexible, independent, and at the same time collaborative (Leonidou et al., 2020).

By increasing investments in high-tech systems involving automation (Vial, 2019), robotics and AI (Vrontis et al., 2021), firms have an alternative for lowering labor costs (Haaker et al., 2021) increasing productivity (Iqbal et al., 2019; Zhou et al., 2020), and, thereby, more capably meeting the expectations stakeholders (Chatterjee et al.,

1 An Overview of Business Advancement Through Technology... 3

2022b) and becoming more competitive (Zhou et al., 2020). These ongoing technological developments also have substantial effects on the nature of the workplace and workforce (Piva & Vivarelli, 2018), i.e., the way in which employees work in organizations (Pereira et al., 2021) as well as the working hours (Dunn, 2020) and conditions under which they do so (Chatterjee et al., 2022b) and relationships in the workplace (employee-supervisory and employee-co-workers relationship) (Pereira et al., 2021). The entire business world is leaning more and more toward it (Hahn, 2020) since greater adoption of these cost-saving mechanisms (Chatterjee et al., 2022a) could improve economic development by boosting efficiency in the workplace (Pereira et al., 2021).

However, it is necessary here to mention that 'AI and robotics must not be categorized as total labor-replacement, since it could only impact certain low-skilled positions' acknowledged by Li et al. (2019; 172). While technological advancements may change the fundamental nature of work (Charalambous et al., 2019) and constitute a serious threat to human employment (Damianidou et al., 2018), they may also generate significant opportunities for human-machine collaboration and integration (Sardi et al., 2021). Within this context, several authors (i.e., Damianidou et al., 2018; Thrassou et al., 2020) support the view that technology can be of great value in facilitating service or sales and providing more pleasant, customized and valued service interactions. As a notable example to these opportunities, smart technologies, especially AI-enabled, can be used to facilitate work activities (Damianidou et al., 2018) and learning (Zarifis & Efthymiou, 2022), regardless of temporal and spatial location (Charalambous et al., 2019). Overall, these examples support the view that the impact of automation technology on staffing decisions (Spenser, 2018) is highly dependent on 'a facility's vertical position in the local marketplace' (Lu et al., 2018; 15), thereby supporting the argument that automate intelligent technologies do not always result in reduced job opportunities.

Machines have always assisted people in producing more output (Pereira et al., 2021). In spite of concerns that automation would eliminate jobs (Spenser, 2018) or bring widespread unemployment (Lu et al., 2018), technology has consistently resulted in the creation of new jobs

(Charalambous et al., 2019). Indeed, history has shown that as productivity increased, so too did employment growth (Iqbal et al., 2019). On the other hand, technological advancements in organizations have enormous influence on employees (Thrassou et al., 2020) concerning the way and manner in which employees view their organization (Zhou et al., 2020) as well as resulting in employees having all types of commitment to an organization (Naim & Lenka, 2018). Damianidou et al. (2018), also noted that multidimensional technology which improves access to information and knowledge sharing as part of technological advances, definitely increases employees' commitment within an organization as their organizational tasks are satisfied. Furthermore, when information is shared with employees (Epaminonda et al., 2020), having the sense of belonging (Thrassou et al., 2020) and attachment (Ogbeibu et al., 2021) which are a part of the commitment component (Damianidou et al., 2018) was discovered.

1.3   Digital HRM

Innovative technologies have also had a profound impact on Human Resource Management (HRM) (Galanaki et al., 2019). Indeed, with the accelerating development and wide application of AI (Verhoef et al., 2021) and other breakthrough technologies (Charalambous et al., 2019), the automation of the administrative components of HRM activities (Spenser, 2018) including the way that organizations attract (Vardarlier, 2020), select (Vrontis et al., 2021), motivate (Li et al., 2019), and retain skilled employees are dynamically transforming on a global scale (Vardarlier, 2020). As organizations compete on the basis of their employees' skills and talents (Naim & Lenka, 2018), HR function and its principal goals have become extremely important in recent years (Zhou et al., 2020). However, technology has changed the way HR practices are now conducted (Zhou et al., 2020), particularly in terms of how organizations acquire, store, use, and distribute information about applicants and workers (Lu et al., 2018).

Adoption of various forms of technology ranging from passive (Charalambous et al., 2019), one-way technologies (e.g., web-based job

1 An Overview of Business Advancement Through Technology... 5

advertising) to more interactive techniques (Turulja & Bajgoric, 2018) (e.g., virtual job fairs) have transformed job application and selection practices throughout the time (Venkatesh et al., 2019; Vrontis et al., 2021). The use of multimedia technologies (Verhoef et al., 2021), online application tracking systems (Zhou et al., 2020), and self-aware/self-learning computing systems (Garg et al., 2021) has resulted in the advancement of such practices. Currently, organizations are using 'web-based application systems that require applicants to apply for jobs online, and use keyword screening systems to determine whether applicants are qualified for the job' (Stone et al., 2015; 219). AI technologies provide opportunities for recruiting process (Dunn, 2020) as these technologies can simulate real work conditions towards evaluation and recruitment (Van Esch et al., 2019). Specifically, the adoption of AI-based technologies in HRM allows organizations to conduct background checks of job applications (Charalambous et al., 2019) and develop compensation packages (Galanaki et al., 2019) for specific positions. AI-enabled recruitment tools and/or platforms can also infer possible behaviors (Van Esch et al., 2019) in terms of job fit and performance (Epaminonda et al., 2020) while being less biased (Damianidou et al., 2018) and more objective than humans (Dunn, 2020).

Consistent with such views, Garg et al. (2021) suggest that machine learning (ML) can greatly benefit HR practitioners and organizations by altering the selection process into a more systematic process (Vrontis et al., 2021) by removing the occurrence of recruiters' biases (Damianidou et al., 2018) or even the methods used by applicants to influence and deviate the selection process (Van Esch et al., 2019). In addition, to select the most talented applicants (Li et al., 2019) from among those who apply for the job, they use electronic selection (e-selection refers to various forms of technology (Zhou et al., 2020)) to determine how well applicants' knowledge (Epaminonda et al., 2020), skills (Favoretto et al., 2022), and abilities (Charalambous et al., 2019) match the job criteria and to facilitate the hiring process (Van Esch et al., 2019), thereby standardizing applicant sourcing and resume screening procedures (Galanaki et al., 2019) for all their subsidiaries. Intelligent algorithms, based on AI and ML, support resolving some of these challenges (Kellogg et al., 2020) while increasing HRM efficiency (Garg et al., 2021) (reduced cost for both applicant and employer (Naim & Lenka, 2018) and effort of data analysis (Mikalef & Krogstie, 2020)) and/or HRM effectiveness (Galanaki et al., 2019) (improved quality of data analysis (Mikalef & Krogstie, 2020)). Undoubtedly, the multiple benefits that AI-based technologies provide to HRM recruiting constitute a positive development for HRM.

As another goal of HRM, HR practitioners must continuously assist their employees in enhancing their knowledge, skills, and abilities through training and development (Zhou et al., 2020). In line with this goal, organizations have adopted a variety of technologies (Hahn, 2020) in an attempt to more effectively deliver (Thrassou et al., 2020) and manage the training process (Vrontis et al., 2021). These attempts, referring to as "e-learning" or "e-training", range from simply providing online training materials (Charalambous et al., 2019), to utilizing a variety of technologies to send course content (Zhou et al., 2020) and support communication (e.g., videoconferencing) (Hoffman et al., 2022). AI is concerned, among others, with 'information processing' (Vrontis et al., 2021), 'logical reasoning' (Pereira et al., 2021) and 'mathematical skills' (Li et al., 2019). According to researchers Vrontis et al., 'AI applications could be of pivotal utility in HRM for training purposes.' (Vrontis et al., 2021; 13). Notwithstanding, AI and ML based applications in HRM create privacy concerns (Themistocleous, 2019) and provide an opportunity for a fruitful discussion of ethical challenges (Piva & Vivarelli, 2018). Notably, direct applications of AI and ML based applications in the employment and HR context, such as the analysis and collection of digital data (Favoretto et al., 2022) to evaluate talent (Mikalef & Krogstie, 2020) and predict work-related challenges (Piva & Vivarelli, 2018), raise various concerns about human privacy (Themistocleous, 2019). Similar privacy concerns occur when picture and/or video recognition used in digital interviews through AI learning (Ferreira et al., 2019) to gather verbal (Mikalef & Krogstie, 2020) and other interpersonal characteristics of applicant (Charalambous et al., 2019) and adjust them to generate a psychological profile (Li et al., 2019) and predict possible job fit (Epaminonda et al., 2020).

In addition to AI an ML, robotic technologies have also brought a number of new learning opportunities to HRM (Galanaki et al., 2019). However, robotic technologies focus on the elimination of repetitive and routine activities handled by human employees (Vrontis et al., 2021), allowing to them the possibility to engage in opportunities to use their knowledge, abilities and skills more effectively (Naim & Lenka, 2018). At the same time, this generates new learning opportunities (Zhou et al., 2020) along with extensive training (Vrontis et al., 2021) for the employees to meet their new duties (altered responsibilities) (Galanaki et al., 2019) and acquire the skills that are necessary to work with a robot (Li et al., 2019).

1.4 Digitization and Working Conditions

As information technology, cloud services and mobile devices enable employees to maintain a constant connection to their workplace (Pereira et al., 2021), and gain access to all kinds of information (Favoretto et al., 2022) and instant messaging services and social networks (Charalambous et al., 2019) allow for direct communication with colleagues and leaders (Venkatesh et al., 2019). Indeed, due to the COVID-19 crisis, organizations have inclined toward platform-orchestrated multi-sided network interactions. Thanks to tech-enabled online communication tools, employees had chance to work more closely in some ways even as they work remotely (Hodder, 2020). It is undeniable that advancements in internet, and more recently mobile technologies (Haaker et al., 2021), have improved the ability of remote working for individuals (Hodder, 2020) and therefore out of usual office hours (Dunn, 2020). Collaboration has also been simpler to achieve (Sardi et al., 2021)—even when colleagues are not physically present in the same place (Naim & Lenka, 2018), with video-conferencing technology (Hoffman et al., 2022) teams can have meetings remotely (Charalambous et al., 2019) and work on the same shared documents at once (Ferreira et al., 2019). They can also use cloud-based file-sharing technologies like Google Drive (Charalambous et al., 2019).

Inevitably, organizations are leaning more and more toward offering flexible working practices (Charalambous et al., 2019) in order to fulfill the needs of employees (Vial, 2019) while reducing the costs associated with having a physical workplace (Pereira et al., 2021). As technology reduces the influence of distance in organizations (Hodder, 2020) that allow employees to work from home (Charalambous et al., 2019), or interact with team members across geographical boundaries (Christofi et al., 2019), organizations are turning to recruiting individuals with specialized skills in remote parts of the world (Van Esch et al., 2019).

The worldwide networks of data sharing, thanks to versatile smart solutions (empowered by AI, the Internet of Things (IoTs), ML, augmented reality (AR), etc.), have led to widespread globalization; resulting in increased geographical mobility (Galanaki et al., 2019; Haaker et al., 2021), resource sharing (Garg et al., 2021), virtual working and teleworking (Charalambous et al., 2019) especially in multinational corporations (Lu et al., 2018). It is obvious that these innovations have profoundly altered the global HRM function (Ferreira et al., 2019). On one hand, there are chances for 'global talent attainment' (Stone et al., 2015), learnings from global HRM practices (Spenser, 2018) and benefits of 'knowledge sharing' across geographies (Christofi et al., 2019; Epaminonda et al., 2020). On the other hand, there are challenges pertaining to managing 'global talent' (Stone et al., 2015), and developing HRM competencies targeting the increasing and strengthening of productivity (Iqbal et al., 2019).

As a result, HR activities include handling changes to work (Piva & Vivarelli, 2018), the workplace and the workforce (Hodder, 2020) that are brought by technological advancement (Hahn, 2020). The principal HR goals of attracting, selecting, motivating and retaining skilled employees in organizations (Vardarlier, 2020; Vrontis et al., 2021) remain crucial, but potentially entail alternative methods (Stone et al., 2015) in the future world of work. For example, as reported by Stone et al. (2015), the idea that technology is altering the way HR processes are managed, particularly in terms of data collection and use (Favoretto et al., 2022) is confirmed as companies have profoundly adopted sophisticated data collection technology (Kellogg et al., 2020) and analytics (Mikalef & Krogstie, 2020) to improve methods of attracting and retaining talent (Vardarlier, 2020).

Furthermore, interactive technologies enabled HR practitioners to enhance interactions (Turulja & Bajgoric, 2018) and communication with their employees (Venkatesh et al., 2019). Emerging technologies, for example, may enable the further development of this trend (Hahn, 2020) by allowing real-time monitoring of employee and workplace data (Mikalef & Krogstie, 2020) through sensors and decision-making (Favoretto et al., 2022) via multifaceted algorithms (Kellogg et al., 2020). At its most drastic, the growth in automation (Spenser, 2018), self-employment (Leonidou et al., 2020), and the gig economy (Dunn, 2020) might result in a considerably reduced permanent workforce (Lu et al., 2018), implying that the role of HR will be radically altered (Van Esch et al., 2019).

1.5 Content and Structure

With these considerations in mind, this book seeks to understand the major implications of changing technology on work and employment. Towards this end, the book presents another 10 chapters, relevant to understanding work and employment in the digital age. The ongoing digitalization offer opportunities as well as challenges to businesses, which vary from simple process improvements, to complex reconfigurations and the emergence of new business models. These changes, nevertheless, entails an alteration of the workplace as we know it, along with the structure and expectations of labor and employment. The woks purposefully cover an array of theoretical, industry and geographic context; and individually and collectively aim to bridge theory and practice to deliver insights from and towards both ends.

Chapter 2, titled 'Research on Robotic Process Automation: Structuring the Scholarly Field' by Dennis Schlegel and Jonathan Wallner, contributes to knowledge by systematically structuring previous work on Robotic Process Automation (RPA) based on a novel classification framework in order to synthesize prior studies and identify research gaps. The results help researchers to gain an overview of existing knowledge and further need for research in order to advance the field and to identify promising future research opportunities related to RPA. The study is based on a systematic literature review of peer-reviewed literature that is used as a basis to develop a conceptual framework to structure the field.

Within the framework of HRM, Chap. 3, (titled: 'The Role of Technology enabled HRM systems in developing Hybrid workplaces: A case study of the Information Technology sector in India' by Sandeep Kulshrestha) examines what technology-enabled systems are being used to facilitate hybrid working. It also explores how they were beneficial to employees and what impact the systems had on employee performance and engagement. The chapter looks at the rationale behind developing technology intensive HRM solutions, how they are deployed, and what the challenges are.

Subsequently, Chap. 4, 'Engineering the metaverse for innovating the electronic business: A Socio-technical perspective' by Giuseppe Festa, Yioula Melanthiou and Pina Meriano, proposes a global framework for definition, conceptualization, and activation of metaverse potentialities, with respect to previous virtual technologies. The term 'metaverse' was first used in a 1992 science fiction novel, "Snow Crash", by Neil Stephenson, about an exploratory, absolutely visionary, journey among what at the time were still considered futuristic technologies (wireless connection, virtual reality, augmented reality, and so on). A SWOT analysis provides a comprehensive vision about the necessity and the opportunity of designing, implementing, and developing metaverse experiences for innovative electronic marketing and management.

Chapter 5 examines the 'Changing technology use and its impact on leadership and hierarchy structure in the virtual workplace'. The authors (Arkadiusz Mironko, Rosemary Muirungi and Anthony Scardino) explain how companies changes their technologies to enable virtual work due to COVID-19. At the same time, put an effort to motivate and lead their teams through various technology modes, including video conferencing, data sharing, voice, and other digital media. However, while technology offers new ways of communicating and doing the job without the necessity of being in the same location, technologies do not guarantee the clarity of communication—losing of gestures and expressions, building trust, and comradery in teams. The chapter offers new insights into how new technology offers new opportunities while at the same time may curtail advancement opportunities for those in lower ranks or early careers.

1 An Overview of Business Advancement Through Technology... 11

Also, in the field of management, Chap. 6, 'Conceptual Mutations of Change Management and the Strategy-Technology-Management Innovation' by Charis Vlados, suggest that the most profound problems for managing change arise from the organization's Stra.Tech.Man physiological core of innovation, which refers to the effective strategy–technology–management synthesis. Upon this theoretical background, a five-step Stra.Tech.Man change management process is proposed for all socio-economic organizations.

Chapter 7, looks at the banking and accounting sectors. This chapter (titled: 'The Spread of Artificial Intelligence and its Impact on Employment: Evidence from the Banking and Accounting Sectors' by Bernardo Batiz-Lazo, Leonidas Efthymiou and Kyra Davies) explores the diffusion of Artificial Intelligence (AI) and its impact on employment in two different sectors, namely 'Accounting' and 'Banking. The chapter presents two studies. The 1st Study, adopts a conceptual approach and examines possible advantages as well as risks of AI on the accounting profession. In Study 2, the analysis explores the use of AI in 'recruitment and selection' in the Banking sector. The analysis, which draws on findings collected through online interviews with Human Resource managers, reveals that none of the five banks participating in the study use AI in their recruitment process. This is attributed to traditional and casual approaches to recruitment, downsizing, restructuring, technical challenges, and ethical considerations. Based on both studies, we are comparing and contrasting the narrative of AI (Accounting) with its actual impact (Banking).

From a Learning and Development (L&D) approach, Chap. 8 is titled 'Machine Learning, Artificial Intelligence and the future of work: impact on HR and learning and development professionals'. The chapter explores how technology is changing the way organisations operate, the effect this is having on its employees and the challenges and opportunities that HR and L&D may face. More specifically, the proposed chapter (by N. Kyriakidou, K Ogbemudia Trem and N. Mahtab) aims to gain an oversight of perceptions of the future use of technology from HR and L&D professionals at different stages in their careers. Then, the findings are used to inform potential knowledge and skills development for delivery to professional practitioners.

Chapter 9 examines 'Technological innovation and performance measurement in the sport sector'. It presents the case of Omega, a Swiss company that offers timing and measurement services at the Olympic Games, as well as the main world sports championships. Using the framework of the Innovation Theory, the chapter (by Mario Nicoliello) illustrates the consequences of the new technological systems both on the technical gesture of the athletes and on the communication language of the sporting event. The research aims to demonstrate how technology can be a driving force both in improving the performance of athletes and in disseminating the sporting event to an ever-increasing audience of users.

In Chap. 10 (titled: Opening up the black box on digitalization and agility: key drivers and main outcomes), the authors investigate the influence of digital transformation on the firm's organizational performance and sustainable development. Salim Chouaibi, Matteo Rossi, Jamel Chouaibi and Alkis Thrassou, carried out a quantitative research, with data collection based on a questionnaire that has been sent via email to Tunisian companies as an example of emerging economy. Drawing on data from 270 Tunisian companies, the chapter shows a growing interest in digital transformation over time. The results suggest that increasing investments in digital transformation and innovation practices tackle the current environment and improved organizational performance and sustainable development.

The final entry, Chap. 11, is titled 'Ecosystem Innovation as the stepping into other people's shoes', by Gianpaolo Basile, Salvatore Esposito De Falco, Sofia Profita and Rosario Bianco. In the last decades, the term "ecosystem" has become central in the management studies and in policy makings. Its rise has mirrored an increasing interest and concern among both researchers and managers with interdependence across organizations and activities. This work presents an ecosystem conceptualization in which it is considered as an affiliation of heterogeneous actors associated in a formal o no formal "collaboration" aimed to produce innovation and value as the answer of social, environmental and economic needs. It presents a clear definition of the ecosystem construct in the network comparison, it highlights the role of the stakeholder engagement theory within collaboration between heterogeneous components and crowdsourcing approach, and, finally, underlines the crowdsourcing approach, supported by ICT, in the ecosystem development.

References

Charalambous, M., Grant, C. A., Tamontano, C., & Michailidis, E. (2019). Systematically Reviewing Remote E-workers' Well-Being At Work: A Multidimensional Approach. *European Journal of Work and Organizational Psychology, 28*(1), 51–73.

Chatterjee, S., Chaudhuri, R., Vrontis, D. (2022a). Examining the Impact of Adoption of Emerging Technology and Supply Chain Resilience on Firm Performance: Moderating Role of Absorptive Capacity And Leadership Support. *IEEE Transactions on Engineering Management,* Vol. ahead-of-print No. ahead-of-print. doi:https://doi.org/10.1109/TEM.2021.3134188.

Chatterjee, S., Chaudhuri, R., Vrontis, D., Thrassou, A. (2022b). Impact of Organizational Dynamic Capability on International Expansion and the Moderating Role of Environmental Dynamism. *International Journal of Organizational Analysis,* Vol. ahead-of-print No. ahead-of-print. doi:https://doi.org/10.1108/IJOA-10-2021-3003.

Christofi, M., Vrontis, D., Thrassou, A., & Shams, S. R. (2019). Triggering Technological Innovation Through Cross-border Mergers and Acquisitions: A Micro-foundational Perspective. *Technological Forecasting and Social Change, 146*, 148–166. https://doi.org/10.1016/j.techfore.2019.05.026

Damianidou, D., Foggett, J., Arthur-Kelly, M., & Wehmeyer, M. L. (2018). Effectiveness of Technology Types in Employment-Related Outcomes for People with Intellectual and Developmental Disabilities: an Extension Meta-analysis. *Advances in Neurodevelopmental Disorders, 2*, 262–272.

Dunn, M. (2020). Making Gigs Work: Digital Platforms, Job Quality and Worker Motivations. *New Technology, Work and Employment, 35*(2), 232–249.

Efthymiou, L. (2018). Worker Body-art in Upper-Market Hotels: Neither Accepted, Nor Prohibited. *International Journal of Hospitality Management, 74*, 99–108.

Efthymiou, L., & Michael, S. (2016). The Cyprus Cash Crash: A Case of Collective Punishment. In B. Batiz-Lazo & L. Efthymiou (Eds.), *The Book of Payments: Historical and Contemporary Views on the Cashless Economy* (pp. 131–140). Palgrave Macmillan.

Efthymiou, L., Orphanidou, Y., & Panayiotou, G. (2020). Delineating the Changing Frontstage and Backstage Segregation in High-end and Luxury Hotels. *Hospitality & Society, 10*(3), 287–312. https://doi.org/10.1386/hosp_00025_1

Epaminonda, E., Chaanine, J., Vrontis, D., Thassou, A., & Christofi, M. (2020). Information Communication Technology, Knowledge Management, Job and Customer Satisfaction: A Study of Healthcare Workers in Lebanon. *Journal of Knowledge Management, 25*(3), 618–641.

Favoretto, C., de Sousa Mendes, G. H., Filho, M. G., de Oliveira, M. G., & Ganga, G. M. D. (2022). Digital Transformation of Business Model in Manufacturing Companies: Challenges and Research Agenda. *Journal of Business & Industrial Marketing, 37*(4), 748–767.

Ferreira, J. J. M., Fernandes, C. I., & Ferreira, F. A. F. (2019). To Be or Not to Be Digital, that is the Question: Firm Innovation and Performance. *Journal of Business Research, 101*, 583–590.

Ferreira, A., & Franco, M. (2019). The Influence of Strategic Alliances on Human Capital Development: A Study Applied to Technology-based SMEs. *EuroMed Journal of Business, 15*(1), 65–85.

Galanaki, E., Lazazzara, A., & Parry, E. (2019). A Cross-National Analysis of E-HRM Configurations: Integrating the Information Technology and HRM Perspectives. In A. Lazazzara, R. Nacamulli, C. Rossignoli, & S. Za (Eds.), *Organizing for Digital Innovation*. Lecture Notes in Information Systems and Organisation (Vol. 27). Springer. https://doi.org/10.1007/978-3-319-90500-6_20

Garg, S., Sinha, S., Kar, A.K., & Mani, M. (2021). A Review of Machine Learning Applications in Human Resource Management. *International Journal of Productivity and Performance Management*, Vol. ahead-of-print No. ahead-of-print. doi:https://doi.org/10.1108/IJPPM-08-2020-0427.

Haaker, T., Ly, P. T. M., Nguyen-Thanh, N., & Nguyen, H. T. H. (2021). Business Model Innovation Through the Application of The Internet-Of-Things: A Comparative Analysis. *Journal of Business Research, 126*, 12–136.

Hahn, G. J. (2020). Industry 4.0: A Supply Chain Innovation Perspective. *International Journal of Production Research, 58*(5), 1425–1441.

Hodder, A. (2020). New Technology, Work and Employment in the era of COVID-19: Reflecting on Legacies of Research. *New Technology, Work and Employment, 35*(3), 262–275.

Hoffman, D. L., Moreau, C. P., Stremersch, S., & Weel, M. (2022). The Rise of New Technologies in Marketing: A Framework and Outlook. *Journal of Marketing, 86*(1), 1–6.

Iqbal, N., Ahmad, M., & Allen, M. M. C. (2019). Unveiling the Relationship between e-HRM, Impersonal Trust and Employee Productivity. *Management Research Review, 42*(7), 879–899. https://doi.org/10.1108/MRR-02-2018-0094

Kellogg, K., Valentine, M., & Christin, A. (2020). Algorithms at Work: The New Contested Terrain of Control. *Academy of Management Annals, 14*(1), 366–410. https://doi.org/10.5465/annals.2018.0174

Kumar, V., Ramachandran, D., & Kumar, B. (2021). Influence of New-Age Technologies on Marketing: A Research Agenda. *Journal of Business Research, 125*, 864–877.

Leonidou, E., Christofi, M., Vrontis, D., & Thrassou, A. (2020). An Integrative Framework of Stakeholder Engagement for Innovation Management and Entrepreneurship Development. *Journal of Business Research, 119*, 245–258.

Li, J. J., Bonn, M. A., Ye, B., & H. (2019). Hotel Employee's Artificial Intelligence and Robotics Awareness and its Impact on Turnover Intention: The Moderating Roles of Perceived Organizational Support and Competitive Psychological Climate. *Tourism Management, 73*, 172–181.

Lu, S. F., Rui, H., & Seidmann, A. (2018). Does Technology Substitute for Nurses? Staffing Decisions in Nursing Homes. *Management Science, 64*(4), 1842–1859.

Mele, C., Polese, F., & Gummesson, E. (2019). Once Upon a Time… Technology: A Fairy Tale or a Marketing Story? *Journal of Marketing Management, 35*(11–12), 965–973.

Mikalef, P., & Krogstie, J. (2020). Examining the Interplay between Big Data Analytics and Contextual Factors in Driving Process Innovation Capabilities. *European Journal of Information Systems, 29*(3), 260–287.

Naim, M. F., & Lenka, U. (2018). Development and Retention of Generation Y Employees: A Conceptual Framework. *Employee Relations, 40*(2), 433–455. https://doi.org/10.1108/ER-09-2016-0172

Ogbeibu, S., Pereira, V., Emelifeonwu, J., & Gaskin, J. (2021). Bolstering Creativity Willingness through Digital Task Interdependence, Disruptive and Smart HRM Technologies. *Journal of Business Research, 124*, 422–436.

Pereira, V., Hadjielias, E., Christofi, M., & Vrontis, D. (2021). A Systematic Literature Review on the Impact of Artificial Intelligence on Workplace Outcomes: A Multi-process Perspective. *Human Resource Management Review,* Vol. ahead-of-print No. ahead-of-print. doi:https://doi.org/10.1016/j.hrmr.2021.100857.

Piva, M., & Vivarelli, M. (2018). Technological Change and Employment: Is Europe Ready for the Challenge? *Eurasian Business Review, 8,* 13–32.

Sardi, A., Sorano, E., Garengo, P., & Ferraris, A. (2021). The Role of HRM in the Innovation of Performance Measurement and Management Systems: A Multiple Case Study in SMEs. *Employee Relations, 43*(2), 589–606. https://doi.org/10.1108/ER-03-2020-0101

Spenser, D. A. (2018). Fear and Hope in an Age of Mass Automation: Debating the Future of Work. *New Technology, Work and Employment, 33*(1), 1–12.

Stone, D. L., Deadrick, D. L., Lukaszewski, K. M., & Johnson, R. (2015). The Influence of Technology on the Future of Human Resource Management. *Human Resource Management Review, 25,* 216–231.

Themistocleous, C. (2019). Customer Data: Contemporary Issues of Privacy and Trust. In D. Vrontis, Y. Weber, A. Thrassou, S. M. R. Shams, & E. Tsoukatos (Eds.), *Innovation and Capacity Building: Cross-disciplinary Management Theories for Practical Applications.* (Palgrave Studies in Cross-disciplinary Business Research, In Association with EuroMed Academy of Business) (pp. 167–184). Palgrave Macmillan.

Thrassou, A., Efthymiou, L., Vrontis, D., Weber, Y., Shams, S. M. R., & Tsoukatos, E. (2022a). Editorial Introduction: Crisis in Context. In D. Vrontis, A. Thrassou, Y. Weber, S. M. R. Shams, E. Tsoukatos, & L. Efthymiou (Eds.), *Business Under Crisis, Volume I: Contextual Transformation.* Palgrave Studies in Cross-disciplinary Business Research, In Association with EuroMed Academy of Business. Palgrave Macmillan. https://doi.org/10.1007/978-3-030-76567-5_1

Thrassou, A., Uzunboylu, N., Efthymiou, L., Vrontis, D., Weber, Y., Riad Shams, S. M., & Tsoukatos, E. (2022b). Editorial Introduction: Business Under Crises: Organizational Adaptations. In D. Vrontis, A. Thrassou, Y. Weber, S. M. R. Shams, E. Tsoukatos, & L. Efthymiou (Eds.), *Business Under Crisis, Volume II: Organisational Adaptations.* Palgrave Studies in Cross-disciplinary Business Research, In Association with EuroMed Academy of Business. Palgrave Macmillan. https://doi.org/10.1007/978-3-030-76575-0_1

Thrassou, A., Uzunboylu, N., Vrontis, D., & Christofi, M. (2020). Digitalization of SMEs: A Review of Opportunities and Challenges. In A. Thrassou, D. Vrontis, Y. Weber, S. M. R. Shams, & E. Tsoukatos (Eds.), *The Changing Role of SMEs in Global Business.* (Palgrave Studies in Cross-disciplinary Business Research, In Association with EuroMed Academy of Business) (pp. 179–200). Palgrave Macmillan. https://doi.org/10.1007/978-3-030-45835-5_9

1 An Overview of Business Advancement Through Technology... 17

Turulja, L., & Bajgoric, N. (2018). Information Technology, Knowledge Management and Human Resource Management: Investigating Mutual Interactions towards Better Organizational Performance. *VINE Journal of Information and Knowledge Management Systems, 48*(2), 255–276.

Van Esch, P., Black, J. S., & Ferolie, J. (2019). Marketing AI Recruitment: The Next Phase in Job Application and Selection. *Computers in Human Behavior, 90*, 215–222.

Vardarlier, P. (2020). Digital Transformation of Human Resource Management: Digital Applications and Strategic Tools in HRM. In U. Hacioglu (Ed.), *Digital Business Strategies in Blockchain Ecosystems* (pp. 239–264). Springer.

Venkatesh, R., Mathew, L., & Singhal, T. K. (2019). Imperatives of Business Models and Digital Transformation for Digital Services Providers. *International Journal of Business Data Communications and Networking, 15*(1), 105–124.

Verhoef, P. C., Broekhuizen, T., Bart, Y., Bhattacharya, A., Dong, J. Q., Fabian, N., & Haenlein, M. (2021). Digital Transformation: A Multidisciplinary Reflection and Research Agenda. *Journal of Business Research, 122*, 889–901.

Vial, G. (2019). Understanding Digital Transformation: A Review and a Research Agenda. *The Journal of Strategic Information Systems, 28*(2), 118–144.

Vrontis, D., Christofi, M., Pereira, V., Tarba, S., Makrides, A., & Trichina, E. (2021). Artificial Intelligence, Robotics, Advanced Technologies and Human Resource Management: A Systematic Review. *The International Journal of Human Resource Management,* Vol. ahead-of-print No. ahead-of-print. doi:https://doi.org/10.1080/09585192.2020.1871398.

Vrontis, D., Thrassou, A., Efthymiou, L., Weber, Y., Shams, R., & Tsoukatos, E. (2022). Editorial Introduction: Business Under Crisis—Avenues for Innovation, Entrepreneurship and Sustainability. In D. Vrontis, A. Thrassou, Y. Weber, S. M. R. Shams, E. Tsoukatos, & L. Efthymiou (Eds.), *Business Under Crisis, Volume III: Avenues for Innovation, Entrepreneurship and Sustainability.* Palgrave Studies in Cross-disciplinary Business Research, In Association with EuroMed Academy of Business. Palgrave Macmillan. https://doi.org/10.1007/978-3-030-76583-5_1

Wisetsri, W., Ragesh, T. S., Isaac, C., Thakur, V., Pandey, D., & Gulati, K. (2021). Systematic Analysis and Future Research Directions in Artificial Intelligence for Marketing. *Turkish Journal of Computer and Mathematics Education, 12*(11), 43–55.

Zarifis, A. & Efthymiou, L. (2022). The Four Business Models for AI Adoption in Education: Giving Leaders a Destination for the Digital Transformation Journey. *IEEE Global Engineering Education Conference (EDUCON)*. Tunisia, 28–31 March 2022.

Zhou, Y., Liu, G., Chang, X., & Wang, L. (2020). The Impact of HRM Digitalization on Firm Performance: Investigating Three-way Interactions. *Asia Pacific Journal of Human Resources, 59*(1), 20–43.

2

Research on Robotic Process Automation: Structuring the Scholarly Field

Dennis Schlegel and Jonathan Wallner

2.1 Introduction

In recent years, Robotic Process Automation (RPA) has gained an increasing amount of attention. RPA provides a software-based method to automate structured and highly rules-based business processes ranging from individual activities to entire end-to-end processes (Lacity & Willcocks, 2016b). Instances of the RPA software, the so called bots, mimic the human workforce by operating on the user interface (UI) of various systems just like humans would do (van der Aalst et al., 2018). The underlying technology of RPA is based on standard software that is developed by large commercial enterprises. Consequently, innovation is largely driven by business firms outside the academic sphere. In contrast, academic

---

D. Schlegel (✉) J. Wallner
Faculty of Informatics, Reutlingen University, Reutlingen, Germany
e-mail: dennis.schlegel@reutlingen-university.de; Jonathan.Wallner@Student.
Reutlingen-University.DE

© The Author(s), under exclusive license to Springer Nature Switzerland AG 2022
A. Thrassou et al. (eds.), *Business Advancement through Technology Volume II*, Palgrave Studies in Cross-disciplinary Business Research, In Association with EuroMed Academy of Business, https://doi.org/10.1007/978-3-031-07765-4_2

literature has lacked attention to RPA, as well as, theoretical and synoptic analysis of the topic (Hofmann et al., 2020; Syed et al., 2020).

Hence, the aim of this paper is to review and structure the latest state of academic research on RPA. Our research aim can be broken down into the following research objectives: First, to develop a classification framework to structure the existing research in the field. Second, to identify research gaps and to derive a future research agenda.

Consequently, in a first step, we have conducted a systematic literature review of scholarly research (Webster & Watson, 2002). First, we have systematically collected and reviewed 87 peer-reviewed papers. Subsequently, we have developed a classification framework based on both, inductive analysis of the research papers, and deductive consideration of seminal frameworks from the Business Process Management (BPM) and Information Systems (IS) discipline. Additionally, we use our analyses to identify research gaps and make suggestions for further research directions.

Previously published literature reviews on RPA have focused on introducing the topic during an earlier stage of its development (Enriquez et al., 2020; Hofmann et al., 2020; Ivančić et al., 2019; Santos et al., 2020; Syed et al., 2020). Given the dynamic nature of the field, there is a clear need to update prior literature reviews. The papers by Syed et al. (2020), Hofmann et al. (2020), Santos et al. (2020), as well as, Ivančić et al. (2019) use literature mostly until 2018. Enriquez et al. (2020) do include studies until 2019, but focus more on a quantitative analysis of the papers' bibliographic data and other attributes, than on a qualitative discussion of the literature.

The remainder of this chapter is organised as follows. The next section explains the research design, before the classification framework is presented in the third section. The fourth section discusses the previous literature, organised by the categories of the framework, before research gaps and future research directions are derived in the fifth section. Finally, we draw a brief conclusion.

2.2 Research Design

The systematic collection of relevant literature regarding the topic closely follows the approach recommended by Webster and Watson (2002) who suggest three steps in determining the source material for the review. In the first step, we started by analysing the leading journals in the field, as they are most likely to contain major contributions (Webster & Watson, 2002). In order to identify the leading journals, we have used the VHB-JOURQUAL ranking for the Business Informatics discipline. We excluded some journals from our search due to an obviously unsuitable specialisation of a journal, the language of the journal not being English, or missing access rights. Overall, in the first step, 48 journals, edited series and proceedings were selected. A keyword search was carried out in these sources using the search strings "Robotic Process Automation" and "RPA" for the years 2010–2020. The following exclusion criteria for papers were defined and manually assessed: papers being *teaching cases* or publications *regarding related topics such as Artificial Intelligence (AI)*, with only little to no regard of RPA. Based on this search method, we identified 37 papers. The second step consists of the backward search, in which 16 additional papers were identified. Finally, a forward search was conducted, examining all articles that cite one of the articles from step one with the help of Google Scholar, resulting in 34 additional papers.

We classify the literature using a qualitative procedure consisting of a combination of inductive and deductive elements. The classification framework consists of two levels. The categories on level 2 were defined and iteratively refined in an inductive procedure, based on the content found in the different pieces of literature. The structure on the first level was deductively inspired by seminal frameworks from the BPM and IS literature. Most notably, the four-phase model of the diffusion of information and communication technology (ICT) in organisations according to Bouwman (2005) was used. It distinguishes between the phases *adoption, implementation, use* and *effects*. It was partially combined with the three-step approach by Geyer-Klingeberg et al. (2018) which suggests the steps *assess, develop* and *sustain* for process automation via RPA. Additionally, individual elements from the BPM lifecycle as described by Dumas et al. (2018) were included.

2.3 Classification Framework

Figure 2.1 presents the classification framework. The figures indicate the number of papers in each category. Details in terms of specific papers assigned to the categories can be found in Table 2.1. On level 1, the framework is phase-oriented, referring to different phases of technology diffusion, with the exception of the general category. The framework consists of the following categories on level 1. The level 2 categories will be discussed in Sect. 2.4.

- **General**: This category covers overarching topics that do not refer to one of the phases of diffusion. It includes general reviews, as well as, project methodologies or challenges regarding RPA in general.
- **Adoption**: In the adoption phase, organisations explore RPA as a new technology and finally decide whether or not to adopt it. Based on the current RPA literature, only the analysis and selection of software vendors falls into this category.
- **Assessment**: In the assessment phase, organisations figure out how exactly to adopt RPA. This includes methods for the selection of

General	Fundamentals and overview	11
	Project methodology and guidance	18
	Challenges	1
Adoption	Software vendor selection	5
Assessment	Process selection criteria and methods	8
	Use cases and application examples	21
	Automated process selection	8
Implementation	Architecture	4
	Automated RPA design and implementation	6
	Automated testing	2
	Intelligent or cognitive RPA	5
Use	Governance and organisation	3
	Process monitoring	2
	Maintenance	1
	Acceptance and trust	2
	Robot-human interaction	3
Effects	Potential and benefits	10
	Risks	1
	Organisational effects	1
	Workforce-related effects	8

Fig. 2.1 Classification framework

suitable processes and use cases, as well as, research on how to automate process selection.

* **Implementation**: Implementation refers to "activities aimed at establishing the actual use of the application in the organisation" (Bouwman, 2005). We have assigned literature to this category that deals with architecture, automating RPA implementation, automating testing of RPA applications and topics related to the cognitive RPA, i.e., the combination of RPA and Artificial Intelligence (AI).
* **Use**: Use refers to questions regarding how and to which extent individuals in an organisation actually use the application, such as acceptance and trust in robots and robot-human interaction. Additionally, in this post-implementation stage, aspects regarding governance and organisation, process monitoring, and maintenance become important.
* **Effects**: This category refers to consequences of RPA. Effects include the potential and benefits of RPA, the risks, as well as organisational and workforce-related consequences.

2.4   Discussion of Previous Research

2.4.1 General

Fundamentals and overview of RPA have been presented by a range of authors. These papers discuss the overall state of the art, functionality, characteristics, or principles of the RPA technology (Asquith & Horsman, 2019; Enriquez et al., 2020; Hofmann et al., 2020; Lewicki et al., 2019; van der Aalst et al., 2018).

Questions of *project methodology and guidance* have been receiving growing attention. In general, the examined papers within this section try to establish guidelines or present their self-developed approaches on how to proceed when adopting RPA in organisations. Upon further examination, it can be noted that various approaches have been suggested, each of them setting different priorities and focal points. For instance, Kirchmer and Franz (2019) as well as Herm et al. (2020), focus on providing overall consolidated approaches, ranging from the implementation to the subsequent governance of RPA initiatives. Although Herm et al. derive general guidelines from 23 case studies whereas Kirchmer and Franz engage in agile approaches, they both aim for flexible approaches that can be adapted to different corporate environments. Another agile-based approach (Ma et al., 2019) focuses on the evaluation of RPA benefits by helping the adopters find the right resources for a smooth RPA adoption.

While all of the examined papers aim for the same objective of providing guidelines, some concepts differ from the rest by focusing on specific sub-topics such providing guidelines for the combination and synergy of RPA and Process Mining (Cabello et al., 2020; Geyer-Klingeberg et al., 2018) or Business Process Management (BPM) (Flechsig et al., 2019; König et al., 2020). Especially Cewe et al. (2018), Koch et al. (2020) and Šimek and Šperka (2019) concepts stand out from the examined literature pool in this category by pointing out rather novel ideas or very specific subjects. Cewe et al. seek to ease the means of process requirement engineering by integrating Test Driven Development (TDD) with RPA development. Koch et al. on the other hand, provide orientation in form of a mock-up for developers by applying a "digital twin" concept for RPA. Šimek and Šperka describe the phases of the pilot project implementation of combining a Robotic Service Orchestration (RSO) Platform. Rutschi and Dibbern (2019, 2020) focus on outlining instructions for the development of different types of robots for different types of automation.

Only a single paper covers the aspect *challenges*, trying to investigate the key drivers and challenges for RPA implementations by conducting a survey that involves shared services leaders and RPA experts (Suri et al., 2017).

2.4.2 Adoption

A crucial step in every successful RPA initiative is the *software vendor selection*. The evaluation of vendors in the literature is based on aspects such as the technical capabilities or tool features. The publications differ in the level of detail and scope of the reviewed tools, ranging from the development of in-depth frameworks to review and assess the current market solutions objectively (Agostinelli et al., 2019; Enriquez et al., 2020), to focusing on the analysis and overview of the few leading vendors (Anagoste, 2017, 2018; Ruchi et al., 2018).

2.4.3 Assessment

The papers in the category *"**process selection criteria and methods**"* deal with the question, what processes in an organisation are suitable for automation with RPA. The authors pursue different approaches in their research. While Anagoste (2018) investigates the automation potential of processes and their respective sub-processes in different areas to infer a list of relevant criteria, Wellmann et al. (2020) collect criteria from the literature, in order to derive an evaluation framework for the viability of RPA. Other authors focus mainly on establishing step-by-step procedural models for the identification and selection of suitable processes (Bourgouin et al., 2018; Kirchmer & Franz, 2019; Timbadia et al., 2020). Few papers go as far as combining the criteria in an overall quantitative model to formalise the selection of relevant processes (Riedl & Beetz, 2019; Wanner et al., 2019). Penttinen et al. (2018), in contrast, outline significant criteria for determining the type of automation – RPA or backend-automation.

With 22 papers contributing to this category, a large body of literature presents different ***use cases and application examples*** for RPA. Although a comprehensive discussion and comparison of use cases is beyond the scope of this paper, it can be summarised that the literature includes specific examples from various industries, such as telecommunications (Lacity & Willcocks, 2016b) or financial services (Lewicki et al., 2019; Marek et al., 2019).

A growing body of literature has examined and provided insights on a more sophisticated approach of identifying suitable processes by means of ***automated process selection***. By recording sequences of user interactions with systems, so called UI Logs, and subsequently further processing these logs via technologies such as process mining (Geyer-Klingeberg et al., 2018; Leno et al., 2020a), machine learning (Leopold et al., 2018) or self-developed solutions (Jimenez-Ramirez et al., 2019;

López-Carnicer et al., 2020), automatable processes can be discovered (Bosco et al., 2019; Leno et al., 2020b, 2020c).

2.4.4 Implementation

An important aspect to consider when implementing RPA in an organisation is the *architecture*, concerning the general enterprise architecture (Auth et al., 2019) as well as existing BPMS structures (König et al., 2020). Auth et al. (2019) specifically discuss the relationship between Enterprise Architecture (EA) and RPA and, while "simple" RPA does not affect backend systems, new market trends that combine RPA with cognitive elements might pose new questions and implications regarding the matter (Auth et al., 2019). Because of its non-complexity and oftentimes implementation through local business units, the lack of consultation and therefore missing governance between the IT department and the RPA-users, needs to be addressed as well, according to Stople et al. (2017).

While today, the standard procedure to implement RPA still requires manual analysis of workflows and programming or customising the software, the examined literature has now put forward a growing number of approaches for the *automated design and implementation*. Even though the authors bring forth different concepts and implementations to tackle the automated design and generation of RPA scripts, the overall functionality is always based on UI logs. While the approaches by Agostinelli et al. (2020) and Gao et al. (2019) use the existing UI logs for further processing, López-Carnicer et al. (2020) "Ui-Logger" concept generates the logs itself and then further processes them. Instead of directly implementing, Leno et al. (2020a, 2020b, 2020c) focus on analysing potential challenges to envision and realise their concept.

A few studies have been published on *automated testing*. This includes the proposal of ideas for model-based testing in RPA projects since classical software tests are mostly not suitable for Robotic Process Automation (Cernat et al., 2020b). Chacon-Montero et al. (2019) have identified the high risk potential of deploying untested robots into production and introduce a prototype for the automated generation of testing environments and test cases.

The category *intelligent or cognitive RPA* investigates the integration of basic RPA with intelligent or cognitive elements such as Artificial Intelligence (AI) or Machine learning (ML). Primary objective of this approach is to advance the automation possibilities of business processes, increasing the number of automatable business process as well as minimising human intervention. Advances in terms of structuring, defining, and reviewing this specific field have been made by providing taxonomic approaches (Martínez-Rojas et al., 2020), differentiating the topic and questioning the general necessity of intelligent RPA (Viehhauser, 2020) as well as conducting surveys to identify open research challenges (Chakraborti et al., 2020). Other studies demonstrate specific action examples such as optical character recognition (OCR) (Anagoste, 2018) and cognitive automated data extractions using neural networks (Houy et al., 2019).

2.4.5 Use

Building *acceptance and trust* towards RPA is an essential step in effectively integrating and sustaining the technology within organisations. Two authors seek to extend the body of literature within this field by developing models for assessing RPA user acceptance (Wewerka et al., 2020) as well as focusing on the factor trust (Syed & Wynn, 2020).

Robot-human interaction focuses specifically on the way humans interact with the software robots. Especially two concepts, the asynchronous and synchronous work with robots and their respective benefits and requirements, are investigated (Cabello et al., 2020). Supplementary to this category there are also fundamental research insights provided on humans working together with AI-centric Robotic Process Automation (Dias et al., 2019).

Another important aspect to consider is the *governance and organisation*. Particularly the fast implementation of RPA challenges existing IT governance structures. The consequences of decentralised RPA management and the relationship between the IT function and local RPA teams are addressed in two papers (Osmundsen et al., 2019; Stople et al., 2017). Plattfaut (2019) shares lessons learned from an in-depth case study, addressing the question how to set up an RPA centre of excellence.

Continuous **process monitoring** of automated processes constitutes a fundamental step to analyse process performance and handle errors. Nowadays, process mining is often used to analyse productive processes. Egger et al. (2020) present a bot log mining approach to integrate processes which have been automated with RPA into process mining. Another study (Geyer-Klingeberg et al., 2018) also discusses combining RPA and process mining, both, for monitoring purposes, but also to analyse automation opportunities in the process landscape.

Sustaining the initially expected benefits from RPA throughout the entire organisation requires a reasoned **maintenance**, especially when the organisation progressively adopts more RPA. Within this context, Noppen et al. (2020) have worked out and evaluated a list of guidelines to help keep RPA solutions maintainable.

2.4.6 Effects

Much work on the **potential and benefits** of RPA has been carried out. The most notable benefits, which are recurring in all papers, are processing time reduction, productivity increase and improvement of compliance. Some studies provide empirical insights on the benefits based on real application scenarios (Vitharanage et al., 2020; Wewerka & Reichert, 2020) or evaluate the literature findings with practical implementations and interviews with experts (Hindel et al., 2020). The majority of examined publications, however, are based on examining previous literature (Aguirre & Rodriguez, 2017; Anagoste, 2018; Radke et al., 2020; Ratia et al., 2018; Sethi et al., 2020; Suri et al., 2017).

Categories/topics that are heavily marginalised, even though they are of high importance, are the thorough analysis of **risks** and **organisational effects**. Only Hindel et al. (2020) analyse the risks of RPA, while Güner et al. (2020) investigate how RPA as a routine capability affects organisational aspects, and BPM practices specifically.

The **workforce-related effects** of RPA have been widely addressed by several of the examined papers. While some studies engage in the investigation of RPA-related effects in the form of job losses in a broader context (Eikebrokk & Olsen, 2019; Riemer & Peter, 2020; Willcocks, 2020), some focus on specific industries or fields of work, such as the Accounting sector (Cooper et al., 2019; Fernandez & Aman, 2018) or Business Process Management (Mendling et al., 2018). Other research shows the impact of RPA on the employment market by analysing required skills and qualifications (Schlegel & Kraus, 2020). Koorn et al. (2018) go as far as developing a framework for the prediction of effects caused by automation.

2.5 Research Gaps and Future Research Directions

2.5.1 Fair View on Benefits Realisation and Challenges

Although many papers provide interesting information on benefits of RPA, there is a lack of robust results on whether the acclaimed benefits hold true in productive contexts. Many of the studies are based on literature reviews that partially include grey literature from RPA vendors, consultants and other advocates of the technology. It is at least questionable whether all of the underlying sources are unbiased. More empirical research, e.g., quantitative survey studies, could help to assess the real value of RPA technology.

On the other side of the coin, challenges and risks of RPA implementations remain underrepresented in the literature. According to some authors, 30–50% of RPA initiatives fail (Kirchmer & Franz, 2019), which implies the necessity for more research into the underlying reasons.

2.5.2 Robust Results on Adoption and Readiness

Reports by consultancies (pwc, 2020) suggest that more than half of German, Austrian and Swiss companies are already using RPA, for example. There are, however, no representative or peer-reviewed results in our literature review. In a similar vein, the question of reasons for or against adoption of RPA is a fundamental issue for further research.

Related to adoption, Syed et al. (2020) furthermore suggest that models for organisational readiness assessment should be developed. In this context, also prerequisites for the adoption of RPA could be examined.

2.5.3 Governing, Organising and Managing RPA

The studies in our sample have dealt with a few aspects related to governance and organisational aspects of RPA. However, many research gaps remain. How to maintain RPA when underlying systems and processes change, is a crucial practical issue, as well as, the related effort and its effect on profitability and benefits of RPA. This highly relevant research question was only addressed by one paper in the sample (Noppen et al., 2020). Similarly, the question of governance and organisational responsibilities regarding RPA should be examined more in detail. Finally, we propose that future studies should target wider organisational effects of RPA, e.g., the impact of RPA adoption on outsourcing and offshoring decisions.

Moreover, future work could investigate organisational capabilities for RPA, as previously suggested by other authors (Syed et al., 2020). The call for more research on monitoring and controlling RPA (Syed et al., 2020), has already partially been addressed by suggesting to combine RPA and process mining (Cabello et al., 2020). More work is necessary to put this interesting approach into a wider context and develop a more holistic perspective on this issue.

2.5.4 Intelligent and Cognitive RPA

The next major advancement of RPA will likely be realised by combining it with AI, enabling it to execute unstructured task and not relying on rule-based procedures (Enriquez et al., 2020). While commercial vendors like UiPath are already offering solutions in this context, there is (again) only little coverage by academic research. There is still a lack of uniform terminology and conceptual structure for this topic. We therefore suggest that future work should start by defining and structuring this area.

2.5.5 Robot-human Interaction

Few papers have dealt with the question of robot-human interaction in the context of RPA. Designing smooth interfaces at the handover point between humans and software in the process, is crucial for a successful RPA implementation and use. In this context, comfortable solutions for non-technical employees in companies are required. Another critical point in RPA operations where human input is required is exception handling. Already in earlier reviews (Syed et al., 2020), other authors have recommended more research in this point. However, little new research has been published on this question in the meantime.

2.6 Conclusion

This paper has investigated the current state of research in the field of RPA. The results suggest that scholarly research has adopted RPA with increasing speed, after having neglected the topic during its early emergence. Besides providing an update about the progress toward closing previously identified research gaps, our discussion has emphasised additional need for research. In order to provide a complete overview of RPA research areas, also including the research gaps identified in this paper, the framework as shown in Fig. 2.2 is proposed.

We are aware that our research may have some limitations. The first is related to the method of the systematic literature review. Since we have decided to focus on ranked journals and conferences based on quality considerations in our first search step, interesting research in less visible publication outlets might have been missed out. Due to the subsequently conducted forward and backward search, however, this effect was mitigated. The second limitation is that new literature is published regularly so that the results regarding research gaps become outdated fast. However, as the classification framework was complemented with categories for research gaps, the framework should remain unaffected by new publications.

32   D. Schlegel and J. Wallner

General	Fundamentals and overview	Areas (partially) covered by existing research
	Project methodology and guidance	
	Challenges	
	Organisational capabilities	*Areas not covered by previous research*
	Success and failure	
Adoption	Software vendor selection	
	Readiness	
	Prevalence	
	Reasons for/against adoption	
Assessment	Process selection criteria and methods	
	Use cases and application examples	
	Automated process selection	
Implementation	Architecture	
	Automated RPA design and implementation	
	Automated testing	
	Exception handling	
	Intelligent or cognitive RPA	
Use	Governanace and organisation	
	Process monitoring	
	Maintenance	
	Acceptance and trust	
	Robot-human interaction	
Effects	Potential and benefits	
	Risks	
	Organisational effects	
	Workforce-related effects	

Fig. 2.2   Final framework

We propose that future studies in the field of RPA should concentrate on addressing the research gaps that were identified in this study. With regard to this research project and developed framework, future work should update the data and research gap regularly and, if necessary, refine the categories of the framework to develop it further.

2.7 Appendix

Table 2.1 Details on classification of papers

Category level 1	Category level 2	Papers
General	Fundamentals and overview	(Anagoste, 2017; Asquith & Horsman, 2019; Enriquez et al., 2020; Hofmann et al., 2020; Ivančić et al., 2019; Lacity & Willcocks, 2016a; Lacity & Willcocks, 2016b; Lewicki et al., 2019; Santos et al., 2020; Syed et al., 2020; van der Aalst et al., 2018)
	Project methodology and guidance	(Cabello et al., 2020; Cewe et al., 2018; Flechsig et al., 2019; Geyer-Klingeberg et al., 2018; Hallikainen et al., 2018; Herm et al., 2020; Kirchmer & Franz, 2019; Koch et al., 2020; König et al., 2020; Lacity & Willcocks, 2016b; Liu & Zhang, 2020; Ma et al., 2019; Marek et al., 2019; Moffitt et al., 2018; Plattfaut, 2019; Rutschi & Dibbern, 2019; Rutschi & Dibbern, 2020; Šimek & Šperka, 2019)
	Challenges	(Suri et al., 2017)
Adoption	Software vendor selection	(Agostinelli et al., 2019; Anagoste, 2017; Anagoste, 2018; Enriquez et al., 2020; Ruchi et al., 2018)
Assessment	Process selection criteria and methods	(Anagoste, 2018; Bourgouin et al., 2018; Kirchmer & Franz, 2019; Penttinen et al., 2018; Riedl & Beetz, 2019; Timbadia et al., 2020; Wanner et al., 2019; Wellmann et al., 2020)
	Use cases and application examples	(Aguirre & Rodriguez, 2017; Anagoste, 2017; Asquith & Horsman, 2019; Cernat et al., 2020a; Cooper et al., 2019; Ebert et al., 2020; Fernandez & Aman, 2018; Hallikainen et al., 2018; Houy et al., 2019; Lacity & Willcocks, 2016a; Lacity & Willcocks, 2016b; Marek et al., 2019; Moffitt et al., 2018; Nauwerck & Cajander, 2019; Ortiz & Costa, 2020; Paulauskaite-Taraseviciene & Kertius, 2020; Sethi et al., 2020; Šimek & Šperka, 2019; Suri et al., 2017; William & William, 2019; Yatskiv et al., 2019)
	Automated process selection	(Bosco et al., 2019; Geyer-Klingeberg et al., 2018; Jimenez-Ramirez et al., 2019; Leno et al., 2020a, 2020b, 2020c; Leopold et al., 2018; López-Carnicer et al., 2020)

(continued)

Table 2.1 (continued)

Category level 1	Category level 2	Papers
Implementation	Architecture	(Auth et al., 2019; Bygstad, 2017; König et al., 2020; Stople et al., 2017)
	Automated RPA design and implementation	(Agostinelli et al., 2020; Agostinelli et al., 2019; Gao et al., 2019; Leno et al., 2020c; Linn et al. n.d.; López-Carnicer et al., 2020)
	Automated testing	(Cernat et al., 2020b; Chacon-Montero et al., 2019)
	Intelligent or cognitive RPA	(Anagoste, 2018; Chakraborti et al., 2020; Houy et al., 2019; Martinez-Rojas et al., 2020; Viehhauser, 2020)
Use	Governance and organisation	(Osmundsen et al., 2019; Plattfaut, 2019; Stople et al., 2017)
	Process monitoring	(Egger et al., 2020; Geyer-Klingeberg et al., 2018)
	Maintenance	(Noppen et al., 2020)
	Acceptance and trust	(Syed & Wynn, 2020), (Wewerka et al., 2020)
	Robot-human interaction	(Cabello et al., 2020; Dias et al., 2019; Sindhgatta et al., 2020)
	Potential and benefits	(Aguirre & Rodriguez, 2017; Anagoste, 2017; Hindel et al., 2020; Radke et al., 2020; Ratia et al., 2018; Sethi et al., 2020; Šimek & Šperka, 2019; Suri et al., 2017; Vitharanage et al., 2020; Wewerka & Reichert, 2020)
Effects	Risks	(Hindel et al., 2020)
	Organisational effects	(Güner et al., 2020)
	Workforce-related effects	(Cooper et al., 2019; Eikebrokk & Olsen, 2019; Fernandez & Aman, 2018; Koorn et al., 2018; Mendling et al., 2018; Riemer & Peter, 2020; Schlegel & Kraus, 2020; Willcocks, 2020)

References

Agostinelli, S., Lupia, M., Marrella, A., & Mecella, M. (2020). Automated Generation of Executable RPA Scripts from User Interface Logs. In A. Asatiani, J. M. García, N. Helander, A. Jiménez-Ramírez, A. Koschmider, J. Mendling, G. Meroni, & H. A. Reijers (Eds.), *Lecture Notes in Business Information Processing. Business Process Management: Blockchain and Robotic Process Automation Forum* (Vol. 393, pp. 116–131). Springer International Publishing. https://doi.org/10.1007/978-3-030-58779-6_8

Agostinelli, S., Marrella, A., & Mecella, M. (2019). Research Challenges for Intelligent Robotic Process Automation. In C. Di Francescomarino, R. Dijkman, & U. Zdun (Eds.), *Lecture Notes in Business Information Processing, Business Process Management Workshops* (pp. 12–18). Springer International Publishing. https://doi.org/10.1007/978-3-030-37453-2_2

Aguirre, S., & Rodriguez, A. (2017). Automation of a Business Process Using Robotic Process Automation (RPA): A Case Study. In J. C. Figueroa-García, E. R. López-Santana, J. L. Villa-Ramírez, & R. Ferro-Escobar (Eds.), *Communications in Computer and Information Science. Applied Computer Sciences in Engineering* (Vol. 742, pp. 65–71). Springer International Publishing. https://doi.org/10.1007/978-3-319-66963-2_7

Anagoste, S. (2017). Robotic Automation Process - The next major revolution in terms of back office operations improvement. In *Proceedings of the 11th International Conference on Business Excellence: Strategy, Complexity and Energy in changing times* (1111th ed., pp. 676–686). de Gruyter. https://doi.org/10.1515/picbe-2017-0072

Anagoste, S. (2018). Robotic Automation Process – The operating system for the digital enterprise. In Proceedings of the 12th International Conference on Business Excellence: Innovation and Sustainability in a Turbulent Economic Environment, Bucharest, Romania.

Asquith, A., & Horsman, G. (2019). Let the robots do it! – Taking a look at Robotic Process Automation and its potential application in digital forensics. *Forensic Science International: Reports, 1.* https://doi.org/10.1016/j.fsir.2019.100007

Auth, G., Czarnecki, C., & Bensberg, F. (2019). Impact of Robotic Process Automation on Enterprise Architectures. In C. Draude, M. Lange, & B. Sick (Eds.), *Lecture Notes in Informatics, Infformatik 2019: 50 Jahre Gesellschaft für Informatik* (pp. 59–65). Gesellschaft für Informatik e.V. https://doi.org/10.18420/INF2019_WS05

Bosco, A., Augusto, A., Dumas, M., La Rosa, M., & Fortino, G. (2019). Discovering Automatable Routines from User Interaction Logs. In T. Hildebrandt, B. F. van Dongen, M. Röglinger, & J. Mendling (Eds.), *Lecture Notes in Business Information Processing. Business Process Management Forum* (pp. 144–162). Springer International Publishing.

Bourgouin, A., Leshob, A., & Renard, L. (2018). Towards a Process Analysis Approach to Adopt Robotic Process Automation. In IEEE (Ed.), *Proceedings of the 15th International Conference on e-Business Engineering (ICEBE)* (pp. 46–53). IEEE. https://doi.org/10.1109/ICEBE.2018.00018

Bouwman, H. (2005). *Information and communication technology in organizations: Adoption, implementation, use and effects*. SAGE.

Bygstad, B. (2017). Generative Innovation: A Comparison of Lightweight and Heavyweight IT. *Journal of Information Technology, 32*(2), 180–193. https://doi.org/10.1057/jit.2016.15

Cabello, R., Escalona, M. J., & Enríquez, J. G. (2020). Beyond the Hype: RPA Horizon for Robot-Human Interaction. In A. Asatiani, J. M. García, N. Helander, A. Jiménez-Ramírez, A. Koschmider, J. Mendling, G. Meroni, & H. A. Reijers (Eds.), *Lecture Notes in Business Information Processing. Business Process Management: Blockchain and Robotic Process Automation Forum* (Vol. 393, pp. 185–199). Springer International Publishing. https://doi.org/10.1007/978-3-030-58779-6_13

Cernat, M., Staicu, A.-N., & Stefanescu, A. (2020a). Improving UI Test Automation using Robotic Process Automation. In Scitepress Digital Library (Ed.), *Proceedings of the 15th International Conference on Software Technologies (ICSOFT 2020)* (pp. 260–267). SCITEPRESS - Science and Technology Publications. https://doi.org/10.5220/0009911202600267

Cernat, M., Staicu, A. N., & Stefanescu, A. (2020b). Towards automated testing of RPA implementations. In S. Getir & P. Nguyen (Eds.), *Proceedings of the 11th ACM SIGSOFT International Workshop on Automating TEST Case Design, Selection, and Evaluation (A-TEST'20)* (pp. 21–24). ACM. https://doi.org/10.1145/3412452.3423573

Cewe, C., Koch, D., & Mertens, R. (2018). Minimal Effort Requirements Engineering for Robotic Process Automation with Test Driven Development and Screen Recording. In E. Teniente & M. Weidlich (Eds.), *Lecture Notes in Business Information Processing. Business Process Management Workshops* (Vol. 308, pp. 642–648). Springer International Publishing. https://doi.org/10.1007/978-3-319-74030-0_51

Chacon-Montero, J., Jimenez Ramirez, A., & Gonzalez Enriquez, J. (2019). Towards a Method for Automated Testing in Robotic Process Automation Projects. In B. Choi, M. J. Escalona, & K. Herzig (Eds.), *IEEE/ACM 14th International Workshop on Automation of Software Test (AST'19)* (pp. 42–47). IEEE. https://doi.org/10.1109/AST.2019.00012

Chakraborti, T., Isahagian, V., Khalaf, R., Khazaeni, Y., Muthusamy, V., Rizk, Y., & Unuvar, M. (2020). From Robotic Process Automation to Intelligent Process Automation - Emerging Trends. In A. Asatiani, J. M. García, N. Helander, A. Jiménez-Ramírez, A. Koschmider, J. Mendling, G. Meroni, & H. A. Reijers (Eds.), *Lecture Notes in Business Information Processing. Business Process Management: Blockchain and Robotic Process Automation Forum* (Vol. 393, pp. 215–228). Springer International Publishing. https://doi.org/10.1007/978-3-030-58779-6_15

Cooper, L. A., Holderness, D. K., Sorensen, T. L., & Wood, D. A. (2019). Robotic Process Automation in Public Accounting. *Accounting Horizons, 33*(4), 15–35. https://doi.org/10.2308/acch-52466

Dias, M., Pan, S., & Tim, Y. (2019). *Knowledge embodiment of human and machine interactions: Robotic-process-automation at the Finland government.* Association for Information Systems (Chair). *ECIS 2019,* Uppsala, Sweden.

Dumas, M., La Rosa, M., Mendling, J., & Reijers, H. A. (2018). *Fundamentals of Business Process Management* (2nd ed.). Springer. https://doi.org/10.1007/978-3-662-56509-4

Ebert, C., Kim, A., & van Genuchten, J. (2020). Technology Trends: Winning With ACES. *IEEE Software, 37*(3), 6–13. https://doi.org/10.1109/MS.2020.2973251

Egger, A., ter Hofstede, A. H. M., Kratsch, W., Leemans, S. J. J., Röglinger, M., & Wynn, M. T. (2020). Bot Log Mining: Using Logs from Robotic Process Automation for Process Mining. In G. Dobbie, U. Frank, G. Kappel, S. W. Liddle, & H. C. Mayr (Eds.), *Lecture Notes in Computer Science. Conceptual Modeling* (Vol. 12400, pp. 51–61). Springer International Publishing. https://doi.org/10.1007/978-3-030-62522-1_4

Eikebrokk, T. R., & Olsen, D. H. (2019). Robotic Process Automation For Knowledge Workers - Will IT Lead To Empowerment Or Lay-Offs? In A. N. Duc, T. R. Eikebrokk, T. V. Johannesen, A. Karlsen, J. Kaasbøll, & P. J. Toussaint (Eds.), *Proceedings from the annual NOKOBIT conference* (Vol. 27., No. 1). Bibsys Open Journals.

Enriquez, J. G., Jimenez-Ramirez, A., Dominguez-Mayo, F. J., & Garcia-Garcia, J. A. (2020). Robotic Process Automation: A Scientific and Industrial

Systematic Mapping Study. *IEEE Access, 8*, 39113–39129. https://doi.org/10.1109/ACCESS.2020.2974934

Fernandez, D., & Aman, A. (2018). Impacts of Robotic Process Automation on Global Accounting Services. *Asian Journal of Accounting and Governance, 9*, 127–140. https://doi.org/10.17576/AJAG-2018-09-11

Flechsig, C., Lohmer, J., & Lasch, R. (2019). Realizing the Full Potential of Robotic Process Automation Through a Combination with BPM. In C. Bierwirth, T. Kirschstein, & D. Sackmann (Eds.), *Lecture Notes in Logistics. Logistics Management* (pp. 104–119). Springer International Publishing. https://doi.org/10.1007/978-3-030-29821-0_8

Gao, J., van Zelst, S. J., Lu, X., & van der Aalst, W. M. P. (2019). Automated Robotic Process Automation: A Self-Learning Approach. In H. Panetto, C. Debruyne, M. Hepp, D. Lewis, C. A. Ardagna, & R. Meersman (Eds.), *Lecture Notes in Computer Science. On the Move to Meaningful Internet Systems: OTM 2019 Conferences* (Vol. 11877, pp. 95–112). Springer International Publishing. https://doi.org/10.1007/978-3-030-33246-4_6

Geyer-Klingeberg, J., Nakladal, J., Baldauf, F., & Fabian, V. (2018). Process Mining and Robotic Process Automation: A Perfect Match. In *CEUR Workshop Proceedings (Chair), BPM 2018*. Sydney, Australia.

Güner, E. O., Han, S., & Juell-Skielse, G. (2020). Robotic process automation as routine capability: A literature review. In Association for Information Systems (Chair), *Proceedings of the 28th European Conference on Information Systems (ECIS): Liberty, Equality, and Fraternity in a Digitizing World*, Marrakech, Morocco.

Hallikainen, P., Bekkhus, R., & Pan, S. (2018). How OpusCapita Used Internal RPA Capabilities to Offer Services to Clients. *MIS Quarterly Executive, 17*(1), 41–52.

Herm, L.-V., Janiesch, C., Helm, A., Imgrund, F., Fuchs, K., Hofmann, A., & Winkelmann, A. (2020). A Consolidated Framework for Implementing Robotic Process Automation Projects. In D. Fahland, C. Ghidini, J. Becker, & M. Dumas (Eds.), *Lecture Notes in Computer Science. Business Process Management* (Vol. 12168, pp. 471–488). Springer International Publishing. https://doi.org/10.1007/978-3-030-58666-9_27

Hindel, J., Cabrera, L. M., & Stierle, M. (2020). Robotic Process Automation: Hype or Hope? In N. Gronau, M. Heine, K. Poustcchi, & H. Krasnova (Eds.), *Proceedings of the 15th International Conference on Wirtschaftsinformatik, Zentrale Tracks: Entwicklungen, Chancen und Herausforderungen der*

Digitalisierung (pp. 1750–1762). GITO Verlag. https://doi.org/10.30844/wi_2020_r6-hindel

Hofmann, P., Samp, C., & Urbach, N. (2020). Robotic process automation. *Electronic Markets, 30*(1), 99–106. https://doi.org/10.1007/s12525-019-00365-8

Houy, C., Hamberg, M., & Fettke, P. (2019). Robotic Process Automation in Public Administrations. In M. Räckers, S. Halsbenning, D. Rätz, D. Richter, & E. Schweighofer (Eds.), *Lecture Notes in Informatics: Vol. 291, Digitalisierung von Staat und Verwaltung* (pp. 62–74) Gesellschaft für Informatik e.V.

Ivančić, L., Suša Vugec, D., & Bosilj Vukšić, V. (2019). Robotic Process Automation: Systematic Literature Review. In C. Di Ciccio, R. Gabryelczyk, L. Garcia-Banuelos, T. Hernaus, M. Indihar Štemberger, A. Kö, & M. Staples (Chairs), *BPM 2019 Blockchain and CEE Forum,* Vienna, Austria.

Jimenez-Ramirez, A., Reijers, H. A., Barba, I., & Del Valle, C. (2019). A Method to Improve the Early Stages of the Robotic Process Automation Lifecycle. In P. Giorgini & B. Weber (Eds.), *Lecture Notes in Computer Science. Advanced Information Systems Engineering* (Vol. 11483, pp. 446–461). Springer International Publishing. https://doi.org/10.1007/978-3-030-21290-2_28

Kirchmer, M., & Franz, P. (2019). Value-Driven Robotic Process Automation (RPA). In B. Shishkov (Ed.), *Lecture Notes in Business Information Processing. Business Modeling and Software Design* (Vol. 356, pp. 31–46). Springer International Publishing. https://doi.org/10.1007/978-3-030-24854-3_3

Koch, J., Trampler, M., Kregel, I., & Coners, A. (2020). 'Mirror, Mirror, On The Wall': Robotic process automation in the public sector using a digital twin. In Association for Information Systems (Chair), *Proceedings of the 28th European Conference on Information Systems (ECIS): Liberty, Equality, and Fraternity in a Digitizing World,* Marrakech, Morocco.

König, M., Bein, L., Nikaj, A., & Weske, M. (2020). Integrating Robotic Process Automation into Business Process Management. In A. Asatiani, J. M. García, N. Helander, A. Jiménez-Ramírez, A. Koschmider, J. Mendling, G. Meroni, & H. A. Reijers (Eds.), *Lecture Notes in Business Information Processing. Business Process Management: Blockchain and Robotic Process Automation Forum* (Vol. 393, pp. 132–146). Springer International Publishing. https://doi.org/10.1007/978-3-030-58779-6_9

Koorn, Jelmer, Leopold, H., & Reijers, H. A. (2018). A task framework for predicting the effects of automation. In *ECIS 2018,* Portsmouth, UK.

Lacity, M., & Willcocks, L. (2016a). A new Approach to Automating Services. *MIT Sloan Management Review, 58*(1), 40–50.

Lacity, M., & Willcocks, L. (2016b). Robotic Process Automation at Telefonica O2. *MIS Quarterly Executive, 15*(1), 21–35.

Leno, V., Augusto, A., Dumas, M., La Rosa, M., Maggi, F. M., & Polyvyanyy, A. (2020a). Identifying Candidate Routines for Robotic Process Automation from Unsegmented UI Logs. In M. de Leoni & A. Sperduti (Chairs), *Process Mining Conference 2020,* Padua, Italy.

Leno, V., Dumas, M., La Rosa, M., Maggi, F. M., & Polyvyany. (2020b). Automated Discovery of Data Transformations for Robotic Process Automation. In D. Zhang, A. Freitas, D. Tao, & D. Song (Eds.), *Proceedings of the AAAI-20 Workshop on Intelligent Process Automation (IPA-20).* arXiv. http://arxiv.org/pdf/2001.01007v1.

Leno, V., Polyvyanyy, A., Dumas, M., La Rosa, M., & Maggi, F. M. (2020c). Robotic Process Mining: Vision and Challenges. *Business & Information Systems Engineering.* Advance online publication. https://doi.org/10.1007/s12599-020-00641-4

Leopold, H., van der Aa, H., & Reijers, H. A. (2018). Identifying Candidate Tasks for Robotic Process Automation in Textual Process Descriptions. In J. Gulden, I. Reinhartz-Berger, R. Schmidt, S. Guerreiro, W. Guédria, & P. Bera (Eds.), *Lecture Notes in Business Information Processing. Enterprise, Business-Process and Information Systems Modeling* (Vol. 318, pp. 67–81). Springer International Publishing. https://doi.org/10.1007/978-3-319-91704-7_5

Lewicki, P., Tochowicz, J., & van Genuchten, J. (2019). Are Robots Taking Our Jobs? A RoboPlatform at a Bank. *IEEE Software, 36*(3), 101–104. https://doi.org/10.1109/MS.2019.2897337

Linn, C., Zimmermann, P., & Werth, D. Desktop Activity Mining -Anew level of detail in mining business processes. In C. Czarnecki, C. Brockmann, E. Sultanow, A. Koschmider, & A. Selzer (Eds.), *Lecture Notes in Informatics, Architekturen, Prozesse, Sicherheit und Nachhaltigkeit.* Gesellschaft für Informatik e.V.

Liu, B., & Zhang, N. (2020). Decision-Making for RPA-Business Alignment. In J. Zhang, M. Dresner, R. Zhang, G. Hua, & X. Shang (Eds.), *LISS2019* (pp. 741–756). Springer. https://doi.org/10.1007/978-981-15-5682-1_54

López-Carnicer, J. M., Del Valle, C., & Enríquez, J. G. (2020). Towards an OpenSource Logger for the Analysis of RPA Projects. In A. Asatiani, J. M. García, N. Helander, A. Jiménez-Ramírez, A. Koschmider, J. Mendling, G. Meroni, & H. A. Reijers (Eds.), *Lecture Notes in Business Information Processing. Business Process Management: Blockchain and Robotic Process*

Automation Forum (Vol. 393, pp. 176–184). Springer International Publishing. https://doi.org/10.1007/978-3-030-58779-6_12

Ma, Y.-W., Lin, D.-P., Chen, S.-J., Chu, H.-Y., & Chen, J.-L. (2019). System Design and Development for Robotic Process Automation. In IEEE Computer Society (Chair), *SmartCloud 2019,* Tokyo, Japan.

Marek, J., Blümlein, K., Neubauer, J., & Wehking, C. (2019). Ditiching Labor-intensive paper-based processes-RPA in a czech insurance company. In J. vom Brocke, J. Mendling, & M. Rosemann (Eds.), *17th International Conference on Business Process Management 2019 Industry Forum* (pp. 16–24). CEUR-WS.org.

Martínez-Rojas, A., Barba, I., & Enríquez, J. G. (2020). Towards a Taxonomy of Cognitive RPA Components. In A. Asatiani, J. M. García, N. Helander, A. Jiménez-Ramírez, A. Koschmider, J. Mendling, G. Meroni, & H. A. Reijers (Eds.), *Lecture Notes in Business Information Processing. Business Process Management: Blockchain and Robotic Process Automation Forum* (Vol. 393, pp. 161–175). Springer International Publishing. https://doi.org/10.1007/978-3-030-58779-6_11

Mendling, J., Decker, G., Hull, R., Reijers, H. A., & Weber, I. (2018). How do Machine Learning, Robotic Process Automation, and Blockchains Affect the Human Factor in Business Process Management? *Communications of the Association for Information Systems, 43.,* Article 19, 297–320. https://doi.org/10.17705/1CAIS.04319

Moffitt, K. C., Rozario, A. M., & Vasarhelyi, M. A. (2018). Robotic Process Automation for Auditing. *Journal of Emerging Technologies in Accounting, 15*(1), 1–10. https://doi.org/10.2308/jeta-10589

Nauwerck, G., & Cajander, Å. (2019). Automatic for the People: Implementing Robotic Process Automation in Social Work. In European Society for Socially Embedded Technologies (Chair), *European Conference on Computer-Supported Cooperative Work,* Salzburg, Austria.

Noppen, P., Beerepoot, I., van de Weerd, I., Jonker, M., & Reijers, H. A. (2020). How to Keep RPA Maintainable? In D. Fahland, C. Ghidini, J. Becker, & M. Dumas (Eds.), *Lecture Notes in Computer Science. Business Process Management* (Vol. 12168, pp. 453–470). Springer International Publishing. https://doi.org/10.1007/978-3-030-58666-9_26

Ortiz, F. C. M., & Costa, C. J. (2020). RPA in Finance: supporting portfolio management: Applying a software robot in a portfolio optimization problem. In *Proceedings of the 15th Iberian Conference on Information Systems and*

Technologies (CISTI) (pp. 1–6). IEEE. https://doi.org/10.23919/CISTI49556.2020.9141155

Osmundsen, K., Iden, J., & Bygstad, B. (2019). Organizing Robotic Process Automation: Balancing Loose and Tight Coupling. In Association for Information Systems (Chair), *Proceedings of the 52nd Hawaii International Conference on System Sciences,* Grand Wailea, Maui, Hawaii, USA.

Paulauskaite-Taraseviciene, A., & Kertius, V. (2020). Service Quotation Generation Using Robotic Process Automation Technology. In A. Lopata, V. Sukacké, T. Krilavičius, I. Vetaite, & M. Woźniak (Eds.), *Proceedings of the Information Society and University Studies 2020* (pp. 115–127). CEUR-WS.org.

Penttinen, E., Kasslin, H., & Asatiani, A. (2018). How to Choose between Robotic Process Automation and Back-end System Automation? In *ECIS 2018,* Portsmouth, UK.

Plattfaut, R. (2019). Robotic Process Automation- Process Optimization on Steroids? In Association for Information Systems (Chair), *ICIS 2019,* Munich, Germany.

pwc. (2020). *Robotic Process Automation (RPA) in der DACH-Region.* https://www.pwc.de/de/rechnungslegung/robotic-process-automation-rpa-in-der-dach-region.pdf

Radke, A. M., Dang, M. T., & Tan, A. (2020). Using robotic process automation (RPA) to enhance item master data maintenance process. *Scientific Journal of Logistics, 16*(1), 129–140.

Ratia, M., Myllärniemi, J., & Helander, N. (2018). Robotic Process Automation - Creating Value by Digitalizing Work in the Private Healthcare? In Association for Computing Machinery (Ed.), *Proceedings of the 22nd International Academic Mindtrek Conference on - Mindtrek '18* (pp. 222–227). ACM Press. https://doi.org/10.1145/3275116.3275129

Riedl, Y., & Beetz, R. K. (2019). Robotic Process Automation: Developing a Multi-Criteria Evaluation Model for the Selection of Automatable Business Processes. In Association for Information Systems (Chair), *25th AMCIS 2019,* Cancún, Mexico.

Riemer, K., & Peter, S. (2020). The robo-apocalypse plays out in the quality, not in the quantity of work. *Journal of Information Technology, 35*(4), 310–315.

Ruchi, I., Riya, M., & Kenali, D. (2018). Delineated Analysis of Robotic Process Automation Tools. In IEEE (Ed.), *Proceeding of the 2nd Internation Conference on Advances in Electronics, Computers and Communications (ICAECC 2018)* (pp. 1–5). IEEE. https://doi.org/10.1109/ICAECC.2018.8479511

Rutschi, C., & Dibbern, J. (2019). Mastering Software Robot Development Projects: Understanding the Association between System Attributes & Design Practices. In Association for Information Systems (Chair), *Proceedings of the 52nd Hawaii International Conference on System Sciences,* Grand Wailea, Maui, Hawaii, USA.

Rutschi, C., & Dibbern, J. (2020). Towards a Framework of Implementing Software Robots: Transforming Human-executed Routines into Machines. *ACM SIGMIS Database: The Database for Advances in Information Systems, 51*(1), 104–128.

Santos, F., Pereira, R., & Vasconcelos, J. B. (2020). Toward robotic process automation implementation: An end-to-end perspective. *Business Process Management Journal, 26*(2), 405–420. https://doi.org/10.1108/BPMJ-12-2018-0380

Schlegel, D., & Kraus, P. (2020). Robotic Process Automation as an emerging career opportunity: An analysis of required qualifications and skills. In D. Vrontis, Y. Weber, & E. Tsoukatos (Eds.), *Proceedings of the 13th Annual Conference of the EuroMed Academy of Business: Business Theory and Practice Across Industries and Markets* (pp. 1083–1097). EuroMed Press.

Sethi, V., Jeyaraj, A., Duffy, K., & Farmer, B. (2020). Embedding Robotic Process Automation into Process Management: Case Study of using taskt. *AIS Transaction on Enterprise Systems, 51*(1). https://doi.org/10.30844/aistes.v5i1.19

Šimek, D., & Šperka, R. (2019). How Robot/human Orchestration Can Help in an HR Department: A Case Study From a Pilot Implementation. *Organizacija, 52*(3), 204–217. https://doi.org/10.2478/orga-2019-0013

Sindhgatta, R., ter Hofstede, A. H. M., & Ghose, A. (2020). Resource-Based Adaptive Robotic Process Automation. In S. Dustdar, E. Yu, C. Salinesi, D. Rieu, & V. Pant (Eds.), *Lecture Notes in Computer Science. Advanced Information Systems Engineering* (Vol. 12127, pp. 451–466). Springer International Publishing. https://doi.org/10.1007/978-3-030-49435-3_28

Stople, A., Steinsund, H., Iden, J., & Bygstad, B. (2017). Lightweight IT and the IT function: Experiences from robotic process automation in a Norwegian bank. In T.-M. Grønli (Ed.), *Proceedings from the annual NOKOBIT conference.* Bibsys Open Journals.

Suri, V. K., Elia, M., & van Hillegersberg, J. (2017). Software Bots - The Next Frontier for Shared Services and Functional Excellence. In I. Oshri, J. Kotlarsky, & L. P. Willcocks (Eds.), *Lecture Notes in Business Information Processing. Global Sourcing of Digital Services: Micro and Macro Perspectives*

(Vol. 306, pp. 81–94). Springer International Publishing. https://doi. org/10.1007/978-3-319-70305-3_5

Syed, R., Suriadi, S., Adams, M., Bandara, W., Leemans, S. J. J., Ouyang, C., ter Hofstede, A. H. M., van de Weerd, I., Wynn, M. T., & Reijers, H. A. (2020). Robotic Process Automation: Contemporary themes and challenges. *Computers in Industry, 115.*, Article 103162, 1–55. https://doi.org/10.1016/j. compind.2019.103162

Syed, R., & Wynn, M. T. (2020). How to Trust a Bot: An RPA User Perspective. In A. Asatiani, J. M. García, N. Helander, A. Jiménez-Ramírez, A. Koschmider, J. Mendling, G. Meroni, & H. A. Reijers (Eds.), *Lecture Notes in Business Information Processing. Business Process Management: Blockchain and Robotic Process Automation Forum* (Vol. 393, pp. 147–160). Springer International Publishing. https://doi.org/10.1007/978-3-030-58779-6_10

Timbadia, D. H., Jigishu Shah, P., Sudhanvan, S., & Agrawal, S. (2020). Robotic Process Automation Through Advance Process Analysis Model. In Y. Robinson & S. Smys (Eds.), *5th International Conference on Inventive Computation Technologies (ICICT)* (pp. 953–959). IEEE. 10.1109/ ICICT48043.2020.9112447.

van der Aalst, W. M. P., Bichler, M., & Heinzl, A. (2018). Robotic Process Automation. *Business & Information Systems Engineering, 60*(4), 269–272. https://doi.org/10.1007/s12599-018-0542-4

Viehhauser, J. (2020). Is Robotic Process Automation Becoming Intelligent? Early Evidence of Influences of Artificial Intelligence on Robotic Process Automation. In A. Asatiani, J. M. García, N. Helander, A. Jiménez-Ramírez, A. Koschmider, J. Mendling, G. Meroni, & H. A. Reijers (Eds.), *Lecture Notes in Business Information Processing. Business Process Management: Blockchain and Robotic Process Automation Forum* (Vol. 393, pp. 101–115). Springer International Publishing. https://doi.org/10.1007/978-3-030-58779-6_7

Vitharanage, I. M. D., Bandara, W., Syed, R., & Toman, D. (2020). An empirically supported conceptualisation of Robotic Process Automation (RPA) benefits. In Association for Information Systems (Chair), *Proceedings of the 28th European Conference on Information Systems (ECIS): Liberty, Equality, and Fraternity in a Digitizing World,* Marrakech, Morocco.

Wanner, J., Hofmann, A., Fischer, M., Imgrund, F., Janiesch, C., & Geyer-Klingeberg, J. (2019). Process Selection in RPA Projects - Towards a Quantifiable Method of Decision Making. In Association for Information Systems (Chair), *ICIS 2019,* Munich, Germany.

Webster, J., & Watson, R. T. (2002). Guest Editorial: Analyzing the Past to Prepare for the Future: Writing a literature Review. *MIS Quarterly, 26*(2), 13–23.

Wellmann, C., Stierle, M., Dunzer, S., & Matzner, M. (2020). A Framework to Evaluate the Viability of Robotic Process Automation for Business Process Activities. In A. Asatiani, J. M. García, N. Helander, A. Jiménez-Ramírez, A. Koschmider, J. Mendling, G. Meroni, & H. A. Reijers (Eds.), *Lecture Notes in Business Information Processing. Business Process Management: Blockchain and Robotic Process Automation Forum* (Vol. 393, pp. 200–214). Springer International Publishing. https://doi.org/10.1007/978-3-030-58779-6_14

Wewerka, J., Dax, S., & Reichert, M. (2020). A User Acceptance Model for Robotic Process Automation. In *24th IEEE International Enterprise Distributed Object Computing Conference (EDOC)* (pp. 97–106). IEEE. https://doi.org/10.1109/EDOC49727.2020.00021.

Wewerka, J., & Reichert, M. (2020). Towards Quantifying the Effects of Robotic Process Automation. In *24th IEEE International Enterprise Distributed Object Computing Conference (EDOC)* (pp. 11–19). IEEE. https://doi.org/10.1109/EDOCW49879.2020.00015

Willcocks, L. (2020). Robo-Apocalypse cancelled? Reframing the automation and future of work debate. *Journal of Information Technology, 35*(4). https://doi.org/10.1177/0268396220925830

William, W., & William, L. (2019). Improving Corporate Secretary Productivity using Robotic Process Automation. In IEEE Computer Society (Chair), *TAAI 2019,* Kaohsiung, Taiwan.

Yatskiv, S., Voytyuk, I., Yatskiv, N., Kushnir, O., Trufanova, Y., & Panasyuk, V. (2019). Improved Method of Software Automation Testing Based on the Robotic Process Automation Technology. In *International Conference on Advanced Computer Information Technologies,* Ceske Budejovice, Czech Republic.

3

The Role of Technology Enabled HRM Systems in Developing Hybrid Workplaces: A Case Study of the Information Technology Sector in India

Sandeep Kulshrestha

3.1 Introduction

The COVID-19 pandemic brought a new paradigm shift in the way the companies strategised running their overall operations in the context of a new reality of the coronavirus pandemic, where uncertainties loomed over the business world. "Working from home" became a reality which was a big challenge for the Human Resource Management (HRM) professionals The Information Technology sector was at the forefront of fostering a model where "working from home" became new normal and many more sectors started the process of working from home. Working for home, although not very new phenomena for the technology sector brought influences on other sectors as well. Online Meeting tools like

---

S. Kulshrestha (✉)
Rectangle Consulting, Hyderabad, India
e-mail: sandeep@rectangleconsulting.com

© The Author(s), under exclusive license to Springer Nature Switzerland AG 2022
A. Thrassou et al. (eds.), *Business Advancement through Technology Volume II*, Palgrave Studies in Cross-disciplinary Business Research, In Association with EuroMed Academy of Business, https://doi.org/10.1007/978-3-031-07765-4_3

Zoom and others became very popular in the business world, with exponential growth (BBC, 2020). Once it was certain that there was no alternative for working from home, companies started thinking on leveraging the technologies for creating seamless systems that would benefit the employees. Human Resources Management (HRM) has to be robust when it comes to managing people and taking care of their work-related needs, while they work from home. While writing this article, the COVID-19 pandemic was existing with different mutants all over the globe. However, in India lockdowns were lifted by July 2021 and when the case load of the disease reduced, many companies were not only encouraging working from home, but they were also gradually opening up their physical office space and asking people to work from office, at least partially (from one to three days in a week). The resultant workplace has now come to be known as a Hybrid workplace, which has a mix of both—working from home and working from a physical office space.

The aim and objectives of this chapter is to explore the role of technology enabled e-HRM (electronic Human Resources Management) systems that helped facilitate a conducive hybrid workplace, especially during the spread of the COVID-19 pandemic. There is a vital need to understand whether technology enabled e-HRM systems indeed impact the workplace in general and organisations overall, in particular. This chapter attempts to assess the scenario in the context of the Information Technology Sector in India. Globally as well as in India, the technology sector looks to be geared up for a Hybrid functioning and hence such studies, like this would be extremely important to understand deeply how the Human Resources professionals, in alignment of technology enabled systems can help their internal customers i.e., the employees of the companies. This chapter may touch upon small nuances of what is happening.

A hybrid workplace is defined as, "a business model combining remote work with office work. It may look different among organisations, but it typically includes the onsite presence of a core group, while others are free to come and go as they please, within reason" (thoughtfarner.com, 2021). In Nutshell, in a Hybrid workplace, there are some employees who necessarily have to go to a physical office, especially those who work in the

3 The Role of Technology Enabled HRM Systems in Developing... 49

daily operations, while there are many others who have the flexibility to visit office depending upon the work requirements.

Historically, e-HRM programs have been in use by the information technology sector, globally as well as in India where software programs like PeopleSoft came into existence in 1987. PeopleSoft changed the landscape of Human Resources which was more of an administrative, pen and paper kind of function. In the western and developed world, if we go back in History, SAP R/2 was launched in 1979 in which HR functionality was integrated in the same database that had other functions such as materials management, financial management and production planning. Human Resources as a function over the years have become more professional and respectful in the new millennia and have adopted best practices as per the change of times.

The e-HRM software has traditionally allowed the employees of the IT sector to work on their devices, whether using internet, intranet, or web portal (Agarwal et al., 2004). The idea of such software was to make employees access HR services seamlessly, in real time.

The pandemic which spread in the early part of 2020 had a profound impact on the professional workplace, so much so that the homes of employees became the new workspaces and there was enhanced focus on employee wellness. (Human Resource Executive, 2021). The research question that the author was probing was to understand if technology could enable HRM systems in a way that they would enable the employees as well as organisations to be efficient in terms of the Hybrid work culture.

The research question that the author is addressing is whether a technology enabled electronic HRM system is useful in a hybrid workplace and if at all such system has a value, what role it plays in helping an efficient running of a Hybrid office.

The information technology sector has been a pioneer in establishing best practices and a large number of companies in the sector had been showcased in the category of "best companies to work for" in majority of the surveys related to best places to work in the last few decades. It was then imperative for the Information Technology sector to come up with innovative electronic HRM systems. The pandemic brought into focus using technology as a leverage to make sure that the employees, as the customers of the Human Resource function work in a congenial environment. This would also make it easier for the management to extract optimal work performance from the employees.

To study this in a holistic fashion, the author conducted interviews with the people in the Human Resources department as well as the employees of different organisations so that the efficacy as well as acceptance of the e-HRM systems can be understood properly.

The post millennials or the Generation Z expected an efficient workplace environment. In that context, a technology enabled HR system was needed, especially after the outbreak of COVID-19 pandemic. This study explores whether such new systems were created and if the answer was in affirmative, what was the role of such systems in developing a hybrid workplace which was need of the hour because of the impact of the pandemic. The need of course was for all employee demographics, not just for the generation Z.

In nutshell, through this chapter, the author is trying to showcase if there were efforts on part of the organisations to implement technology enabled e-HRM systems and in what way they helped create a Hybrid workplace. The author also studied the genesis or the need of a Hybrid work place and how it shaped out during the era of COVID-19 pandemic.

The rationale for this study is related to the reality that the Hybrid work is going to stay, and it is not perfect. Managers are not having enough ways to measure employee performance, for example (theconversation.com, 2021). Also, the traditional management concepts and academic and application-oriented fields like Organisational Behavior and Organisational Psychology have to modify the approaches based on these new workplace realities and that includes the role of electronic HRM systems. This paper is hence important to give a context to one important aspect of any organisation and that is the management of human resources.

3.2 Literature Review

As looking at the future of work through a Hybrid model of work perspective is fairly new, most of the literature available on this matter is about what companies have been doing in the last two years, in the shadow of the pandemic. Working from home as a model has been existing since many years, in the Information Technology sector but considering Hybrid model was a relatively new idea that is now being considered by many corporations worldwide. In fact, at the time of writing this article many companies are still running their operations in a work from model itself (flexjobs, 2021).

According to (techtarget.com, 2021), there are fourteen Hybrid workplace technologies that would power the future of work. The list goes like this: Application Tracking System (For recruitment, where all stakeholders related to the interview process including the candidate are located remotely), Collaboration tools (useful for progress on common team projects, also including cloud storage and document syncronisation), Communication Platforms (platforms like slack are used for employees and teams to communicate), Document Management, Human Capital Management (for overall human resources management needs), Office capacity management tools (to understand how many employees are entering and existing a physical office in a particular day or the month), Automation of office cleaning (Technologies like Artificial Intelligence can be used to alert the cleaning staff or the robots for a physical office space to be cleaned or sanitised), Employee learning applications (as employee training is useful for re-skilling them, such applications would be useful), Mobile tools (although they are already in use, these are equally important for an effective hybrid workplace), Onboarding Applications (tools like cloud based remote on-boarding), Performance Management tools, Reservations System (if the organisation offers reserving hotel rooms whenever the employees are in a physical office), Security software (which is very important in remote as well as Hybrid working) and video conferencing software (where new features include understanding facial expressions and body language).

The five major tech categories to support Hybrid work, (reworked.co, 2021) would include the following;

1. Digital Adoption Platforms: Realtime education and learning would be useful in enabling new behaviors for the employees. Walk me (walkme.com) is an example.
2. Machine Learning workflow: Workers would be able to automate their jobs themselves and can focus more on areas like strategic decision making and engaging with co-workers (example: IBM Watson Orchestrate)
3. People Analytics: For remote workers, this is a tool to optimise and analyse their work better, especially for the remote workers. Activetrak (activetrak.com) is an exaample
4. Low code for citizen developers: This would be able to assist employees to easily build solutions based on existing apps and data. (Example: Microsoft Power apps)
5. Work coordination: In a Hybrid work situation, all employees are located at various places. Through work coordination companies can help coordinate the work of many employees around a central project or task and also help in execution. Smart sheet is one example for work coordination software.

There is a significant change in conventional human resources and its changing pattern towards digital human resources through a cloud-based networking system. The human resource field has shifted from conventional operation to mobile device-based operation. Social and mobile functionality is considered an important need for recruitment selection. (Saini, 2018). It is observed that HRM functions can be transformed and integrated in digital forms within organisations. In current practices, the most widely used e-HRM functions are: E- HR Planning, acquiring HR (recruitment and selection), developing HR (training and development, career management), rewarding HR (performance evaluation, compensation and benefits), protecting HR (health and safety, employee relations/legal issues). (Fındıklı et al., 2015).

In the field of Human Resource Management (HRM), technology has made a paradigm shift from administration or personnel management to strategic HRM. Technology and HR together assist in cost reduction and efficiency along with a lot of opportunities and challenges. It enables managers in taking quick strategic decisions by providing real time information. The use of technology supports HR strategies, policies, and practices within the organisation. (Rawat et al., 2015).

3.3 Methodology and Research Context

Qualitative methodology was chosen to undertake this research and the author took 22 interviews with the people who were in the forefront of Human Resources role and the employees who were the users of electronic HRM systems.

For data collection, total sample size was 22 employees in different Information Technology Companies in India. The employees who were working in the areas of human resources or talent management were twelve in number while the remaining ten were executives working in the Information Technology sector, employed in different work areas including software testing, business development, operations etcetera.

The methodology included survey questionnaire and personal interviews with all respondents. The survey questions included questions around new role of Human Resources in terms of leveraging technology with a strategy to create an effective hybrid workplace and what new interventions were employed to make e-HRM systems conducive for a hybrid workplace. This data helped the author in understanding the role of technology enabled e-HRM systems in terms of productivity, overall impact, and employee satisfaction.

Also, as the concept of Hybrid workplace is new, the author considered available qualitative information on how technology has been leveraged in the past couple of years to facilitate effective Hybrid workplace functionality in terms of Human Resource Management and its ancillary functions like Recruitment (or talent acquisition), On-Boarding, Performance management, team collaboration, employee engagement, retrenchment and so on.

The covid-19 pandemic brought into focus the innovative way to conduct business and as soon as the Indian Government declared the first lockdown in mid-march 2020, all of the companies in the Information Technology sector asked the employees to work from home. Working from home became a norm for such companies for a long time (more than a year). While the employees of many companies are still completely working from home, there are various companies which have adopted a new hybrid way of working, where employees work few days in a week based in their offices and remaining days they work from home. In some companies (part of the study) employees work 2–3 days in a week from office, while in other companies they work for a day in office and remaining days from home.

The Hybrid workplace brings a question into focus and that is about the role of Human Resources function in an Organisation. Human Resources has become more of an enabler of best practices, rather than being a historical function of hiring people, appraising employee performance and handling grievances. As the Hybrid workplace is also a workplace of the future, the HR leaders are increasingly getting prepared for having this kind of work arrangement to stay for many more years to come (factorialhr.com, 2021). There is also a visible trend in the corporate world where many human resources leaders are in fact taking this seriously, with new job titles such as Head of Hybrid work or Head of Dynamic Work etcetera being offered. The organisations create these new job roles so that core technology enabled tools can be created (Reworked. co, 2021).

Also, the businesses and companies had less of a choice during the COVID-19 pandemic but to allow employees to work for home and explore the Hybrid workplace as a viable option. With leveraging of technologies like cloud based HRM systems, companies had time in hand to focus on enhancing the employee experience in terms of Human Resource initiatives. With many roles of Human Resources including onboarding, performance review, payroll, leave request management and so on becoming automated, the role of HR is minimum in terms of a physical pen and paper effort, in these areas (empuls.io, 2022). In terms of the research question, great amount of thinking is happening in organisations with reference to technology, innovation, best practices development and overall effectiveness in the HR role.

3 The Role of Technology Enabled HRM Systems in Developing... 55

In terms of the general workplace scenario in India, many companies feel that Hybrid working is a temporary measure while some companies are considering looking at this from a long term perspectives and setting up policies and procedures to implement Hybrid working permanently. (SHRM, 2021). According to a Survey published by the National Association of Software and Service companies in India (NASSCOM, 2021), almost half of the Information Technology workforce is expected to return for work in a Hybrid mode—up to three days in a week. The advantage of the Information Technology sector lies in its flexibility in adapting to change and during the course of the interviews with respondents; this fact emerged as one of the most evident.

Not surprisingly, around 88% Business leaders are seriously investing in hiring specialists and consultants to help design new workplace policies that would help them create new policies and structures in the post pandemic world. India is also leading in the APAC region when it comes to offering flexibility at workplace (LinkedIn, 2021) This study, commissioned by LinkedIn also shows concerns of the business leaders in terms of lower efficiency, lesser collaboration within employees and a dent in the customer experience. According to the LinkedIn study, Companies are rethinking about their working models, cultures, and company values. And as they do, they're realising that hybrid work is increasingly becoming a permanent part of the picture — more than half respondents (51%) said that offering hybrid, remote, and flexible working options was the way their companies would be operate going forward.

In the workplace pulse survey undertaken by the global consulting firm Price Waterhouse Coopers along with NASSCOM (National Association of Software and Service Companies) (The Economic Times, 2021) it was found that in a complete work from model, one in four employees felt that their productivity had gown down and that their physical and mental wellbeing had declined. The overloaded schedules of employees (which sometime included back-to-back meetings stretching for hours was a big barrier in being effective at workplace. The PWC NASSCOM survey also talks about tools like productivity analysis would be able to improve employee experience, giving insights on where companies would need to redesign work processes.

It's no surprise, given the massive changes in the global economy, that the need to upskill and reskill feels especially urgent to leaders, with close to three-quarters (72%) believing that training is necessary for people to build the skills needed to work effectively in the new hybrid and flexible work environments. In this context, Business leaders are trying to understand the strengths as well as pitfalls of Hybrid work.

During the pandemic, businesses (especially in the Information Technology sector) were able to maintain continuity and equilibrium because they took steps to adopt digital solutions, tools and interventions over the last couple of years. The transition from physical office to working from home and Hybrid working was made easier because of these digital tools. The objective of the businesses was to keep the momentum of productivity and collaboration go on in full swing. Digital tools helped transition to a remote and hybrid way of working to help increase productivity and collaboration. These were the trying times for the companies and employees were trained with newer skills to get adapted to the new workplace design. One of the respondents in this study (in the business development area) said in the interview that initially when lockdown happened because of the pandemic, all people in her team were jittery and worried about their future. However, there were assurances from the Human Resources professionals that the company would the best it can to maintain the continuity of work.

The question nevertheless emerges about what an engaging workplace is so that people look forward to attending work even when it means that there would be a virtual work environment only. When employees are self-motivated to come to work every day, the possibility is higher that they would give their best to work and as a resultant action, they would be effective and efficient as well. Once employees would be totally interested and hence would love coming to work, the customers, managers and the stakeholders would be happy. Hence, the essence of an effective workplace is that it would make employees feel committed towards work. This applies to working from Physical office, working from home or a hybrid model, where employees work from home as well as from their office. This is the essence of an effective workplace, and all our tools and processes must be geared towards these goals. An organisation can also be looked at as a place for collaboration, teamwork, innovation, and creativity The question emerges if such kind of workplace can be created at homes of the employees where collaboration and teamwork is possible. While researching for this article, it emerged that employees were not fully happy and satisfied with hundred percent work from home model and craved for a human touch. In this context, a Hybrid office seemed like a natural option for many.

This article hence tries look at different research contexts to showcase a holistic picture on the need of Hybrid workplaces and in what way technological inputs are enabling such Hybrid workplace that is collaborative, efficient and is able to enhance customer experience.

3.4 The Pre-pandemic Workplace

In the pre-pandemic (pre-March 2020) era, e-HRM systems were in place in terms of either one function in the overall Enterprise Resource Planning (ERP) software or standalone HR software that could take care of recruitments, payroll, learning and development, leave records and other routine as well as operational matters related to HR. HR dashboards were also in operation during the pre-pandemic days and they still have a presence in the e-HRM ecosystem.

One of the prevalent e-HRM software was Adrenalin (By Polaris Financial Technology). This software was customisable as per the client needs. The other prevalent software was Empower HRMS which had various modules for separate HR functions including attendance, leave, payroll, staff attendance etcetera (Agarwal et al., 2004).

The use of Technology in HR was well established for the purpose of HR operational processes and allowing distributed access to employees and managers (Raja et al., 2020).

In pre pandemic phase, we cannot for sure say that workplaces were really effective in terms of various factors including employee engagement, productivity, innovation, scope for creativity etc. The Human Resource leaders are still pondering over this question about how the new processes can help create effective Hybrid workplace systems. According to Rob Goffee, Professor of Organisational Behavior at London Business School, (Harvard Business Review, 2013), there are various factors that constitutes an effective workplace. One of the key ingredients, he argues is "letting people be", which in nutshell means giving importance to the individual traits which people possess and let them explore their creativity. Another thing he emphasizes in the article quoted his about the free flow of information which should be happening in Organisations. Information flow leads to transparency and trust. Professor Goffee also points out the fact in his article that companies should formulate such tools within companies that would be able to magnify employee's strengths. An Organisational culture where strengths are valued is a great win-win for both the company's management as well as its employees.

The author through the interviews of the respondents found that the pre-pandemic workplace was not significantly different except for the fact that there was better interaction with people at the personal level. The interactions in the era of the pandemic have turned digital and people are using tools like WebEx, Zoom, Google meet and so on.

Also, in many Organisations, a HR dashboard has been a very useful tool. A HR dashboard is basically the on-screen interactive display of Human Resources reports as well as data analytics (hrmsworld.com, 2019). For a Human Resources professional, a dashboard shows a real time information on work related issues like Managing Key Performance areas of employees, understanding various indicators including recruitment and retrenchment, mapping of employees' satisfaction and so on.

The Human Resources dashboard is a part of e-HRM systems that makes managers as well as the team members understand the workflow in real time including tasks they are handling, team collaboration status, along with status of new hires, retrenchments, employee engagement and so on. All the individuals who participated in this study were using some kind of a dashboard. While the Human Resources teams were using HR Dashboards, those in other job roles had different kinds of productivity tools.

In an article in the Forbes magazine in 2014, Josh Bersina, leading analyst in Human Resources, talent, leadership, and HR technology had said that the Human Resources technology landscape, worth $15 billion market in software, was exploding with growth, newer opportunities, and innovation. When he wrote that article, more than 100 new startups in social and referral recruiting, talent analytics, assessment science, online

3 The Role of Technology Enabled HRM Systems in Developing...

learning, and mid-market core HR systems started their operations to develop new tools to help manage employee communications, engagement, recognition, and workplace wellness were having great demand. According to his estimation, the top 50 HR technology deals in 2014 were over $560 million. Hence, besides being tools to enhance productivity and effectiveness, investing in Human Resources Technology innovations is a big business.

HR people have to be curious about the recent trends in technology. It is not always required to follow each trend, but it is needed to be choosy and wise when technological trends are being followed. It is a responsibility of HR department to select a right technology for their organisation. (Rawat et al., 2015).

3.5 Findings

Hybrid workplaces in the Information Technology sector in India was thought of as a viable option when the Government started opening different sectors of the economy. Companies which are researched as part of this chapter had a clear strategy in mind, in late summer of 2020 to work towards developing and sustaining Hybrid way of working but they were not interested to open the workplace for a Hybrid set-up yet, till the time they were certain that they were sufficiently equipped with standard operating procedures, best practices and the relevant employee training. The companies were waiting for a clearer picture in terms of the pandemic. When the vaccination was first announced in April 2021 in India, all the companies that were researched made it mandatory for the employees to necessarily get vaccinated. India had the second wave of COVID-19 affecting it in late April 2021 and it continued till late June of 2021.

22 Individuals participated in the study and the break-up of their area of work can be seen in the following Table 3.1.

6 of human resource participants in this study said that the HR modules in the Human Resources software were modified to address employee requirements in context to Hybrid workplace. They mentioned that there was a specific employee helpdesk created to take care of employee needs. The modification in HR modules included emphasis on collaboration

Table 3.1 Survey/Interview participants' overview

Are of work	Number of respondents
Human Resources Management	12
Operations	3
Business Development	2
IT Consulting	3
Software Testing	2

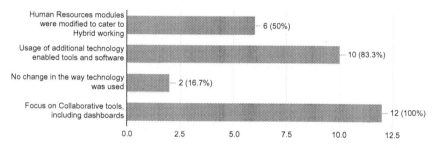

Chart 3.1 Graphical representation to the data collected from the Human Resources respondents

suites that incorporated both work from home and the physical workplace. 10 Human resources participants said that they were using more technology enabled software including slack while the remaining 2 mentioned that there was almost no change in terms of technology usage. 3 Human Resources professionals aid that they have been using collaborative tools developed by their own company while the remaining said that they were outsourcing those from outside tech vendors.

All Human resources executives who participated in the study said that they were focusing more on collaborative tools in the future, combined with a dashboard, for an effective Hybrid work situation. They were exploring all cloud based collaborating tools which also categorised co-workers into "working from home" and "working from a physical office workstation". The graphical representation to the data collected from the Human Resources respondents is given below (Chart 3.1):

All human resources participants also mentioned that their respective companies were creating a strategic framework for a Hybrid work situation, where technology would play a key role.

3 The Role of Technology Enabled HRM Systems in Developing... 61

While in the non-HR domain, it was 6 people who said they were using additional software including collaborative tools and video conferencing tools. Remaining were used to remote working technologies in the past and were continuing at the time of writing this article as well.

7 Human Resources and 4 in the non-HR domain employees felt that the human touch was missing and that they would prefer a hybrid model than working from home. Others in the study thought they were fine with either remote work or Hybrid.

8 Human Resources professional informed that their companies focused to facilitate work life balance. In the area of work-life balance, employees used to get alerts for breaks for meditation or for coffee while working on their home-based workstations. 2 managers from non-HR areas also used to ask their teammates about what they did to take breaks in between meetings. These discussions used to happen on Friday evenings before the end of a workweek. All Human resources executives who participated in the study were of opinion that their respective companies were seeking more ideas from both the technology and HR domains to explore newer technological inputs, for the near future.

Overall, it was brought to knowledge that collaboration tools were given more importance than other areas of Human Resources Management. Online application Tools like Slack was used widely by the individuals who participated in the study. Hence, technology enabled e-HRM systems were more focused on workplace collaboration, whether employees were working from home or were part of the Hybrid set-up. The study clearly showcases that there was a substantial role of e-HRM systems to create an effective Hybrid workplace and the companies were having a strategic road map to explore newer technologies which would make their work processes better, in the future, while reviewing the external environment which was created because of the pandemic.

3.6 Limitations

There are limitations in the study mainly because of these reasons;

1. Information Technology companies in India, like their counterparts in other countries have been using e-HRM tools since a long time, that were enabled by technology, but a Hybrid work situation is fairly new and availability of complete data in this regard is challenging.
2. Information Technology companies in India are still testing and exploring new tools and interventions that would enhance productivity of their workforce and hence the data is insufficient in that regard. More data will emerge when the companies adapt to new systems and processes.
3. There is a scope of a larger study, in a bigger time frame to come to a complete understanding of how technology enabled e-HRM systems have delivered in terms of expectations.
4. A bigger study with a larger sample size can bring better results to understand how Hybrid workplace is powered by technology enabled e-HRM systems.

3.7 Conclusion

Organisations in the Information Technology sector, in India gradually geared up for Hybrid work during the covid-19 pandemic. The information technology sector in India, based on the sample size, did play an important role in creating systems for Hybrid workplace. The systems and tools primarily focused on collaboration between employees, using cloud computing effectively. Also, it was found in the study that the organisations were seriously interested to invest in the right technology that could aid employees become productive. Besides this, companies also invested in work life balance which was also necessary to create a right kind of work culture. Overall, there was immense focus on using technology for either enhancing existing collaborative tools or creating new collaborative tools. In conclusion, the role of technology is immense in creating systems for an effective Hybrid workplace, but wider research would open more avenues to explore this topic.

References

Agarwal, M., et al., (2004). *E-HRM and Recent Strategies: New Spice for HR Practitioners*. Global Journal of Finance and Management. Accessed December 17, 2021, from https://www.ripublication.com/gjfm-spl/gjfmv6n6_11.pdf

Alawadhi, N. (2021, November 01). *Hybrid to be new norm for return to work, finds Nasscom-indeed study*. Business Standard. Accessed January 25, 2022, from https://www.business-standard.com/article/economy-policy/hybrid-to-be-new-norm-for-return-to-work-finds-nasscom-indeed-study-121110100541_1.html

Anand, S. (2021, December 3). *Approaches to hybrid work policies in India*. SHRM. Accessed December 30, 2021, from https://www.shrm.org/shrm-india/pages/approaches-to-hybrid-work-policies-in-india.aspx

Basu, S. (2021, March 16). *Pandemic has accelerated digital upskilling, but key groups still miss out: PwC Survey*. The Economic Times. Accessed January 25, 2022, from https://economictimes.indiatimes.com/jobs/pandemic-has-accelerated-digital-upskilling-but-key-groups-still-miss-out-pwc-survey/articleshow/81530860.cms

Courtney, E. (2021, January 04). *The Benefits of Working from Home: Why the Pandemic isn't the Only Reason to Work Remotely*. Flexjobs.com. Accessed December 17, 2021, from https://www.flexjobs.com/blog/post/benefits-of-remote-work/

Fındıklı, et al. (2015). *Exploring the Outcomes of Electronic Human Resource Management (E-HRM)?* Sciencedirect. Accessed January 25, 2022, from https://www.sciencedirect.com/science/article/pii/S1877042815052453?via%3Dihub

Foxall, D. (2019, January 21). *Maximizing the effectiveness of your HR analytics dashboard*. Hrmsworld.com. Accessed December 27, 2021, from https://www.hrmsworld.com/maximizing-hr-analytics-dashboard.html

Goffee, R. et al., (2013). *Creating the Best Workplace on Earth*. Harvard Business Review. Accessed December 17, 2021, from https://hbr.org/2013/05/creating-the-best-workplace-on-earth

Lane, R. et al., (2021, January 28). *4 ways organization design can enable the Hybrid workplace*. Human Resource Executive. Accessed December 18, 2021, from https://hrexecutive.com/4-ways-organization-design-can-enable-the-hybrid-workplace/

Lobosco, M. (2021, September 09). *The Future of Work is Flexible: 71% of Leaders Feel Pressure to Change Working Models.* LinkedIn. Accessed December 29, 2021, from https://www.linkedin.com/business/talent/blog/talent-engagement/future-of-work-is-flexible

Mitchell, A. (2021, October 22). *The future of work is hybrid – here's an expert's recommendations.* Theconversations.com. Accessed February 22, 2022, from https://theconversation.com/the-future-of-work-is-hybrid-heres-an-experts-recommendations-167432

Nicastro, D. (2021, July 13). *Emerging Software Needs for the Hybrid Workplace.* Reworked.co. Online at: https://www.reworked.co/digital-workplace/emerging-software-needs-for-the-hybrid-workplace/

Raja, V. A. J. et al., (2020, March 11). *E-HRM in Software Organizations.* International Journal of Management Research and Development. Accessed December 18, 2021, from https://papers.ssrn.com/sol3/papers.cfm?abstract_id=3536141

Rangarajan, J. (2022, January 21). *Evolving role of HR in the future Hybrid Workforce.* Empuls Blog. Accessed January 21, 2022, from https://blog.empuls.io/role-of-hr-in-future-hybrid-workforce/

Rawat, P. et al., (2015). *Influence of Technology on Human Resource Management.* MIT-SOM PGRC KJIMRP 1st International Conference (Special Issue). Accessed December 17, 2021, from http://khoj.mitsom.edu.in/index.php/KHOJ/article/viewFile/107768/75836

Saini, S. (2018, April 01). *Digital HRM and its Effective Implementation: An Empirical Study.* Semantic Scholar. Accessed December 21, 2021, from https://www.semanticscholar.org/paper/Digital-HRM-and-its-Effective-Implementation%3A-An-Saini/51d785461a769772cde018f547864be70dd35f9e

Sherman, N. (2020, June 02). *Zoom sees sales boom amid pandemic.* BBC News. Accessed December 21, 2021, from https://www.bbc.com/news/business-52884782

St-Jean, E. (2021, July 01).*14 hybrid workplace technologies to power future of work.* Techtarget.com. Accessed December 29, 2021, from https://searchhrsoftware.techtarget.com/feature/Hybrid-workplace-technologies-to-power-future-of-work

Symonds, C. (2021, November 25). *Finding a Balanced Hybrid Work Schedule.* Factorialhr.com. Accessed December 17, 2021, from https://factorialhr.com/blog/hybrid-work-schedule/

Unknown. (2021, August 23). *The hybrid workplace: Is this the future of work?* Thoughtfarmer.com. Accessed December 17, 2021, from https://www.thoughtfarmer.com/blog/hybrid-workplace/

4

Engineering the Metaverse for Innovating the Electronic Business: A Socio-technological Perspective

Giuseppe Festa, Yioula Melanthiou, and Pina Meriano

4.1 Introduction

The term 'metaverse' derives from the combination of two words ('meta', from Greek μετά, and 'verse', from Latin *versus*), whose meaning could be expressed as "to go beyond". To be more precise, considering its first use and description in the science fiction novel entitled "Snow Crash" (1992),

---

G. Festa (✉)
Department of Economics and Statistics, University of Salerno, Salerno, Italy
e-mail: gfesta@unisa.it

Y. Melanthiou
Department of Public Communication, Faculty of Communication and Media Studies, Cyprus University of Technology, Limassol, Cyprus
e-mail: yioula.melanthiou@cut.ac.cy

P. Meriano
Inside Marketing, Naples, Italy
e-mail: pina.meriano@insidemarketing.it

© The Author(s), under exclusive license to Springer Nature Switzerland AG 2022
A. Thrassou et al. (eds.), *Business Advancement through Technology Volume II*, Palgrave Studies in Cross-disciplinary Business Research, In Association with EuroMed Academy of Business, https://doi.org/10.1007/978-3-031-07765-4_4

by Neil Town Stephenson, it outlines the idea of going beyond the real world and somehow, beyond real life.

In "Snow Crash", Stephenson deals with an exploratory, absolutely visionary, journey across what by that time was considered as futuristic technology (wireless connection, virtual reality, augmented reality, and so on). Among those various prophetic inspirations there was also the idea of 'metaverse', i.e., the global result of a technological evolution that could allow a highly immersive virtual experience in three dimensions (3Ds), which today the big-tech companies are trying to recreate for mainly (but not only) commercial purposes (Smart et al., 2007).

The concept of metaverse is constructed around the individual-user, and then it could be well-explained by the description of the main character's experience, i.e., «… a computer-generated universe that his computer is drawing onto his goggles and pumping into his earphones» (Stephenson, 1992, p. 24); in this respect, the metaverse is a virtual world, which people can enter using general or specific electronic devices. Stephenson also deals with a lot of similarities with reality, but he underlines that in the metaverse each object «… does not really exist—it's just a computer-graphics protocol written down a piece of paper somewhere—none of these things is being physically built. They are, rather, pieces of software, made available to the public over the worldwide fiber-optics network» (*ibidem*).

People from all over the world can enter the metaverse by virtue of a computer-graphic representation: their 'characters' can be represented in a 3D space in the form of an 'avatar' (i.e., the virtual alias of a person who exists in the real world), and then they can explore virtual spaces, interacting with other avatars and implementing several activities, such as visiting houses, enjoying entertainment, and developing business: in other words, living a kind of parallel, but also integrated and/or enriched life (Damar, 2021).

The idea or the vision of people entering virtual reality using external devices (e.g., special gloves for touching or special glasses for watching, and so on) and connecting from everywhere in the world was already explored in some movies, like "Tron" (1982) by Steven Lisberger, "The Lawnmower Man" (1992) by Brett Leonard, and "Ready Player One" (2018) by Steven Spielberg (who adapted Ernest Cline's science fiction novel "Player One" in his film). However, all these perspectives associate virtual reality especially with game activities, which is quite different from the original vision of Stephenson.

In fact, since the term 'metaverse' was coined, Stephenson's ideas influenced and shaped actual and potential development in the technological field; many scholars and enthusiasts about technology have used—and are still using—this neologism in different contexts and with different meanings, and some of them have tried—and are still trying—to develop the software technologies and the hardware devices required for its creation, because it represents a tremendous opportunity to evolve the environment of connections and interactions among people, at social, technological, and economic level. In the progress of time, Stephenson's vision of the metaverse also expanded, and today, by virtue of the available technology, it includes the idea of a computerized integration of physical world objects and digital world activities, a sort of liquid IoT (Internet-of-Things), enabling a continuous, enlarged, and profound interaction between the real world and the virtual world (Carmigniani & Furht, 2011).

Starting from the above considerations, this study aims to provide a global vision about potential definition, conceptualisation, and activation, in the business perspective, of the metaverse potentialities, analysing the differences of the world of metaverse with respect to 'previous' virtual technologies. The structure of the chapter is the following: after a literature review in the field, focusing on the characteristics of the metaverse and its physiological trans-conceptual dimension, the investigation, adopting a narrative approach with exploratory intention, and moving from relevant business experiences, aims to delineate an overall SWOT (Strengths, Weaknesses, Opportunities, and Threats) analysis, as final outcome, which has been engineered to outline a socio-technological overview about the necessity and the opportunity to design, to implement, and to develop metaverse experiences for innovative electronic marketing and management.

4.2 Literature Review

Although the interest of the scientific community for this field of research has been growing in recent years, the metaverse can be undoubtedly considered as a novel topic. In fact, a pilot investigation on the most important scientific databases (Scholar, Scopus, and Web Of Science) has revealed the existence of relatively few publications about (more specifically, 9420 documents from Scholar, 218 from Scopus, and 164 from Web of Science as results from the query about "metaverse" on the 22nd of January 2022; naturally, results may vary over time).

This novelty has suggested the opportunity of conducting an exploratory analysis of the various literature in the field. More specifically, two possible focuses of investigation have been assumed as potentially the most interesting, i.e., the effort of examining the main characteristics of a potential definition of the metaverse, and the intuition about the possible—or perhaps inevitable—hybrid dimension of the metaverse.

4.2.1 Beyond the 'Standard' Conception of Virtual Reality: A Definition of Metaverse

Critical voices argue that metaverse is just a term currently used to rebrand virtual reality, which in the past, to be honest, often failed to keep up with the expected ambitions. In fact, in different studies different authors adopt different meanings, uses, and definitions of metaverse, dealing only with aspects that are strictly related to virtual reality; in those situations, metaverse appears only as an innovative concept to capture a potential new trend, which in truth refers to the same matter, i.e., virtual reality. Naturally, metaverse is closely related to the idea of artificial representation, but it has much wider meaning, embedding altogether virtual reality, augmented reality, and hybrid reality, enabling the activation of a digital world of connections, interactions, and developments that are potentially hyperbolic, i.e., theoretically infinite in their possible operations, applications, and most of all, combinations.

As a consequence, there is not yet a standard definition of metaverse, most of all because of its novelty and its physiological dynamics, but

4 Engineering the Metaverse for Innovating the Electronic... 69

among the most adopted definitions, some define the metaverse as the next version of the Internet, and perhaps the Web more specifically, especially in combination with the mobile dimension of the access to the 'network of the networks'. However, this seems not the right direction for designing a potential understanding of metaverse: for example, in fact, Matthew Ball (2021) underlines that metaverse will not replace the Internet, but instead, it would most probably transform it in an iterative way similar to how the mobile Internet did.

In fact, personal computers allowed people to be connected to the Internet only in certain places and at certain times, in a completely different way than mobile devices allow, permitting people to get continuous access, in any place and at any time. Furthermore, the metaverse could immerse everyone in a sort of 3D—and even more Ds—version of the Internet, without the need to 'access' (in the logging meaning), but rather 'existing' inside it at any time, exploiting connections in real time with an enormous number of users; in the metaverse there would be a continuity of data related to identity, history, activity, and so on, and any information would be persistent even in the moments when people would only be in the real world (today, this concept would be expressed by saying "when people log out").

Thus, the current conception of Internet, Web, and so on is on the point of changing, and similarly there will be changes (evolutions? revolutions?) as concerns the site interface, the hypertext navigation, the data visualisation in terms of text, images, videos, and so on, with subsequent impact on the evolution of the internet marketing applications (Shams, 2019); for example, 3D hyperlink functionality will allow to traverse virtual world contexts (Lombardi & Lombardi, 2010). In this scenario, virtual reality will play a central role, but many aspects of the 'current' virtual reality will profoundly evolve.

Moreover, while each virtual world exists on its own, the metaverse by definition will consist of an integrated network of complex 3D virtual worlds; in this network, the technology of virtual worlds does not correspond to closed systems, but it will rather be complemented by many other technologies. Nowadays, to have a draft understanding of this conception, it is possible to think about similar experiences in the virtual worlds that are specifically designed for the gaming field.

70 G. Festa et al.

Furthermore, in addition to this view of the metaverse as an interconnection of virtual 3D worlds, it is important to point out that it should be also based on an extremely enriched hybrid reality (i.e., a combination or fusion of real world and virtual reality), to allow operating simultaneously in different but intertwined spaces. In this respect, it is to highlight that in the metaverse physical environments, objects, and activities would be blended to virtual ones.

From another point of view, it is possible to evoke that the metaverse will consist of smart spaces, as a sort of mirror and/or integrated world in which physical and digital layers are strongly intermingled (Ricci et al., 2015). Thus, it would be necessary to develop, enable, and improve advanced middleware technologies (Fuller et al., 2020) that would be capable to exploit the aforementioned IoT in combination with Artificial Intelligence (AI) and holography, only to mention some evident applications or representations, so that human beings can see through a display (as part of a different futuristic device) objects that concern reality but that do not physically exist in the real world.

As arguable from many of the above considerations, the development of the metaverse necessarily requires open systems. Nowadays, most probably, at least to the best of the knowledge that is achievable outside the scientific laboratories, at public or private level, which are secretly working on the metaverse (for example, Facebook, considering that in 2021 Mark Zuckerberg has communicated the next evolution of the social network into a/the metaverse), only professional graphic creators seem able to develop digital twins and other computer science environments that are useful for representing real objects in the metaverse, but naturally, to make it more accessible to every user, simpler user interfaces are required, impacting in an absolute unpredictable way the world of UGC (User Generated Content) (Ondrejka, 2005).

On these bases, it seems possible to elaborate a potential conceptual overview of the metaverse, trying to include all its main characteristics; in this respect, the metaverse could be expressed as a synchronous, persistent, interoperable, and open (not proprietary) network, representing a hybrid world between reality and virtuality in which people (i.e., users represented by avatars) are fully immersed, continuously interacting and switching from reality to virtuality using innovative electronic devices, participating in any kind of activities together with an unlimited number of other users (avatars) in real time, feeling a sense of transparent, convergent, and empowered presence. According to this perspective, some conceptual coordinates seem to emerge.

- Innovative hardware and software infrastructures will be necessary for entering, using, and exploring the Internet to ensure continuity of access and stability of connection, but also to collect, transmit, and enrich any kind of data, transactions, and services in a continuous and persistent manner (Park & Kim, 2022).
- Innovative Internet services will be necessary for constantly adopting applications, platforms, and connections that would be completely based on standards—not necessarily open from the introduction, but that naturally will become more and more open—that can ensure the continuous integration of data, transactions, and services (Kim, 2021).
- Innovative formats, (aforementioned) standards, and protocols will be necessary to preserve privacy and security of the data that in any case will be at the basis of the hyperbolic operations, activities, and utilities that will be deployed in the metaverse, whatever platform or network of platforms may be interested (Di Pietro & Cresci, 2021).
- Innovative technologies, probably ever more miniaturized, will be necessary, to allow people/users/avatars to exist, operate, and interact in a hybrid reality, experiencing a life in which real world and virtual world continuously coexist (Nuncio & Felicilda, 2021).
- Innovative possibilities, ways, and models about business (from an economic point of view) will be necessary, exactly as will happen about information services, entertainment experiences, and social life, with the only limit that most probably will be represented by the invention, creativity, and fantasy of the users/avatars, who will explore, experience, and live new concepts of lifestyle, unpredictably combining their relationships together with technology and sociality (Trkman & Černe, 2021).

4.2.2 From Immersive Simulation to Emersive Experience: A Trans-conceptual Vision of the Metaverse

In general, and thus without specific reference to the business world, the new technological universe that most probably will arise in the near future will have significant applications for the development of the quality of life of people, for example in terms of accessibility to activities, services, and utilities (Duan et al., 2021). In fact, according to Meta Inc., i.e., the current and future evolution of Facebook, the «... metaverse is the next evolution of social connection» (Facebook.Com, 2021); in this perspective, social life and community building could be more inclusive and beneficial, providing this new environment with a hybrid place to exist in not only for what one can operate, but also for what one can live.

The metaverse, as a sort of integrated electronic ecosystem, will then be interoperable at digital and social level, because it is co-constructed by each user/consumer/citizen; naturally, this aspect is existing since the Web 2.0, ma it is evident that the potentialities of the UGC in the metaverse are almost without limit. The related experience 'emerges', and in this respect 'emersive' seems the most appropriate characteristic of the metaverse, as a kind of amplified life, or better still a hyper-life (and not only a hyper-reality, by virtue of its hybrid nature), and the meaning of concepts such as liquidity, life-logging, and ubiquity (Jacquemard et al., 2014) could acquire a different, powerful, and enlarged sense, continuously providing, amplifying, and innovating experiential interconnected activities.

In truth, the reasoning about the combination between real and digital is not completely new, also at business level: the diffusion of the Internet, of the mobile Internet, and of the social networks has induced many scholars to reflect upon the transition from 'off-line' to 'on-line' to 'on-life', and this dimension (on-life), firstly coined by Floridi (2015), seems an intriguing starting point for envisioning the trans-conceptual sense of metaverse. In this respect, it could be possible that these innovative digital environments could represent a tremendously innovative evolution of Baudrillard's vision about hyperreality (1983), remaining exposed to

4 Engineering the Metaverse for Innovating the Electronic...

manipulation from a negative point of view, but providing capacity to manipulation from a positive point of view, implementing a sort of continuous lifelong login.

Moreover, some scholars conceive the metaverse as a kind of embodied Internet, probably to emphasize how deep, engaging, and potential the related hybrid life could be, but also to highlight the wearable digital devices that will be necessary, like the aforementioned gloves and glasses. After wearing the appropriate technology, which today could still seem a sort of obstacle, but which evidently in the near future will be more and more accessible (as happened for laptops, tablets, smartphones, and so on), the user/avatar is able to experience login, immersion, persistence, ubiquity, and life-logging, elevating the aforementioned on-life to hyper-life (cf. Fig. 4.1), co-constructing and co-participating, amplifying the experience of the metaverse in all the possible contexts that could emerge at digital, social, and human level, thus providing a trans-conceptual vision.

In fact, it is to highlight that in the aforementioned novel "Player One" (2011), Ernest Cline presents a virtual reality entertainment universe called 'OASIS', an acronym for Ontologically Anthropocentric Sensory Immersive Simulation; from a computer science point of view, the metaverse could be defined most probably as something similar, but always

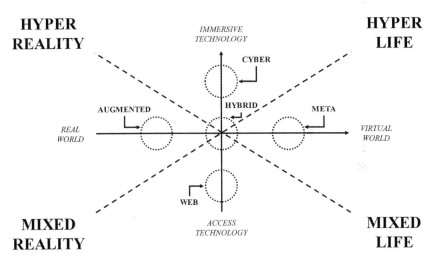

Fig. 4.1 A trans-conceptual vision of the metaverse (Author's elaboration)

considering that the metaverse by its own nature is beyond everything that exists today (*meta*). In this respect, the concept of immersion, which is already so profound, also in technological terms (e.g., virtual community, virtual reality, augmented reality, and so on) could also be evolved in an innovative dimension, i.e., 'emersion', with 'emersive' that could represent a sort of post-immersive conception (Bernard & Andrieu, 2014; Engeln et al., 2018; Keck et al., 2014; Midol et al., 2017; Ramos & Dunne-Howrie, 2020; Wijers, 2018).

According to a technological progress, even though only hypothetically, the real world should 'evolve' more and more towards a virtual world (as happened for example to many commercial activities, like bookstores, travel agent's, financial services, and so on), naturally leveraging on access technologies (what is possible even today when logging in) and on immersive technologies (what will be possible only tomorrow when life-logging). From this vision, which is represented in Fig. 4.1 by the two conceptual axes, the mixed reality that is possible even today (e.g., virtual payments in physical stores to buy physical products) can evolve towards mixed life from a social perspective (e.g., the personal branding that a person may increase on social networks) and towards hyperreality from a technological perspective (e.g., virtual payments in virtual stores to buy physical and/or virtual products); at the same time, the hyperreality can evolve towards hyperlife from a social perspective (e.g., the experience of hosting avatars in a virtual house to show a Non-Fungible Token—NFT artwork).

4.3 Methods

As previously highlighted, the novelty of the topic has suggested to adopt for the current study a narrative approach with exploratory intention, mostly pursuing an abductive inquiry (Kosterec, 2016). More specifically, after the examination of the most accredited business experiences about the metaverse, thus adopting a sort of grounded investigation, the research has then developed a conceptual tool, namely a SWOT analysis, to provide a general overview about the potential applications of the metaverse, which have been then discussed.

4.4 The Grounded Investigation: Relevant Business Experiences in the Field (Past, Current, and Future)

As continuously highlighted above, the term 'metaverse' is often abused to refer to various virtual reality worlds; however, some corporate experiments, although related to a very early stage of a 'real' metaverse, have already been started, even though the success of the term, as aforementioned, is mainly due to the announcement in 2021 by Mark Zuckerberg with reference to the future evolution of the Facebook platform, symbolically and operatively expressed by the launch of Meta Inc.

As regards more specifically digital 3D virtual environments, which most probably have been the first ecosystems for which innovative technological possibilities have been developed, it is possible to mention several business cases. Some of these are accessible even using well-known—and above all, already available—computer interfaces.

According to a chronological point of view, for example, an embryonic form of 'mirror world', which already mixes real and virtual dimensions, is Google Earth, launched in 2001, which today is a kind of virtual representation of the planet that combines real (historical) data and virtual information, loading them altogether in real time (Earth.Google.Com). Most probably, however, the first application of the concept of 'metaverse', with main reference to virtual reality experiences in videogames and similar, is Second Life, launched in 2003, with apparent enormous potentiality at the beginning, but with minor success in the progress of times (SecondLife.Com).

Subsequently, other brands related to the field of virtual reality and augmented reality videogames have developed further similar experiences, integrating innovative or at least new functionalities; some examples in this respect are "Roblox" and "Garry's Mod" (launched in 2006), "Minecraft" (2011), "Grand Theft Auto V" (2013), "Pokémon Go" (2016), "Fortnite" (2017), "Super Mario Maker 2" (2019), and "Animal Crossing: New Horizons" (2020). These videogames environments show the effort that companies such as Epic Games, Niantic, Nintendo, Nvidia, and Sony (among many others) have been generating to create more and more engaging gaming experiences.

In fact, each of the abovementioned videogames has some specific traits: some allow the players to create their own levels using the resources available on the platform and, if desired, they can also publish them for other users to play (i.e., "Super Mario Maker 2"); others are based on geolocated augmented reality with GPS (Global Positioning System) (i.e., "Pokémon Go"); others can adapt the experienced context, for instance, to the seasons of the northern and/or southern hemispheres by virtue of the current location of the player (i.e., "Animal Crossing: New Horizons"). More in general, many of them allow the players to customise the appearance of their own characters (avatars) to choose peculiar characteristics (i.e., facial features, clothes, hairstyles, and so on), and sometimes it is also possible to generate some kind of holographic portrait, thus permitting a sort of mix between real (or desired) life and the consequently projected virtual experience.

A very peculiar element to further consider is that some of the abovementioned videogames support local and on-line cooperative play, have open interfaces (with features accessible to both professional creators and users with no experience in programming and computer graphic design, like for example the functions enabling to create worlds in "Fortnite" using the "Unreal" engine), have been engineered as cross-platforms, and are capable to host live events such as concerts (i.e., singers like Ariana Grande or musicians like Marshmello in "Fortnite"). Very importantly, almost all of these games have adopted currencies (also cryptocurrencies, using the blockchain) that can be used while playing (often to buy premium items) that correspond to real money purchases outside the game (i.e., "Miglia Nook" in "Animal Crossing: New Horizons", "V-buck" in "Fortnite", and so on); more particularly, in "Grand Theft Auto V" (GTA V) the characters have their own smartphones that can be used to contact friends, to access the Internet (e.g., to read their emails or even to buy vehicles), and to enter a specific social network called "LifeInvader".

Naturally, several companies and not only those associated with the gaming industry have been trying to experiment and develop immersive (virtual, augmented, or hybrid) experiences to explore the potential applications of the metaverse for their business. However, considering the great

4 Engineering the Metaverse for Innovating the Electronic... 77

Table 4.1 Some business experiences in the metaverse (Authors' elaboration)

Gaming industry	Non-gaming industry
• Roblox (Roblox)	• Google Earth
• Garry's Mod (Facepunch)	• Second Life
• Minecraft (Mojang)	• IBM
• Grand Theft Auto V (Rockstar North)	• Siemens
• Pokémon Go (Niantic)	• Implenia
• Fortnite (Epic Games)	• Ericsson
• Super Mario Maker 2 (Nintendo)	• Nike
• Animal Crossing: New Horizons (Nintendo)	• Hyundai
• (Nvidia)	• Adidas
• (Sony)	• Vans
	• Gucci
	• Microsoft
	• Facebook (Meta)

impact of the metaverse in the gaming industry, which will also emerge as a strength in the following SWOT analysis, it seems useful to provide (cf. Table 4.1) a list of some entrepreneurial experiences in the world of metaverse, distinguishing between gaming and non-gaming industries.

According to the chronological order that has been reported in Table 4.1, in 2007 IBM developed private collaboration spaces in Second Life, demonstrating a tremendous potential in connecting workers and employees, and allowing their interactions from anywhere in the world; more specifically, IBM has collaborated with Second Life to explore a journey between two different virtual worlds, realizing the first virtual teleportation, in which an avatar from a Second Life test world was transported to a virtual world managed by IBM; in this respect, "Big Blue" seems to appear as the first (or undoubtedly one of the earliest) major companies to create formal guidelines (i.e., a virtual world policy of conduct) to regulate virtual worlds.

In 2008, Siemens, in partnership with the University of Cincinnati, explored potential digital twins, investigating more specifically how to turn real environments, platforms, and models into 3D representations, to enable real-time customer feedbacks that could be 'really' generated in a 'virtual' dimension. In the same year, Implenia (a Swiss building service provider) developed an interconnection between a real object and its virtual counterpart, as a sort of amplified smart-home model, to control doors, lights, and other elements of a real-world dollhouse through interactions with its virtual version.

To provide more updated, advanced, and applicable examples, in 2021 Ericsson has created virtual versions of cities (building digital twins using Omniverse) to figure out how to best implement its 5G networks, and large companies in the world like Nike, Hyundai, Adidas, Vans, Gucci, and many others have implemented actions to be prepared for the future of the metaverse, trying to experiment with virtual environments (also, but not only, in a gaming perspective), testing hybrid experiences, and paying attention to NFTs. More in general, nowadays the term 'metaverse' has begun to be more widespread and used both by the media and in the business world, with several companies announcing investments and projects related to this new technological dimension.

For example, Microsoft is working on the development of the metaverse; after the "Windows Mixed Reality" (formerly "Windows Holographic") platform, they announced "Mesh for Teams", designed to enable "… presence and shared experiences from anywhere—on any device—through mixed reality applications" (Microsoft.Com > Mesh). Furthermore, platforms like Decentraland (for the selling and the buying of plots of land) and Cryptovoxels (based on and powered by the Ethereum blockchain to buy plots of land, open stores, and create art galleries) have been conceived, engineered, and launched, with tremendous expectations (naturally, to be verified at the test of time).

However, 2021 is 'the' year of the metaverse most of all because the name of Facebook Inc. has been changed to Meta Inc., to underline the intent to invest in the development of the metaverse. Zuckerberg has already launched the "Horizon Workroom", which is a platform for smart working in virtual reality, the "Oculus Quest 2", which is an innovative virtual reality viewer, and many collaboration projects to improve the applications of virtual, augmented, and immersive technologies in various fields (hoping for ever more 'emersive' functionalities).

In 2021, moreover, news related to the development of the metaverse arrived not only from private companies, but also from public authorities. For example, the Seoul Metropolitan Government announced the launch of a digital platform with the aim of creating a metaverse ecosystem for accessing in traditional and innovative modalities some of the activities, services, and utilities that regard all the areas of its municipal administration (English.Seoul.Go.Kr).

4.5 The Conceptual Development: A SWOT Analysis for the Governance and the Management of the Metaverse

On the basis of the above reasoning, it is possible to delineate a potential framework, from a qualitative point of view, with the intention of understanding the main characteristics of the metaverse as an innovative business opportunity. In this respect, a SWOT analysis (cf. Table 4.2) seems the most suitable tool to elaborate.

All the elements that have been reported in Table 4.2 have been object of analysis in the previous considerations, and thus it seems not necessary to describe them with further details. However, some reflections seem opportune with specific reference to the potential threats.

In fact, the digital divide is currently a serious problem, because great part of the global population has relevant obstacles in accessing today the cyberspace, which is naturally less heavy of what could emerge in the metaverse; the risk in this direction is that marginalized economies of the

Table 4.2 Tentative SWOT analysis about metaverse as business opportunity (Authors' elaboration)

Strengths	Weaknesses
• Interoperability	• Necessity for improved technology
• GUI (Graphic User Interface) as never before	• Absence of definitions and standards
• Experience as never before	• Security and privacy issues
• Previous experience in the gaming industry	• Risk of social alienation
• Hyperbolic (infinite) applications	• Suspect about manipulation (dystopia)
• Mixed/Hybrid/On-Life convergence	• Suspect about the 'new old thing'
Opportunities	**Threats**
• Availability of some sufficient technology (devices, storages, connections, and so on)	• Current digital divide
	• Cybersecurity
• Availability of some innovative technology (IoT, AI, blockchain, and so on)	• Suspects about potential future standards
	• Probable shortage of competence of the users (in terms of data protection and in terms of business development)
• New (infinite) opportunities of business	

world could be even more marginalized with respect to the future technology, and thus national and most of all international interventions in this respect are fundamental. At the same time, paradoxically but evidently, the regions that are more developed from a technological point of view, and that most probably will firstly access the metaverse, are daily under the attack of cyber-criminals, and an innovative digital ecosystem like the metaverse will be undoubtedly more exposed to major offense, also because there is no certainty about potential future technological standards; thus, most probably the metaverse will have to proceed altogether with the improvement of digital security, even though it is to consider that the very early users could be attracted by the fascination of the metaverse, decreasing their psychological levels of attention.

Accordingly, there is a high probability that those users, from a personal and professional point of view, will be not ready to carefully manage the protection of the data and the development of the business, thus provoking some failures at individual and/or corporate level, as in truth always happens with an innovative technology, but with the risk of amplifying the perception of the above-reported weaknesses. However, it is always to remember that every innovation, at social, technological, and economic level, presents some risks and costs, which in truth, from an overall evaluation of the above SWOT analysis, seem potentially minor, also because these risks already exist, while the potential benefits of the metaverse and related advantages are yet to come.

4.6 Findings' Discussion about Potential Business Applications of the Metaverse

Several scholars have investigated about the opportunities of the development that could affect metaverse in many different fields, from commerce and retailers to arts and museum experiences (Hazan, 2008), human interactions such as team collaboration (van der Land et al., 2011), education (Collins, 2008), and so on. Most of all, as above analysed, many companies have already started experimenting the metaverse from a business point of view, mainly exploring the commercial potential that could offer, but in truth it is evident that all the activities of the value chain can be involved by the metaverse representation, both at internal and (above all) at external level, 'metaversing' the digital enterprise inside (Business Process Management, Business Process Reengineering, Enterprise Resource Planning also as industrial evolution first of Material Requirement Planning and then of Manufacturing Resource Planning) and outside (Supply Chain Management, Customer Relationship Management, and Enterprise Relationship Management), implementing and somehow overcoming the holistic change conceptually deriving from digital transformation (Kokuytseva et al., 2022); moreover, all social and economic sectors may be affected by the metaverse, with consequent impact on their change, evolution, or even revolution.

In fact, in addition to accessibility, inclusiveness, and sociability, the metaverse represents a tremendous opportunity for the business world, at theoretical (scientific possibilities of conception with metaverse) and practical (managerial opportunities of innovation with metaverse) level. Most probably, the characterising element in this respect will be represented by the 'emersive' nature of the metaverse, which will influence the subsequent 'emersive' propension of business models, methodologies, and solutions.

For example, only to cite the potential application that could emerge about the marketing mix, as concerns the product management, new ideas could be developed starting from consumer data and feedbacks that can be collected in real-time, during the tests in which the users/avatars are experiencing the product (in the form of concept tests, or product tests, or even market tests); furthermore, new products could be conceived at digital level, like NFTs, which already exist today, but which will enormously benefit in the metaverse. As concerns the price management, new pricing strategies, tactics, and operations could be conceived combining real and virtual worlds in continuous interaction (to test and/or to promote offerings).

As concerns the communication management, the promotion could be much more personalized, using Big Data that have never been generated before, and/or in modalities that have never been conceived before, advertising offerings via synesthetic messages, and promising an explosion of experiential marketing (Cuomo et al., 2021a, 2021b); in this respect, it is also to consider the tremendous opportunities that could emerge, according to an 'emersive' perspective, combining metaverse with neuromarketing (they both need specific electronic devices, which maybe in the future—or even today?—can be integrated in the same viewer, capable of being altogether an eye reader and an eye tracker). At last, as concerns the distribution management, still today the most relevant business examples of metaverse, as aforementioned, regard commercial environments, at least from a structural point of view, providing innovative e-commerce, mixing retailing points-of-sales at physical and digital level (but going extremely beyond the clicks and mortar dimension: Christoforou & Melanthiou, 2019), activating smarter payments with cryptocurrencies, and so on; but also from a systemic point of view, it can be mentioned that maybe, in the metaverse there will be experiences that cannot be experienced only virtually, for example, the wine tasting, but being the metaverse also mixed or hybrid, it will be possible to combine innovative uses, for example smart tasting with and in the metaverse, living totally amplified sensory experiences.

4.7 Conclusion

Although there are still some voices that seem reluctant to accept the idea of metaverse, not considering it as a 'real' innovation, mainly because nowadays it is difficult to understand precisely and in advance the future technological experiences and developments that may derive, it is to highlight that the metaverse could have limit only in terms of invention, creativity, or even fantasy, also from a business point of view. Undoubtedly, there are still many technical impediments to the large adoption and vast diffusion of the metaverse, but it is evident that its underlying idea, whatever the possible technological solutions may be at the end, is powerful and physiologically intended to succeed, since it is based on an innovative universe where people/users/avatars may benefit activities, services, and utilities exploiting the continuous evolution of technology, so benefiting access in real time, even at the same time, of any person in the world, with a contextual sense of continuity.

In this respect, the metaverse requires exceptional technical advancements and a lot of standard formats, protocols, and platforms, hopefully more and more open, because a holistic approach of communication seems almost inevitable, like in the case of the Internet protocols, for example, even though until now the big companies that have started as first movers some business experiments about the metaverse are understandably not oriented in this direction. There are also many fears about the metaverse, impacting most of all privacy and security issues, but also other uncertainties—for example, the potential digital divide that could regard the users—are under investigation, concerning also psychological, social, and human issues, since visionary universes like the metaverse have often been presented in dystopian science fiction books, amplifying an unrealistic and worrying perception of such technological evolutions.

However, the great majority of scholars, experts, and professionals consider since today the metaverse as a potential epochal transformation and emerging technologies (5G, IoT, cloud, Big Data, AI, blockchain, augmented reality, virtual reality, and so on) suggest that a very early stage of the metaverse—a sort of «... digital "big bang" of our cyberspace» (Lee et al., 2021)—could be not so far away in the future. Business operators, whatever role they could act, are then inevitably forced to get prepared, to govern this technological revolution on the point of starting, avoiding the very concrete risk of remaining floored for having disregarded to act ambidextrously—i.e., exploring the technology and exploiting the technology—when there still was the possibility (that is, today).

In line with these considerations, this study could provide a double contribution. First, as concerns the trans-conceptual vision that has been adopted to imagine—and potentially engineer—a metaverse experience in terms of hybrid reality; and second, as concerns the SWOT analysis focusing on the current and future issues that could be related to the incoming diffusion of the metaverse, having in mind a business-oriented application, but moving more in general from a socio-technological perspective.

References

Ball, M. (2021, June 29). Framework for the Metaverse. *MatthewBallVC*, https://www.matthewball.vc/all/forwardtothemetaverseprimer.
Baudrillard, J. (1983). *Simulations*. Semiotext (e).

Bernard, A., & Andrieu, B. (2014). *Manifeste des arts immersifs*. PUN – Editions Universitaires de Lorraine.

Carmigniani, J., & Furht, B. (2011). Augmented Reality: An Overview. In B. Furht (Ed.), *Handbook of Augmented Reality* (pp. 3–46). Springer.

Christoforou, T., & Melanthiou, Y. (2019). The Practicable Aspect of the Omni-Channel Retailing Strategy and Its Impact on Customer Loyalty. In A. Thrassou, D. Vrontis, Y. Weber, S. M. R. Shams, & E. Tsoukatos (Eds.), *The Synergy of Business Theory and Practice* (pp. 239–260). Palgrave Macmillan.

Collins, C. (2008). Looking to the Future: Higher Education in the Metaverse. *Educause Review, 43*(5), 1–8.

Cuomo, M. T., Colosimo, I., Ricciardi Celsi, L., Ferulano, R., Festa, G., & La Rocca, M. (2021a). Enhancing Traveller Experience in Integrated Mobility Services via Big Social Data Analytics. *Technological Forecasting and Social Change, 176*(2022), 1–7.

Cuomo, M. T., Tortora, D., Foroudi, E., Giordano, A., Festa, G., & Metallo, G. (2021b). Digital Transformation and Tourist Experience Co-Design: Big Social Data for Planning Cultural Tourism. *Technological Forecasting and Social Change, 162*(2021), 1–9.

Damar, M. (2021). Metaverse Shape of Your Life for Future: A Bibliometric Snapshot. *Journal of Metaverse, 1*(1), 1–8.

Di Pietro, R., & Cresci, S. (2021, December 12–15). Metaverse: Security and Privacy Issues. *Proceedings of the Third IEEE International Conference on Trust, Privacy and Security in Intelligent Systems, and Applications*, Virtual Event, University of Pittsburgh, PA, USA.

Duan, H., Li, J., Fan, S., Lin, Z., Wu, X., & Cai, W. (2021, October 20–24). Metaverse for Social Good: A University Campus Prototype. *MM '21: Proceedings of the 29th ACM International Conference on Multimedia*, Virtual Event China.

Engeln, L., Hube, N., & Groh, R. (2018). Immersive Visual Audio Design: Spectral Editing in VR. *AM'18: Proceedings of the Audio Mostly 2018 on Sound in Immersion and Emotion*, Article No. 38, pp. 1–4, https://doi.org/10.1145/3243274.3243279.

Floridi, L. (2015). *The Onlife Manifesto: Being Human in a Hyperconnected Era*. Springer.

Fuller, A., Fan, Z., Day, C., & Barlow, C. (2020). Digital Twin: Enabling Technologies, Challenges and Open Research. *IEEE Access, 8*(2020), 108952–108971.

Hazan, S. (2008, September 15–18). Musing the Metaverse. *Annual Conference of CIDOC*, Athens, Greece.

Jacquemard, T., Novitzky, P., O'Brolcháin, F., Smeaton, A. F., & Gordijn, B. (2014). Challenges and Opportunities of Lifelog Technologies: A Literature Review and Critical Analysis. *Science and Engineering Ethics, 20*(2014), 379–409.

Keck, M., Lapczyna, E., & Groh, R. (2014). Revisiting Graspable User Interfaces. In A. Marcus (Ed.), *Design, User Experience, and Usability. Theories, Methods, and Tools for Designing the User Experience. DUXU 2014. Lecture Notes in Computer Science* (Vol. 8517, pp. 130–141). Springer.

Kim, J. (2021). Advertising in the Metaverse: Research Agenda. *Journal of Interactive Advertising, 21*(3), 141–144.

Kokuytseva, T. V., Ovchinnikova, O. P., & Kharlamov, M. M. (2022). Approaches to the Digital Transformation of High-Tech Companies in Russia Under the Crisis: Problems and New Opportunities. In D. Vrontis, A. Thrassou, Y. Weber, S. M. R. Shams, E. Tsoukatos, & L. Efthymiou (Eds.), *Business Under Crisis - Volume II* (pp. 161–184). Palgrave Macmillan.

Kosterec, M. (2016). Methods Of Conceptual Analysis. *Filozofia, 71*(3), 220–230.

Lee, L.-H., Braud, T., Zhou, P., Wang, L., Xu, D., Lin, Z., Kumar, A., Bermejo, C., & Hui, P. (2021). All One Needs to Know about Metaverse: A Complete Survey on Technological Singularity, Virtual Ecosystem, and Research Agenda. *Journal of Latex Class Files, 14*(8), 1–66.

Lombardi, J., & Lombardi, M. (2010). Opening the Metaverse. In W. Bainbridge (Ed.), *Online Worlds: Convergence of the Real and the Virtual (Human-Computer Interaction Series)*. Springer.

Midol, N., Chenault, M., & McEwen, L. (2017). Introduction to Consciousness-based Practices. *Staps, 117–118*(3–4), 5–21.

Nuncio, R. V., & Felicilda, J. M. B. (2021). Cybernetics and Simulacra: The Hyperreality of Augmented Reality Games. *Kritike, 15*(2), 39–67.

Ondrejka, C. (2005). Escaping the Gilded Cage: User Created Content and Building the Metaverse. *NYLS Law Review, 49*(1) Article No. 6, 1–23.

Park, S.-M., & Kim, Y.-G. (2022). A Metaverse: Taxonomy, Components, Applications, and Open Challenges. *IEEE Access, 10*(2022), 4209–4251.

Ramos, J. L., & Dunne-Howrie, J. (2020). The post-immersive manifesto. *International Journal of Performance Arts and Digital Media, 16*(2), 196–212.

Ricci, A., Piunti, M., Tummolini, L., & Castelfranchi, C. (2015). The Mirror World: Preparing for Mixed-Reality Living. *IEEE Pervasive Computing, 14*(2015), 60–63.

Shams, S. M. R. (2019). Industry and Managerial Applications of Internet Marketing Research. In A. Thrassou, D. Vrontis, Y. Weber, S. M. R. Shams, & E. Tsoukatos (Eds.), *The Synergy of Business Theory and Practice* (pp. 161–184). Palgrave Macmillan.

Smart, J., Cascio, J., & Paffendorf, J. (2007). Metaverse Roadmap. Pathways to the 3D Web. A Cross-Industry Public Foresight Project. https://www.metaverseroadmap.org/MetaverseRoadmapOverview.pdf (pp. 1–28).

Stephenson, N. (1992). *Snow Crash*. Bantam.

Trkman, P., & Černe, M. (2021). Humanising Digital Life: Reducing Emissions While Enhancing Value-Adding Human Processes. *International Journal of Information Management.*, ahead-of-print (ahead-of-print), 1–4. https://doi.org/10.1016/j.ijinfomgt.2021.102443

van der Land, S., Schouten, A. P., van der Hoof, B., & Feldberg, F. (2011). Modeling the Metaverse: A Theoretical Model of Effective Team Collaboration in 3D Virtual Environments. *Journal of Virtual Worlds Research, 4*(3), 1–16.

Wijers, E. (2018). Emersive Storytelling: An Exploration of Animation and the Fourth Wall as a Tool for Critical Thinking. *Animation Practice, Process & Production, 7*(1), 41–65.

5

The Changing Technology Use and its Impact on Leadership and Hierarchy Structure in the Virtual Workplace

Arkadiusz Mironko, Rosemary M. Muirungi, and Anthony J. Scardino

5.1 Introduction

How can teams perform well in the technology-driven virtual work environment? Early studies indicate that organizational structures in the virtual world are getting flattened (Lee, 2021a, 2021b). Flat corporate structures develop more functional teams (Yu et al., 2019); they also reduce layered and cumbersome decision making. According to Greer as

A. Mironko (✉)
Management and Entrepreneurship, Indiana University East, Richmond, IN, USA
e-mail: amironko@iu.edu

R. M. Muirungi
Gonzaga University, Spokane, WA, USA
e-mail: muriungi@gonzaga.edu

A. J. Scardino
Felician University, Rutherford, NJ, USA
e-mail: scardinoa@felician.edu

© The Author(s), under exclusive license to Springer Nature Switzerland AG 2022
A. Thrassou et al. (eds.), *Business Advancement through Technology Volume II*, Palgrave Studies in Cross-disciplinary Business Research, In Association with EuroMed Academy of Business, https://doi.org/10.1007/978-3-031-07765-4_5

found in the article by Walsh (2017), egalitarian teams were more focused on the group because they felt like "we're in the same boat, we have a common fate" (p. 2). It elevates the employees' level of responsibility in the organisation. It has the potential to remove excess layers of management and improves the coordination and speed of communication between employees. There may be fewer levels of management encouraging an easier decision-making process among employees.

In the face of tumultuous and changing virtual times, such as the COVID-19 pandemic, a decision to strategically posture incremental and radical innovations requires a dramatic departure from the status quo. Many organisations are shifting to restructuring their modus operandi to allow for an easier flow of communication and efficiency. Given a myriad of obstacles thwarting a budding entrepreneur's idea generation and exploitation in large, unwieldy structures, emphasis justifiably rests with encouraging and nurturing opportunity-seeking behaviors (Dess et al., 1999). As well, increased global competition, the influence of technology, and the immediate access to global resources have driven massive changes in the way companies develop products, search for talent, and engage customers (Anandarajan et al., 2006) and this includes virtual connections.

In a flat organizational structure, the manager has more responsibility as the number of people directly supervised is significant and people at lower levels rely on him/her/them for support, guidance, help, and direction. This type of structure is created to empower employees so that they can take independent decisions. A prevalent thought is that a flat structure is best for small and start-up organizations as it is designed to minimize bureaucracy. The fact that this worked at times within the parameters of smaller firms and start-ups, there is an opportunity for stronger research that can be expanded to traditional companies and organizations. With a flat structure, there is a risk for generalization and confusion if the company fails to hone and specifically direct team goals and talents. Organizations with a flat structure find success when they allow specialists to pursue passion projects that serve the organization with team support. That means dividing up into smaller units.

There are many reasons for the implementation of a flat corporate structure as proposed above. Nonetheless, within the context of this

5 The Changing Technology Use and its Impact on Leadership... 89

chapter, we will focus on two primarily, as they seem intricately connected to the virtual world. The first is "clear and direct communication." There is no mid-level management, and this ensures direct contact between the top and lower levels. This is a bonus for the company because when information passes through several layers, the chances of misuse or distorted information is high. In a flat organizational structure, this is not the case, and hence the flow of information is clear and precise with little chance of miscommunication. The second reason closely reviewed is that a flat corporate structure "encourages collaboration". In a flat organizational structure, the employees belong to the same playing field, hence the potential for real collaboration in the virtual world can prove to be advantageous.

One of the disadvantages of such an implementation is the creation of power struggles in a flat organizational structure since employees are empowered to make independent decisions. A clear disadvantage is too much autonomy and no concept of leadership in place, therefore, making it challenging for employees to step up due to the leadership gap. Many employees may not have a direct boss (leader) to report to, which may cause confusion and a struggle for power due to dearth of proper clarifications and role confusion in the flat organizational structure. As well, employees must undertake several responsibilities at a single time, and this creates difficulty in their minds about their actual role and accountability in the company. Further, given a flat organizational structure with potentially overlapping and ill-defined organizational role boundaries, personal (Tierney & Farmer, 2002; Wood & Bandura, 1989) and relational factors (Dienesch & Liden, 1986; Liden & Maslyn, 1998), the role of the leader seems to be more important than ever.

The era of COViD-19 has shown the possibilities that abound for businesses to shift work from operating in brick-and-mortar facilities to a virtual landscape. While the concept of telecommuting had been around for years (Contreras et al., 2020), most businesses offered this as an alternative working method that was utilized only in specific contexts and by certain categories of workers (Guyot & Sawhill, 2020). Come 2020 and the Coronavirus pandemic forced most businesses and their workers to move the workplace to their homes by capitalizing on technological advances (Towler, 2020) that made it possible to work remotely

(Emond & Maese, 2020; Guyot & Sawhill, 2020). In this chapter, we explore how leadership plays out in an evolving workplace. In subsequent sections we examine the existing literature and its direction, then briefly analyze our findings, and offer conclusions. The structure of this chapter will allow for the reader to best understand transformative leadership in a new paradigm shift within an organization's structure and levels of autonomy that enhance a virtual workplace.

5.2 Existing Literature and Research Direction

Some studies suggest that ameliorating time constraints for creative thinking impacts individuals beyond their time within the organization itself; a finding which is crucial to practical efforts seeking the development of an entrepreneurial edge, particularly as technological diffusion becomes more central to global competitive industry change (Bettis & Hitt, 1995). Creativity is a process, often lengthy and somewhat chaotic, that requires focused and thoughtful rumination for the fruition of product or technology (Brazeal et al., 2014).

Flatter organizations offer a new set of management actions, more teamwork, less bureaucracy, better communications, opportunities for professional development, and greater job satisfaction. The effectiveness of this change critically depends on the attitudes and perceptions of the people working in flatter organizations (Powell, 2002). These findings from the exploratory survey reinforce the views (Powell, 2002) that flatter structures, often empowered using technology tools, may well promote the image of empowerment at the expense of the actual practice of empowerment.

The studies of virtual teams from a few decades back focus on business efficiencies, leveraging remote workforce for purposes of outsourcing, downsizing, and using the remote skilled workforce to promote innovation (Chesbrough & Teece, 1998; Teece, 2018). The early studies of virtual teams in the COVID-19 era find that virtual events, such as conferences, are far more convenient, and deliver a high-quality

5 The Changing Technology Use and its Impact on Leadership... 91

conference experience that is often more egalitarian, equitable, and diverse than in-person conferences (Price, 2020). Also, virtual work from home becomes less costly, more environmentally friendly, and sets a stage for more egalitarian organizational structures (Lee, 2021a, 2021b). These and other studies take into the account the efficiencies driven by the technological tools available (Grewal et al., 2020)

Although technology offers many benefits for both automation of manufacturing and office related tasks as well as capability to imitate, at least to some extent, face to face interaction, collaboration, and communication, it does not eliminate the need for being in the same room or building. In the same way as "death of distance" of the 1980s did not eliminate the need for person-to-person communication and travel (Florida et al., 2021). Available technologies, although they cannot completely replace the need for in-person presence at work (Nohria & Eccles, 2000), they can certainly augment the way employees and leaders perform their jobs (Oudshoorn, 2008).

To be effective in the long-term, global virtual teams need to maintain a high level of aspiration towards common goals. Aspiration creates the highest levels of engagement, it is what separates the best leaders from everyone else, and it is what employees want most in their leaders. Bain & Company's research by Horwitch and Callahan (2016) identified 33 distinct and tangible attributes that are statistically significant in creating inspiration in others. Empowerment, vision, and direction are a few of those elements that drive the performance of teams and offer an opportunity to reflect on one's work and impact (Horwitch and Callahan, 2016); Mironko, 2019), which is an important part of one's performance.

Virtual teams use information technology to enable member interaction (Maduka et al., 2018; Martins et al., 2004). Virtual leadership refers to "a social influence process mediated by AIT (advanced information technology) to produce a change in attitudes, feelings, thinking, behavior, and/or performance with individuals, groups, and/or organizations" (DasGupta, 2011). Leading virtual teams necessitates a combination of leadership styles, competencies, and characteristics that assure effective tele-working (Maduka et al., 2018). According to Purvanova & Kenda (2018), "virtual leadership differs from traditional leadership in how virtual leaders go about achieving results" (p. 3). The business environment propelled ever faster by new technologies enables virtual teams and leaders to be more responsive to the rising speed in decision-making and responsiveness. Specifically, technological innovations in telecommunication, data transfer, design, production, often prove important under the conditions of Volatility, Uncertainty, Complexity, and Ambiguity (VUCA). The VUCA framework allows leaders and teams to anticipate and prepare solutions where they do not have sufficient information to make decisions, such as in a developing crisis or unexpected scenario which many virtual teams and their leaders face (Mironko et al., 2021; Vrontis et al., 2022).

Some of the leadership styles that are applicable to virtual teams include transformational (Bass & Riggio, 2008; Purvanova & Bono, 2009), collaborative (Archer & Cameron, 2009; Kramer & Crespy, 2011), empowering (Hill & Bartol, 2016; Lorinkova et al., 2013) and adaptive (Nelson & Squires, 2017). Transformational leaders value their team members and motivate them to be their best selves (Bass & Riggio, 2008). Virtual teams adapt the characteristics of transformational leadership such as self-management, strong vision, and facing challenges (Molina, 2020). Collaborative leadership embraces everyone's input and fosters quick problem resolution (Kelly, 2020; Kramer & Crespy, 2011). Empowering leadership encourages employees to engage in decision-making and power-sharing (Lorinkova et al., 2013). Adaptive leadership is suited to complex situations where finding solutions that are multi-faceted and collaborative is crucial (Nelson & Squires, 2017).

Organizations that are versatile continually scan their operating environments and adjust accordingly. The COVID-19 health pandemic demonstrated how leading in moments of crisis and disruptive change is an ever-evolving phenomenon. While the initial projections were that the pandemic would be short-lived, the health crisis has proved to be a protracted affair (Webster, 2021) with far reaching socio-economic implications (Bashir & Shahzd, 2020; Kaiser, 2020). With constantly emerging variants such as Delta and Omicron (Webster, 2021), the world might as well prepare for the reality of COVID-19 being the norm in the foreseeable future (Bidmead & Marshall, 2020; Bloom, 2022a). Within the organizational context, exploring models of leadership that keep pace

5 The Changing Technology Use and its Impact on Leadership...

with complex business environments (Kaiser, 2020; Pavlica et al., 2011) will aid in effectively dealing with the challenges those environments pose.

From a technology perspective, organizations overcame the challenges posed by COVID-19 on the workforce to lead in disruptive and complex environments (Bushe & Marshak, 2016; Hawryszkiewycz, 2021; Kaiser, 2020) by capitalizing on technology (Prasad et al., 2020). One of the most immediate changes in the workforce post-COVID-19 was the shift towards remote work (Bloom, 2022a; Galanti et al., 2021) as a means to minimizing physical contact between people in the workplace and managing the spread of the Coronavirus. By embracing technology that enabled a digital workspace (Sébastien et al., 2020), such as applications and software for video-calls (Zoom and so on), document sharing (Dropbox and others), and communication (Microsoft teams and so forth), many organizations continued their operations without a physical presence in offices. As a result, they were able to adapt a working from home culture (Wang, Liu, Qian, and Parker, 2020).

Versatility in organizations and how well they respond to disruption in their environment can be associated with versatile leadership which considers multiple alternatives and mindsets in managing crisis (Pavlica & Jarosová, 2014) The speed at which an organization responds to change can either make or break it (Kaiser, 2020; Katare et al., 2021) and is a key attribute of versatile leaders. Versatility in leadership also improves team dynamics in disruptive moments by way of increased adaptability, productivity, and effectiveness (Kaiser, 2020). To this end, several considerations come to mind in the transition to a fully or hybrid virtual work environment. Some of the questions organizational leaders need to consider include: What does access to technology involve (and imply) for different professions and occupational groups? What will the digital infrastructure look like? How will organizational performance be measured in the virtual workplace, especially in the areas of employee engagement and well-being, given the stress associated with the isolation experienced when working virtually? The post-pandemic work environment has evolved into what Bloom (2022b) refers to as the "three-tier workforce—fully-in-person (50%), hybrid (40%), and fully remote (10%). Depending on the industry and organization's mandate, decisions on what categories of employees should work under the three tiers—fully remote, hybrid, or fully in-person-need to be considered.

The foregoing implies that organizations require the knowledge and skills (Kaplan & Kaiser, 2003; Schröder, 2014) to compete effectively in the virtual landscape. By extension, a review of the competencies that are critical for versatile organizations and individuals (Sloan, 1994) in an increasingly complex and disruptive society, is worthy of consideration. Competencies such as building trust, team integration, effective communication, and an awareness of technological trends are crucial for virtual leadership (Contreras et al., 2020; Maduka et al., 2018). Personal characteristics that contribute to effective leadership of virtual teams include self-efficacy, hope, optimism, and resilience (Maduka et al., 2018). Communication effectiveness is a key attribute of leadership and is measured by the speed messages are transmitted, clarity, and efficiency of communication, and is a predictor of leader performance (Neufeld et al., 2010). Acknowledging that you cannot just take what works with "in-person" interactions and have everyone do that makes you pay closer attention to the specific requirements and challenges of virtual teams.

Leaders as an "Agent of Change" have evolved to what has become an "Agent of Connection". (Zofi, 2012). Leadership in the virtual workplace has reflected the paradigm shift that has occurred, bringing a new order of business relationships and a new definition for the role of the leader. The very nature of a dispersed team means that virtual leaders can no longer successfully manage through command-and-control techniques (Zofi, 2012). Leadership takes confidence in their team and should have tenacity to integrate people, despite time and space constraints. Team members may be out of sight, but they cannot be out of mind (Zofi, 2012).

Building leadership capability is a keystone of the art of change leadership. Organizations that focus on educating and building leadership skills as a consistent focus, not only set vision for change, but also execute it because of the focus on developing their leaders' and teams' skill sets (Cran, 2015).

We reviewed the studies identifying the technological impact on the changing leadership role and changing hierarchical structures in the virtual work environments. The studies reviewed offered intriguing insights into how advanced technology offers new opportunities for large and established organizations, while at the same time curtailing advancement opportunities for those in lower ranks, at the start-up stage/early careers or are small in size.

We categorized the findings and observations contained in the studies reviewed to determine new trends and upcoming challenges in dealing with the changes in leadership and the hierarchy structure in the virtual workplace.

5.3   Analysis of the Findings

Hierarchical attitudes die hard. Only after years of organizational change are companies starting to experience the benefits of flatter structures and achieving an internal change of culture (Hooper & Potter, 2000). Ideally a change in culture must come before restructuring (Powell, 2002), and therefore leadership needs to embrace the cultural shift and flatten the structure for greater connection to a virtual world. This model of a flat corporate structure reduces stress and gives independence in work to the benefit of the organization (Umai Rani et al., 2019). It appears that this shift of a flatter structure and connectivity in the new virtual landscape is in the early stages of full development and needs more research and reflection. However, leadership, organizational culture, and power distance will certainly determine whether this more autonomous structure can be effective. Some studies suggest that while a flatter hierarchy can improve ideation and creative success with recent growth in the flat business market, credibility and trust are key drivers for businesses to be successful (Covey, 2006). Leadership can be determined to be a real conduit to its successful implementation. Flat organizations are structures with minimal to no middle management, often empowering employees to take on more responsibility.

Flatter, less hierarchical organizational structures lead to more effective coordination of shared leadership in virtual teams (Nordbäck & Espinosa, 2019). In teams that are more diverse, the participants are less likely to share the same leadership expectations. Shared leadership may either be advantageous or be detrimental to team success (Nordbäck & Espinosa, 2019). An additional advantage of virtual working environments is access to a remote workforce (Chesbrough & Teece, 1998; Mironko, 2020) which allows for leveraging costs and resources while potentially increasing diversity of teams, especially in case of sourcing workforce from abroad.

This new work environment is most likely here to stay, and companies are trying to figure out ways that they can augment their leadership styles that accommodate the virtual operation of a business. Hierarchical, authoritarian, and egalitarian models are being tested to create efficient work environments that deliver value to employees and customers. Thus, the use of new technologies, or wider adaptation of the existing technologies, demonstrates the crossing of the chasm in trust in teams as well as the trust between managers and employees. While technology offers new ways of communicating and doing the job without the necessity of being in the same location, technologies do not guarantee the clarity of communication. For example, the loss of gestures and body expressions, building trust, and comradery in teams.

In a world where business operating environments are becoming more complex, the hierarchical organizational structures of yesteryears are not responsive enough in times of uncertainty or ambiguity that often demand quick decision-making (Walsh, 2017). Leaders today must think on their feet and empower their teams to generate solutions for hiccups that arise at work. As Contreras et al. (2020) contend, "if companies do not respond to crises and adapt to the new conditions, they are likely to disappear" (para 2). Innovation is a key aspect of problem resolution and never has this been so true than in virtual leadership (Contreras et al., 2020). With companies competing to implement new technologies based on Artificial Intelligence (AI) and expanding capability of Automation (IA) (Coombs, 2020) many workers, including knowledge workers, may face job cuts or require re-skilling.

5.3.1 Challenges of Virtual Teams

There is substantial evidence that one of the things that determines how effective a group or team will be is the quality of its communications (Nydegger & Nydegger, 2010). One of the fundamental differences between colocation and virtual teams is communication. In a study

5 The Changing Technology Use and its Impact on Leadership... 97

conducted by Lepsinger and DeRosa (2010) various factors that touch on communication attributed to a higher percentage of the challenges of virtual teams as presented in Table 5.1. These included lack of face-to-face contact with team members at 46% and limited sharing of information at 21%.

Further, Bjørn & Ngwenyama (2009) point out another element related to communication that is very important in the virtual group environment—translucence. This refers to a real-time design software, features that permit invisible social cues to become visible making it easier for members to understand the subtleties and deeper meanings of the work they are doing together. Translucence is a vitally important element in collaborative technologies and should be made available in a "low-effort, seamless way" that does not interfere with the primary tasks (Ebling et al., 2002). With the relative absence of typical non-verbal and paraverbal cues in the virtual team, translucency in the technology realm makes true collaboration much easier and more efficient.

5.3.2 Strategies for Leading Virtual Teams

Some of the strategies advanced for leading virtual teams (Maryville University, n.d.; Ehrmantraut, 2020; Larson et al., 2020; Robison & Hickman, 2020; Sull et al., 2020) include transparency (access to information and frequent communication); inclusion (valuing team member insights and creating opportunities for virtual social interaction); creativity (encouraging idea generation by team members); empathy (providing social and emotional support and promoting work-life integration for

Table 5.1 Top challenges of virtual teams

Lack of face-to-face contact with team members	46%
Lack of resources	37%
Time zone differences hinder our ability to collaborate	29%
Team members are on more than one team and cannot devote enough time to this team	27%
Team members do not share relevant information with one another	21%
Lack of skill training	20%

Adopted from Lepsinger and DeRosa (2010). Data represents percentage of responses

employee well-being); individualized coaching (engage workers at their level); clear expectations (rules of engagement for performance, maintaining productivity, and engagement); support to workers (flexibility in work schedules, providing technology for remote work, and regular check-ins). Table 5.2 captures some of these strategies, corresponding actions, and related outcomes.

5.4 Discussion and Conclusion

A common feature of today's organizations is the shift to more organic structures (Contreras et al., 2020), a reality that is becoming the norm for organizations in the digital era (Neufeld et al., 2010; Uhl-Bien et al., 2007), particularly those with a more dispersed workforce and transnational presence (Maduka et al., 2018).

Some of the pre-COVID-19 research shows that flat corporate structures can develop more functional teams (Yu et al., 2019). Other studies demonstrate that hierarchical structures in organizations have merits by providing necessary direction, motivation, conflict reduction, among other benefits.

In the pandemic age, a reimagined workplace (Alexander et al., 2020; PWC, 2021) has made many companies consider remote work for survival (Contreras et al., 2020). A Gallup Survey in 2020 revealed that the world of work would have been adversely affected if the technology that allowed for telework did not exist. Virtual leadership is an opportunity to reimagine the future of employment and careers (Hite & McDonald, 2020). As the world shifts to a more digital working environment, equity considerations in terms of accessibility to the virtual space come to mind. The resources that make a digital workspace possible are not necessarily available to every worker (Askin et al., 2021). Organizations working in remote areas or in neighbourhoods with populations without access to the internet, or the equipment required to do so, have the additional burden of ensuring that this does not affect the organization and employees adversely. It is a well-documented fact that many small businesses and organizations that did not have the technological platform to immediately shift to a remote working environment when COVID-19 hit, were

5 The Changing Technology Use and its Impact on Leadership... 99

Table 5.2 Strategies employed in leading virtual teams with actions and outcomes

Strategies employed	Action	Outcome
Transparency	Access to information and frequent communication	Trust
Inclusion	Evaluating team member insights and creating opportunities for virtual social interaction	Increased employee engagement and well-being
Creativity	Encouraging idea generation by team members	More inclusive decision-making and a feeling of ownership in organisation's core mandate
Empathy	Providing social and emotional support and promoting work-life integration for employee well-being	Healthy workforce
Individualized coaching	Engage workers at their levels	Individual staff development contributing to enriched communities of practice and a learning organisation
Set clear expectations	Rules of engagement for performance, maintaining productivity, and engagement	Improved communication; better flow of work; and a more productive workforce striving towards the same vision and common goals.
Support to workers	flexibility in work schedules, providing technology for remote work, and regular check-ins	Improved employee wellbeing contributing to a more engaged workforce and a growing organisation.
Shift to more organic structures	Make dispersed workforce feel like a team	A sense of belonging; potential for serving more clients given the virtual operating environment.

Possible actions and outcomes based on adaptation of strategies advanced for leading virtual teams (Ehrmantraut, 2020; Larson et al., 2020)

either forced to shut down or to quickly embrace technology for their survival (Fabiel et al., 2020). The lessons learned from the experiences of such organizations can be instrumental in informing the future of the digital workspace (Jain, 2020; Kaiser, 2020; Katare et al., 2021; Lau, 2020).

Studies taken during the Coronavirus pandemic age indicate that most organizations and workers will shift to remote work entirely or partially in the future (Contreras et al., 2020; Mexi, 2020). According to a McKinsey Report in 2020, some industries such as call centers, customer service, contact tele-sales, publishing, public relations (PR), marketing, research and information services, information technology (IT), and software development are likely to maintain a virtual workforce (Alexander et al., 2020) in the foreseeable future, and not require their employees to work from the office (Rudolph et al., 2020). Another group of industries indicates a desire to bring their virtual workers back—finance companies, schools, and academic institutions, among others.

In addition to the structural changes being made to shift to the virtual workplace, other changes need to be considered. These include work design and operating routines (Nediari et al., 2021; Parker, 2020), development of policies and mechanisms that support employee engagement, performance, and their well-being while working remotely. Not much research abounds on how technology affects survival of businesses (Abed, 2021) and how the remote working landscape has evolved to navigate behavioural aspects that influence relationships in virtual settings. For example, the notion of time and space blurs in the digital space (Collins, 2008) making it challenging for organizations to determine how employees manage their time and organize work. Some behaviours that may pose a challenge in the digital workplace include cyber bullying, misuse, or abuse of organizational resources and time (Shrivastava & Singh, 2021). This is an area that requires further exploration given the direction the post-COVID workplace is heading.

Although we can anticipate changing work environments in the near- and long-term future, we will have plenty of opportunities to observe which structures will transform and succeed and which ones will not. The post-COVID economic recovery and the reluctant return to the office is a strong signal for the change in management and leadership of companies (Florida et al., 2021). The savings in operational costs accrued from teleworking are immense and the flexibility enjoyed by workers to choose the hours and the place they work from contribute to their well-being

5 The Changing Technology Use and its Impact on Leadership... 101

(Ozimek, 2020). As the world navigates the shift to a more virtual work environment, a corresponding shift in how "virtuality may change leadership itself" needs to be explored further (Purvanova and Kenda (2018). We can be certain that new business and communication strategies enabled by technological innovations will challenge the existing leadership and management structures when embarking on the new future of work.

References

Abed, S. S. (2021). A Literature Review Exploring the Role of Technology in Business Survival During the Covid-19 Lockdowns. *International Journal of Organizational Analysis*. https://doi.org/10.1108/IJOA-11-2020-2501

Alexander, A., De Smet, A., & Mysore, M. (2020). *Reimagining the Post Pandemic Workforce*. McKinsey & Company. Recuperado de: https://www.mckinsey.com/business-functions/organization/ourinsights/reimagining-the-postpandemic-workforce

Anandarajan, M., Teo, T. S. H, & Simmers, C. A. (2006). *The Internet and Workplace Transformation*. New York: Routledge.

Archer, D., & Cameron, A. (2009). *Collaborative Leadership: How to Succeed in an Interconnected World*. Elsevier.

Askin, N., Babb, M., Darling, P., Dingwall, O., Finlay, L., Finlayson, K., Haas, C., & Osterreicher, A. (2021). Not Virtual Enough: A Virtual Library's Challenges During the COVID-19 Pandemic. *The Canadian Journal of Library and Information Practice and Research, 16*(1), 1–7.

Bashir, M., Benjiang, M. A., & Shahzd, L. A. (2020). A Brief Review of Socio-economic and Environmental Impact of Covid-19. *Air Quality, Atmosphere & Health, 13*, 1403–1409.

Bass, B. M., & Riggio, R. E. (2008). *Transformational Leadership*. Taylor Y Francis e-Library.

Bettis, R. A., & Hitt, M. A. (1995). The new competitive landscape. *Strategic Management Journal, 16*(1), 7–19.

Bidmead, E., & Marshall, A. (2020). Covid-19 and the 'New Normal: Are Remote Video Consultations Here to Stay? *British Medical Bulletin*, 1–7.

Bjørn, P., & Ngwenyama, O. K. (2009). Virtual Team Collaboration: Building Shared Meaning, Resolving Breakdowns and Creating Translucence. *Information Systems Journal, 19*(3), 227–253.

Bloom, N. (2022a). I've Been Studying Work-From-Home for Years. Here's What's Coming. *BARRON'S*. Retrieved form https://www.barrons.com/articles/ive-been-studying-work-from-home-for-years-heres-whats-coming-51641330825

Bloom, N. (2022b). The Three-Tier workforce. https://www.cutoday.info/THE-corner/The-Three-Tier-Workforce

Brazeal, D. V., Schenkel, M. T., & Kumar, S. (2014). Beyond the Organizational Bounds in CE Research: Exploring Personal and Relational Factors in a Flat Organizational Structure. *Journal of Applied Management and Entrepreneurship, 19*(2), 78–106.

Bushe, G. R., & Marshak, R. J. (2016). The Dialogic Mindset: Leading Emergent Change in a Complex World. *Organizational Development Journal, 34*(1), 37–65.

Chesbrough, H. W., & Teece, D. J. (1998). When is Virtual Virtuous? Organizing for Innovation. *The Strategic Management of Intellectual Capital, 27*, 65–73.

Collins, F. (2008). Digital Selves: Preparing Graduates for the Virtual Workplace. In *EdMedia+ Innovate Learning* (pp. 5853–5858). Association for the Advancement of Computing in Education (AACE).

Contreras, F., Baykal, E., & Abid, G. (2020). *E-Leadership and Teleworking in Times of COVID-19 and Beyond: What We Know and Where Do We Go.* Fron.

Coombs, C. (2020). Will COVID-19 be the Tipping Point for the Intelligent Automation of Work? A Review of the Debate and Implications for Research. *International Journal of Information Management, 55*, 102182.

Covey, S. R. (2006). Leading in the knowledge worker age. *Leader to Leader, 2006*(41), 11–15.

Cran, C. (2015). The Art of Change Leadership: Driving Transformation in a Fast-paced World. Wiley.

DasGupta, P. (2011). Literature Review: E-leadership. *Emerging Leadership Journeys, 4*(1), 1–36.

Dess, G. G., Lumpkin, R. D., & McGee, J. E. (1999). Linking Corporate Entrepreneurship to Strategy, Structure, and Process: Suggested Research Directions. *Entrepreneurship: Theory and Practice, 23*(3), 85–102.

Dienesch, R., & Liden, R. C. (1986). Leader-member Exchange Model of Leadership: A Critique and Further Development. *Academy of Management Review, 11*(3), 618–634.

5 The Changing Technology Use and its Impact on Leadership... 103

Ebling, M. R., John, B. E., & Satyanarayanan, M. (2002). The importance of translucence in mobile computing systems. *ACM Transactions on Computer-Human Interaction, 9*(1), 42–67.

Ehrmantraut, R. (2020). Tips to Adapt Your Leadership Style to a Virtual Environment. *Human Resources Director (HRD)*. Retrieved from https://www.hcamag.com/ca/specialization/hr-technology/tips-to-adapt-your-leadership-style-to-a-virtual-environment/240434

Emond, L., & Maese, E. (2020). *Evolving COVID-19 responses of the world's largest companies*. Gallup. Retrieved from Evolving COVID-19 Responses of World's Largest Companies (gallup.com).

Fabiel, F. N., Pazim, K. H., & Langgat, J. (2020). The Impact of Covid-19 Pandemic Crisis on Micro-enterprises: Entrepreneurs' Perspective on Business Continuity and Recovery Strategy. *Journal of Economics and Business, 3*(2), 837–844.

Florida, R., Rodríguez-Pose, A., & Storper, M. (2021). Cities in a Post-COVID World. *Urban Studies*, 00420980211018072.

Galanti, T., Guidetti, G., Mazzeir, E., Zappalà, S., & Toscano, F. (2021). Work from Home During the COVID-19 Outbreak. *Journal of Occupational and Environmental Medicine, 63*(7), 426–432.

Grewal, D., Hulland, J., Kopalle, P. K., & Karahanna, E. (2020). The future of technology and marketing: A multidisciplinary perspective. *Journal of the Academy of Marketing Science, 48*(1), 1–8.

Guyot, K. & Sawhill, I. V. (2020). Telecommuting Will Likely Continue Long after the Pandemic. Brookings. Retrieved from https://www.brookings.edu/blog/up-front/2020/04/06/telecommuting-will-likely-continue-long-after-the-pandemic/

Hawryszkiewycz, I. T. (2021). Organizations in a Complex World. In *Transforming Organizations in Disruptive Environments* (pp. 3–19). Palgrave Macmillan.

Hill, N. S., & Bartol, K. M. (2016). Empowering Leadership and Effective Collaboration in Geographically Dispersed Teams. *Personnel Psychology, 69*, 159–198. https://doi.org/10.1111/peps.12108

Hite, L. M., & McDonald, K. S. (2020). Careers after COVID-19: Challenges and Changes. *Human Resource Development International, 23*(4), 427–437.

Hooper, A., & Potter, J. (2000). *Intelligent Leadership - Creating a Pattern for Change*. Random House.

Horwitch, M., & Callahan, M. W. (2016). How leaders inspire: Cracking the code. Bain & Company. Retrieved from v5-Inspirational leadership-cover pages.indd (bain.com).

Jain, M. (2020). The Next Normal: Building Resilience in the post-COVID-19 Workspace. *Digital Debates, 23*, 23–35.

Kaiser, R. B. (2020). Leding in an Unprecedented Global Crisis: The Heightened Importance of Versatility. *Consulting Psychology Journal: Practice and Research, 72*(3), 135–154.

Kaplan, R. E., & Kaiser, R. B. (2003). Developing Versatile Leadership. *MT Sloan Management Review*, 20–26.

Katare, B., Marshall, M. I., & Valdivia, C. B. (2021). Bend or Break? Small Business Survival and Strategies During the COVID-19 Shock. *International Journal of Disaster Risk Reduction, 61*, 1–8.

Kelly, L. (2020). *How to Adapt your Management Style for Motivated Remote Teams*. Peoplegoal. Retrieved from https://www.peoplegoal.com/blog/how-to-adapt-your-management-style-for-motivated-remote-teams

Kramer, M. W., & Crespy, D. A. (2011). Communicating Collaborative Leadership. *The Leadership Quarterly, 22*(5), 1024–1037.

Larson, B. Z.; Vroman, S. R. & Makarius, E. E. (2020). A Guide to Managing Your (Newly) Remote Workers. *Harvard Business Review*. Retrieved from https://hbr.org/2020/03/a-guide-to-managing-your-newly-remote-workers

Lau, A. (2020). New Technologies used in COVID-19 for Business Survival: Insights for the Hotel Sector in China. *Information Technology & Tourism, 22*, 497–504.

Lee, M. R. (2021a). *Leading Virtual Project Teams: Adapting Leadership Theories and Communications Techniques to 21st Century Organizations*. CRC Press.

Lee, S. (2021b). The Myth of the Flat Start-up: Reconsidering the Organizational Structure of Start-ups. *Strategic Management Journal*. https://doi.org/10.1002/smj.3333

Lepsinger, R., & DeRosa, D. (2010). *Virtual Team Success: A Practical Guide for Working and Leading from a Distance*. Center for Creative Leadership.

Liden, R. C., & Maslyn, J. M. (1998). Multidimensionality of Leader-Member Exchange: An Empirical Assessment through Scale Development. *Journal of Management, 24*, 43–72.

Lorinkova, N. M., Pearsall, M. J., & Sims, H. P. (2013). Examining the Differential Longitudinal Performance of Directive Versus Empowering Leadership in Teams. *Academy of Management Journal, 56*(2), 573–596.

Maduka, N., Edwards, H., Greenwood, D., Osborne, A., & Babatunde, S. (2018). Analysis of Competencies for Effective Virtual Team Leadership in Building Successful Organisations. *Benchmarking, 25*(2), 696–712. ISSN 1463-5771.

Martins, L. L., Gilson, L. L., & Maynard, M. T. (2004). Virtual Teams: What Do We Know and Where Do We Go from Here? *Journal of Management, 30*(6), 805–835.

Maryville University (n.d.). *Virtual Leadership Styles for Remote Businesses.* Retrieved from https://online.maryville.edu/blog/virtual-leadership/

Mexi, M. (2020). The Future of Work in the Post-COVID-19 digital era. *United Nations Research Institute for Social Development (UNRISD).* Retrieved from https://www.unrisd.org/covid-19-digiwork

Mironko, A. (2019). On-site Applied Learning with the Use of Mixed Methods as a Reflective Learning Model in International Business. In *The Palgrave Handbook of Learning and Teaching International Business and Management* (pp. 401–419). Palgrave Macmillan. https://doi.org/10.1007/978-3-030-20415-0_19

Mironko, A. (2020). To Make or to Serve–Industrial Specialization Drivers of Foreign Subsidiaries in Service and Manufacturing Sectors Across Agglomerations in a Transition Economy. *International Journal of Business and Applied Social Science, 6*(3). https://doi.org/10.33642/ijbass.v6n3p1

Mironko, A., Muriungi, R., & Scardino, A. (2021). The Future Agenda for International Leadership Research and Practice. In Y. Tolstikov-Mast, F. Bieri, & J. L. Walker (Eds.), *Handbook of International and Cross-Cultural Leadership Research Processes.* Routledge.

Molina, G. (2020). *Characteristics of Transformational Leadership in Remote Organizations.* Distant Job. Retrieved from https://distantjob.com/blog/transformational-leadership-remote-organizations/

Nediari, A., Roesli, C., & Simanjuntak, P. M. (2021). Preparing Post Covid-19 Pandemic Office Design as the New Concept of Sustainability Design. *IOP Conference Series: Earth and Environmental Science, 729*(1), 1–9.

Nelson, T., & Squires, V. (2017). Addressing Complex Challenges through Adaptive Leadership: A Promising Approach to Collaborative Problem Solving. *Journal of Leadership Education, 16*(4), 111–123. https://doi.org/10.12806/V16/I4/T2. Retrieved from https://journalofleadershiped.org/wp-content/uploads/2019/02/16_4_squires.pdf

Neufeld, D., Wan, Z., & Fang, Y. (2010). Remote Leadership, Communication Effectiveness and Leader Performance. *Group Decision and Negotiation, 19*(3), 227–246.

Nohria, N., & Eccles, R. (2000). Face-to-face: Making network organizations work. In N. Nohria & R. C. Eccles (Eds.), *Technology, Organizations, and Innovation: Critical Perspectives on Business and Management* (pp. 1659–1681). Harvard Business School Press.

Nordbäck, E. S., & Espinosa, J. A. (2019). Effective Coordination of Shared Leadership in Global Virtual Teams. *Journal of Management Information Systems, 36*(1), 321–350. https://doi.org/10.1080/07421222.2018.1558943

Nydegger, R., & Nydegger, L. (2010). Challenges In Managing Virtual Teams. *Journal of Business & Economics Research (JBER), 8*(3). https://doi.org/10.19030/jber.v8i3.690

Oudshoorn, N. (2008). Diagnosis at a Distance: The Invisible Work of Patients and Healthcare Professionals in Cardiac Telemonitoring Technology. *Sociology of Health & Illness, 30*(2), 272–288.

Ozimek, A. (2020). *The future of remote work.* Retrieved from https://papers.ssrn.com/sol3/papers.cfm?abstract_id=3638597

Parker, L. D. (2020). The Covid-19 Office in Transition: Cost, Efficiency and the Social Responsibility Business Case. *Accounting, Auditing and Accountability Journal, 33,* 1–32.

Pavlica, K. & Jarosová, E. (2014). Versatile Leadership and Organizational Culture. Conference Paper. *European Conference on Management, Leadership & Governance,* 221–229.

Pavlica, K., Kaiser, R. B., & Jarosová, E. (2011). Versatile Leadership, LVI and their Application. *Chinese Busines Review, 10*(12), 1181–1190.

Powell, L. (2002). Shedding a Tier: Flattening Organizational Structures and Employee Empowerment. *The International Journal of Educational Management, 16*(1), 54–59.

Prasad, K. D. V., Mangipudi, M. R., Vaidya, R. W., & Muralidhar, B. (2020). Organizational Climate, Opportunities, Challenges and Psychological Wellbeing of the Remote Working Employees During COVID-19 Pandemic: A general Linear Model Approach with Reference to Information Technology Industry in Hyderabad. *International Journal of Advanced Research in Engineering and Technology (IJARET), 11*(4), 372–389.

Price, M. (2020). Scientists discover upsides of virtual meetings. *Science, 368*(6490), 457–458. https://doi.org/10.1126/science.368.6490.457

Purvanova, R. K., & Bono, J. E. (2009). Transformational leadership in context: Face-to-face and virtual teams. *Leadership Quarterly, 20*, 343–357.

Purvanova, R. K. & Kenda, R. (2018). Paradoxical Virtual Leadership: Reconsidering Virtuality through a Paradox Lens. *ResearchGate.*

PWC. (2021). It's Time to Reimagine Where and How Work Will Get Done: *PwC's US Remote Work Survey* - January 12, 2021. Retrieved from https://www.pwc.com/us/en/library/covid-19/us-remote-work-survey.html

Robison, J. & Hickman, A. (2020). *COVID-19 Has My Teams Working Remotely: A Guide for Leaders.* Gallup. Retrieved from https://www.gallup.com/workplace/288956/covid-teams-working-remotely-guide-leaders.aspx

Rudolph, C. W., Allan, B., Clark, M., Hertel, G., Hirschi, A., Kunze, F., et al. (2020). Pandemics: Implications for Research and Practice in Industrial and Organizational Psychology. *Industrial and Organizational Psychology, 14*(1–2), 1–35.

Schröder, T. (2014). Didactical Concept of Work-based Training in a Virtual Work Space. *US-China Education Review, 4*(7), 441–448.

Sébastien, J., Ouahabi, A., & Thierry, L. (2020). Remote Knowledge Acquisition and Assessment During the COVID-19 Pandemic. *International Journal of Engineering Pedagogy, 10*(6), 120–138.

Shrivastava, S., & Singh, K. (2021). Workplace deviance in the virtual workspace. *Strategic HR Review, 20*(3), 74–77. https://doi.org/10.1108/SHR-09-2020-0083

Sloan, E. B. (1994). Assessing and Developing Versatility: Executive Survival Skill for the Brave New World. *Consulting Psychology Journal: Practice and Research, 46*(1), 24–31.

Sull, D., Sull, C. & Bersin, J. (2020). Five Ways Leaders Can Support Remote Work. *MIT Sloan Management Review.* Retrieved from https://sloanreview.mit.edu/article/five-ways-leaders-can-support-remote-work/

Teece, D. J. (2018). Business Models and Dynamic Capabilities. *Long Range Planning, 51*(1), 40–49.

Tierney, P., & Farmer, S. M. (2002). Creative self-efficacy: Its potential antecedents and relationship to creative performance. *The Academy of Management Journal, 45*(6), 1137–1148.

Towler, A. (2020). *Leading Virtual Teams: How to Lead in the 21st Century Knowledge Economy.* Retrieved from https://www.ckju.net/en/dossier/leading-virtual-teams-how-lead-21st-century-knowledge-economy

Uhl-Bien, M., Marion, R., & McKelvey, B. (2007). Complexity Leadership Theory: Shifting Leadership from the Industrial Age to the Knowledge Age. *The Leadership Quarterly, 18*(4), 298–318.

Umai Rani, P., Cynthia, A. R., Priyankaa, S., & Murugan Kandaswamy, K. (2019). A Flat Organizational Model for Agile Workforce with Reference to Holocracy. *International Journal of Recent Technology and Engineering, 8*(2S8), 1525–1527.

Vrontis, D., Thrassou, A., Weber, Y., Shams, S. M. R., Tsoukatos, E., & Efthymiou, L. (2022). *Business Under Crisis: Organisational Adaptations* (Vol. II), Palgrave Studies in Cross-disciplinary Business Research, In Association with EuroMed Academy of Business, ISBN 978-3-030-76574-3). Palgrave Macmillan.

Walsh, D. (2017). Written Rethinking Hierarchy in the Workplace. *Insights by Stanford Business.* https://www.gsb.stanford.edu/insights/rethinking-hierarchy-workplace

Wang, B., Liu, Y., Qian, J., & Parker, S. K. (2020). Achieving Effective Remote Working During the COVID-19 Pandemic: A Work Design Perspective. *Applied Psychology: An International Review, 70*(1), 1–44.

Webster. (2021). COVID-19 Timeline of Events. *Nature Medicine, 27,* 2052–2061.

Wood, R., & Bandura, A. (1989). Social Cognitive Theory of Organizational Management. *Academy of Management Review, 14*(1), 361–384.

Yu, S., Greer, L. L., Halevy, N., & Van Bunderen, L. (2019). On Ladders and Pyramids: Hierarchy's Shape Determines Relationships and Performance in Groups. *Personality and Social Psychology Bulletin, 45*(12), 1717–1733.

Zofi, Y. S. (2012). *A Manager's Guide to Virtual Teams* (1st ed.). American Management Association. Retrieved January 12, 2022, from New York: American Management Association.

6

Conceptual Mutations of Change Management and the Strategy–Technology–Management Innovation

Charis Vlados

6.1 Introduction

Change management does not constitute an "ever-settled" scientific field so that there are clear and strictly defined thematic boundaries and methodological prerequisites; there are no "generally accepted principles" on the subject. In contrast, change management theory and practice arise through the convergence and interconnection of various social sciences disciplines and interdisciplinary conceptual traditions (Augsburg, 2010; Frodeman et al., 2019; Hacklin & Wallin, 2013). Although this is its

---

C. Vlados (✉)
Department of Economics, Democritus University of Thrace, Komotini, Greece

School of Business, University of Nicosia, Nicosia, Cyprus

School of Social Sciences, Business & Organisation Administration, Hellenic Open University, Patras, Greece
e-mail: cvlados@econ.duth.gr

© The Author(s), under exclusive license to Springer Nature Switzerland AG 2022
A. Thrassou et al. (eds.), *Business Advancement through Technology Volume II*, Palgrave Studies in Cross-disciplinary Business Research, In Association with EuroMed Academy of Business, https://doi.org/10.1007/978-3-031-07765-4_6

110   C. Vlados

strength and charm, tracing its theoretical foundations and perspectives is still a significant challenge (Burnes, 2009). On top of that, the multitude of related disciplines studying the subject—management, business strategy, economics, sociology, social psychology, and other related fields—makes it even more challenging to summarise the fundamental theoretical background, as this has been shaped in recent decades.

6.1.1 Purpose

With these remarks on the cross-disciplinary nature of change management in mind, this chapter aims to examine fundamental corresponding approaches that the widely exercised practice appears to assign value. This aim will be accomplished by their distinguished contribution and accentuating their potential drawbacks. In this context, our research question is: Where do some cardinal change management analytical schemes seem to focus? Is a theoretical layout synthesising the explicative dimensions of strategy, technology, and management comparatively more fertile? We advocate that the dialectical conception that interweaves these three spheres seems to fabricate a structure that appears imperative for advancing today's business research in innovation and change management (Vlados, 2021). To this end, we examine how this recalibrated explanatory approach in Stra.Tech.Man terms can readjust and fertilise the current change management comprehensions and practices.

6.1.2 Methods

This theory-building article will elliptically examine notable change management viewpoints to offer an overview of relatively recent developments on the subject, intending to arrive at a new, repositioned theoretical framework (Mohajan, 2018; Snyder, 2019). In the second section, significant perspectives of change management are presented, which have been widely accepted in today's business practice and scholarly literature (learning organisation and systems thinking, organisation's reinvention, paradigm-shift and change in the organisation's mind, maintaining balance and results-based change management, leading change, and doing business in the age of chaos). In the third section, a critical review of the modern change management approaches is attempted (Grant & Booth, 2009). The fourth concluding section suggests a new perspective of organisational innovation and change in the synthesis of strategy, technology, and management.

6.2 Literature Review

P. Senge's work follows a similar research orientation to the Japanese philosophical approach to management, specifically in the "fifth discipline" (Senge, 1990). According to this perspective, the term five disciplines is an expression of new learning skills that appear in modern organisations. These dexterities refer to having a purpose and creating commonly accepted visions. Also, they are concerned with the ability to conceive broader patterns and their interdependency by developing systems thinking. Finally, new learning skills are the outcome of augmented reflective capabilities so that people can be increasingly aware of their assumptions (Gibson, 1998).

For Senge, the concept of systems is crucial to the "dance of change," which becomes faster and more challenging nowadays (Senge, 1999). A system is anything that acquires substantiality through its parts' underlying interactions, including all organisations across the planet. Systems are defined by the fact that their elements have a shared purpose and behave in ordinary ways precisely because they relate to that purpose. According to Senge, four primary challenges exist in the initiation of any change: a) an interest in change, b) the right time for change has arrived, c) there is help to support the change, and d) as the obstacles to a change are removed, no unfamiliar problems deriving from this process will become unbearable. It is further argued that business organisations are institutions that help us realise the global systems perspective. As interdependence and interconnectivity proliferate globally, the business organisation becomes more complex and dynamic, imposing a radical overhaul on how we have traditionally learned to see things—an immediate transition to a "new paradigm" (Thakkar, 2021). Senge also notes that the reason for not introducing changes into an organisation stems from the fact that some persons pose questions and resist change, requiring thus additional time (Senge, 2008). Therefore, only a few traditional organisations will manage to survive this delicate transition that inevitably arises. Those who successfully carry out this process will maintain a unique competitive advantage, using human imagination and intelligence in ways no traditional and authoritarian organisation can (Ghannay & Mamlouk, 2012). To this end, and according to Jacques (2006), people in various hierarchical levels are differentiated according to how far they can see in the future. Thus, hierarchy is legitimised because it can see more clearly the possible impact of decisions than the people closely related to the actual process of daily implementation.

To reinforce an organisation's change management capabilities, its people should start participating fully in the planning process; they must treat this participation as a learning procedure, which refers to continuous cultural development that improves all mental models in decision-making (Andrikopoulos, 2009; O'Donovan, 2008). Overall, Senge's work appears open to understanding modern challenges of managing change—to the extent that it offers a systems-based approach that underlines the significance of radically transforming the way organisations perceive reality. It helps to avoid simplification in change management because business transformation does not merely require accelerating the process or intensifying past and inadequate forms of organisation (Jones & Recardo, 2013). The following subsections investigate similar systemic considerations in change management, developed in the context of different scientific traditions and interpretative approaches.

6.2.1 Change and the Risk of Reinventing the Organisation

According to Goss et al. (1993), managers seeking a more radical change in their organisation's capabilities must not just improve; they must reinvent the organisation. When a decision for reinvention is taken, this must uncover and then change the invisible assumptions on which decisions and actions are based. This challenging task of reinvention involves bringing together critical groups of actors who will create a sense of urgency, deal with conflicts, and reveal weaknesses. Contemporary reality raises the standards for effective leadership at an unprecedented height. Building competitive advantage is a challenging process that increasingly leads to blaming the company's administration for inefficiency, poor handling, and inadequate strategic programs. Besides leadership, this problem is rooted in the foundational organisational competencies, in how organisations can create and manage subtle or significant changes. It seems that most organisations must change what they are and discover what they are not (Leavy, 2014; McKenzie & Aitken, 2012).

According to the approach of organisational reinvention, everything is about context. The context changes what everyone in the organisation sees, and executives often do not dare to eliminate the ineffective framework they created. To this end, a refreshing vision must remind everybody that old certainties and routines must be continuously questioned. The manager oriented towards reinvention must overcome the past, venturing on an unknown journey and not that "gentle." Inventing a healthy future is critical because this change manager must not describe a prospect based on existing beliefs about how things already work in the business or focus on situations impossible to be diffused and implemented. Pragmatism is needed; otherwise, communicating such a "reinvention" may reinforce the path towards an uncertain future. In this context, a new declaration must be well formulated and simple, while a vision must offer an extensive description of the desired situation, considering how the organisation functions at all levels (Kantabutra & Avery, 2010; Kirkpatrick, 2016).

Overall, perseverance and flexibility are significant features for all activities required for reinventing an organisation (Englehardt & Simmons, 2002). This approach is invaluable for understanding change management and further implications since it underlines the inherent risk in any new organisational framework, attributing significance to past developments and today's competitive survival (Gill, 2002; Grote & Künzler, 2000). It helps us realise that organisational change requires courage and leadership to make the "operation" successful.

6.2.2 Paradigm Shift and Change in the Mind

S. Covey's (1989a) approach offers significant insight into the context of change management. This paradigm shift (in terms of organisations) refers to shifting from the human relations and resources models—according to which we must treat people well and use them—to a radically new management philosophy based on a method of personal improvement. Covey suggests seven habits that highly effective people have in common as their change mechanisms in both their personal and corporate life. These are the following: "be proactive; begin with the end in mind; put first things first; think the win/win scenario always; seek to understand first, before making yourself understood; learn to synergise; sharpen the saw." Covey (2004) also adds an eighth principle later in this organisational paradigm shift, expressed as "finding your voice and inspiring others to find theirs." In another book called "principle-centred leadership," Covey (1989b) presents a more specific perspective on how this paradigm shifts in organisations. According to the suggested theoretical framework, the first concern of management must be to create a workforce that has been transferred with a part of the organisation's authority, having shared visions and beliefs around a system of principle-based values. Covey argues that the fundamental paradigm must be shifted for most corporations, noting that most businesses are trying to introduce modern technologies and terminologies by keeping their old "philanthropic" and authoritarian paradigms. Shifting the paradigm altogether is not easy, especially at the organisation-wide level. However, it is not impossible, especially when it can be the only success for companies operating in today's globalised economy (Friedman, 1999; Levitt, 1983).

From a similar research orientation, R. Martin (1993) suggests that organisations need to "change their minds," noticing how disappointing it is when large corporations that go through a crisis take the same actions that once led them to become big, often causing a "resistance to change" syndrome (Coch & French Jr, 1948; Georgalis et al., 2015; Oreg, 2003). The secret to overcoming this syndrome is to stop the excuses and pay attention to the company's development before the crisis. In trying to remove this syndrome's adverse effects, structuring "steering mechanisms" is critical. These mechanisms can often be inadequate due to problematic feedback, leading managers to ignore complaints and other forms of unwelcome feedback that could be precious if used appropriately. In an ideal organisational setup, steering mechanisms report on changes in the market and continuously force the company to respond and learn. Martin also argues that change managers must be accurate about their organisations' psychodynamics and technical analyses. In this context, shaping a path of rigorous strategic debate is crucial. The executive needs to clarify that the organisation is in crisis and determine what the company did right in the first place. In this debate, all senior managers must express their personal views on the company's vision—and everyone must feel secure to express themselves freely. Martin concludes that companies need to "burn themselves down" and rebuild their strategies, roles, and practices every few years.

These approaches to change management are a significant basis for understanding the "resistance to change" manifested within all organisations. It could be said that this management theorising is in direct contrast to the mechanistic character of classical management since it conceptualises today's manager as a "gardener" instead of an "engineer" (Burns & Stalker, 2011; McNamara, 2009). They help avoid misconceptions on managing change without affecting past successful organisational elements and processes.

6.2.3 Maintaining Balance in the Change Process and the Significance of Swift Results

According to J. Duck (1993), it is crucial to maintain organisational balance in any change process. The author suggests introducing new management methods, discouraging breaking down changes into small chunks and focusing on the necessary embracement of all parts in the effort. It is argued that change management means achieving critical balance, controlling discussion, creating a suitable organisational framework, and managing emotional relationships. This transformation always has a human-centric imprint, and change management is unlike any other corresponding task within all organisations because of its complexity and criticality. It is further argued that modern change management must be based on effective messaging and continuous communication. This reporting should be a priority for every manager in the company's hierarchy, as unsuccessful communication means ineffective change management. In this context, all group members must first be communicated (and eventually persuaded by) the company's vision and accepting this perception will lead to new attitudes within the organisation, causing their behaviour to change and their performance to improve. However, in large corporations, employees have often experienced various change programs, so they are now cautious. To this end, senior management should better start by calling for a change in behaviour that will lead to improved production in broad terms so that enthusiasm and faith can follow.

From a converging perspective, Schaffer and Thomson (1992) focus on the significance of tangible results for a change program's overall success. They find that most corporate improvement programs negatively affect functional and financial performance because management focuses on activities rather than results. In the opposite direction, an alternative method for improvement and development programs is suggested based on results and focused on achieving specific, measurable operational improvements in the short run. It is noted that the second strategy is more effective, although both methods aim at reinforcing the company's competitiveness. It is argued that result-based organisational transformation bypasses lengthy preparatory work, focusing on achieving immediate and measurable benefits. The primary advantages of the results-based method are four: companies introduce management and process innovations only when they are needed; empirical control reveals what works and what does not; frequent reinforcement revitalises the improvement process; management creates a routine learning procedure, taking advantage of lessons learned from earlier phases of the program.

These approaches shed light on significant aspects of the change management process within modern organisations, even though they seem to diverge in methodological terms. From a joint perspective, it could be said that claiming organisational balance and achieving tangible results through practical solutions can be simultaneously implemented within organisations. Moreover, in their conceptual background, the two

6 Conceptual Mutations of Change Management...   117

approaches take for granted that any change process requires total organisational commitment (Nordin, 2012; Raja & Palanichamy, 2011). In this interpretive direction, the following subsection shows how leadership affects the overall course of the organisation.

6.2.4 Change and Leadership

J. Kotter's (1996) relevant perspective is one of the most well-known approaches in organisational change management. The author suggests an eight-step process for successfully assimilating change into an organisation, arguing that an omission or inadequate handling of these could damage the change procedure's effectiveness. The eight-step process is as follows:

1. Create a sense of urgency: A false reassurance can waste of valuable reaction time, and too often, a sense of urgency is absent at the beginning of a change program.
2. Form a guiding coalition: The leadership's inadequate commitment to excellence through renewal can delay and significantly hamper the work for change.
3. Develop an inspired vision: In failures of change programs, various tactics and partial plans exist without sharp foresight.
4. Convey the new vision: Change cannot be effectively implemented if employees do not know when they will need to make sacrifices for functional changes, are unaware of why this change is necessary, and when their efforts will pay off.
5. Empower others to enact the vision: Too often, either implicitly or explicitly, senior management can obstruct the employees' desire to implement the new understanding.
6. Generate short-term wins: Swift results and interim success can psychologically strengthen and encourage an organisation during its transformation.
7. Sustain acceleration of the vision: Any hasty declaration that the "war of change" has been won can be disastrous as it can lead to a relaxation of efforts when these endeavours should be intensified.

8. Institute permanent change: Transformation is assimilated when it becomes a settled method of action, that is, a profound "philosophy" of conceiving things within the organisation.

Kotter (1995) also notices that organisations often fail to successfully manage change because they cannot avoid critical errors that usually involve "bypassing" or improperly incorporating the aforementioned change management phases. In essence, it seems that Kotter's approach is a well-grounded guide to effective change management within modern organisations. It is clear (suggests structured steps), coherent (every step follows a successive pattern), comprehensive (raises most of the internal issues of organisational change), and realistic (recognises why a transformation program can fail). If it involves a relative weakness this derives from its exclusively internal perspective, a trait that also appears in recent approaches to leading change (Thrassou et al., 2018; Vrontis et al., 2018). The external organisational environment's specific dynamics and the corresponding business strategy are hardly considered (Ismail & Kuivalainen, 2015).

6.2.5 Chaotics and Doing Business in the Age of Turbulence

Various modern approaches to change management seem to be primarily inward-oriented. However, the idiosyncratic global environment cannot be omitted without affecting each change management model's comprehensiveness. Kotler and Caslione (2009) focus on the underlying global crisis of the 2000s, arguing that contemporary business reality is characterised by "chaos." The authors suggest solutions organisations can implement for responding to this unprecedented situation, noting that the new era requires a unique organisational action. Any traditional and hierarchically rigid model cannot adapt in this age of turbulence. In contrast, the modern way of approaching, dealing with, and exiting turbulence requires courage, aggressiveness, and determination instead of old-style anticipation, shrinking, and conservatism. In this context, the authors

6 Conceptual Mutations of Change Management... 119

present ten fundamental mistakes and best business practices amid this "global chaos":

(a) Duplication of capabilities: Companies must do their best to avoid duplication between their suppliers and distributors by focusing on cutting overlaps and costs.

(b) The complexity of contracts: Companies must have simple agreements based on the trust they built over time, including executing contracts with the cooperation of suppliers and distributors on a day-to-day basis and emphasising continuous improvement.

(c) Insufficient performance rating systems: Companies must make significant efforts to obtain supplier and distributor performance measurement systems that are easy to understand and get direct feedback.

(d) Inadequate product development/specification: Companies should ask suppliers and distributors to suggest modifications for improving products and reducing costs.

(e) Single dimensional selection process: Companies should choose suppliers exclusively through supplier departments and distributors via sales divisions, making their choices based on information gathered from the company's inter-functional teams.

(f) Maintaining physical separation from primary suppliers and distributors: Shared infrastructure and facilities promote better communication between suppliers, distributors, and the company, while the knowledge of all sides helps the firm and ensures better control over its interests within the supplier and distributor operations.

(g) Maintaining too many suppliers: To improve their management, companies must increasingly supply from a sole source or a reduced number of suppliers, thus securing their customer base so that limited resources can be focused on an easily managed number of suppliers.

(h) Maintaining the wrong suppliers and distributors: Companies do not have to wait too long to break off relations with suppliers and distributors of low or marginal performance, or their relationship with the company is irreparable.

(i) Not investing in training for suppliers and distributors: By training their suppliers and distributors, companies reduce operating costs and increase sales while increasing the quality of products and services provided to the company and its customers.

(j) Not investing in communications with suppliers and distributors: Companies use various methods to improve communication with suppliers and distributors while reducing inferior quality communications and offering feedback opportunities on issues of mutual interest (Fig. 6.1).

All these findings specify the need for a reconfirmed strategy, technology, and management (the Stra.Tech.Man organisational generator, as explained in the concluding section) for dealing with the co-determined chaotic conditions that emerge in contemporary global dynamics (external environment). Overall, these aspects and best practices highlighted by Kotler and Caslione converge that any fragmentary, opportunistic, and hasty response is inadequate for responding to the pressing challenges and growing uncertainty a modern organisation faces. Their suggestions focus on change management dynamics, "condemning" organisational

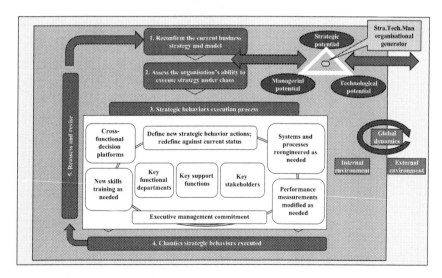

Fig. 6.1 Strategic behaviour, technological and managerial potential within the chaos of contemporary global dynamics, based on Kotler and Caslione (2009)

6 Conceptual Mutations of Change Management...   121

inertia, myopic conservatism, submissiveness, and strategic cowardice in dealing with chaotic global conditions (Laudicina & Peterson, 2016).

6.3 Analysis of Findings

Without a doubt, change management literature appears to be quite diverse. Are immediate results or quick wins the primary motors of change management within an organisation? Is it patience, slow cultivation of organisational abilities, or "strategic perseverance" that distinguishes successfully managed transformations? Do instantaneous leaps defeat the continuous evolutionary transformation and corporate mutation? Is change a "bottom-up" or "top-down" process? Is effective change management a birth of democracy and co-decision or an expression of robust and enlightened central leadership? We do not find any easy or one-way answers to these questions:

* As business consultants, we have repeatedly faced how pursuing only immediate results can adversely affect organisational change. We do not question the significance of a fast-paced administrative manoeuvre. However, we also have witnessed procrastination and "tail chasing" within various organisations where no further effort can save them.
* We also have seen that hasty solutions lead to added tensions and unnecessary conflicts, increasing uncertainty and exacerbating instability during the organisation's transition to the new reality. Quick-change plans can often destroy the present "healthy metabolism" of the organisation. Simultaneously, we have experienced situations where the long-term expectation of creating a learning and participatory organisation remains only a lengthy wish list that can accompany the organisation until its decay.
* Deciding the best alternative between a significant leap or continuous and mutational organisational improvement is challenging. Various organisations might manage a significant transformational leap while others succeed by following the humble path of day-to-day progress.
* Likewise, no sufficient arguments suggest any unilaterality of the "bottom-up" or "top-down" approach to change. On the contrary, most

successful transformation endeavours are due to bottom-up and top-down affective action—at every hierarchical level.

Therefore, as it seems, change management becomes perceived as a cross-disciplinary field in the presented related literature. Some authors appear to focus either on the commanding role of technology, the need for dynamic strategic rebalancing, or the overhauling effort of management. At best, the attempted synthesis appears to involve only two of these change rudiments. Hence, bearing this shortage in mind, the concluding section functions as a resynthesis endeavour, arguing that managing change must integrate the organisation's strategy, technology, and management.

6.4 Conclusion: Towards a Restructured Perspective of Organisational Change (Strategy–Technology–Management Synthesis)

We argue that effective change management needs a way of thinking deriving primarily from dialectics—the thesis–antithesis–synthesis amalgamation. A dialectical synthesis where the ongoing birth of evolutionary conflict occurs between the "thesis" that denotes the previous states of affairs and the "antithesis" that signifies the continuous subversion of the earlier regimes (Morabito et al., 2018). To overcome this antithesis, the modern manager of change must elucidate before any action the primary "physiological" goals of change in "Stra.Tech.Man" terms, meaning the synthesis of strategy, technology, and management (Vlados, 2019a):

* Strategy: "Where am I? Where do I want to go? How do I go there? Why?"
* Technology: "How do I draw, create, compose, diffuse, and reproduce my knowledge and expertise? Why?"
* Management: "How do I use my available resources? Why?"

There is no linearity in this understanding of managing change; no firm is an unwitting machine but a "living organisation" (de Geus, 2002; Kelly, 1994; Meyer & Davis, 2003). It has specific limits of "physiology," determined by the way innovative evolutionary synthesis is achieved in "Stra.Tech.Man" terms (Vlados & Chatzinikolaou, 2019). Moreover, any attempt to manage change within all organisations must consider the "livingness" of the external environment, which co-evolves with the corresponding internal environment. This coevolution between the internal and external organisational environment is critical to delimit the environmental boundaries in "Stra.Tech.Man" terms for all socioeconomic organisations—and not just for large companies, as usually advocated in popular change management approaches.

Specifically, innovation in Stra.Tech.Man terms concerns how each socioeconomic organisation manages to match its existing production potential (supply side) with the corresponding demand dynamics (Di Stefano et al., 2012; Peters et al., 2012). From the "technology bunching strategy" perspective (Grappes technologiques), a concept developed by GEST (1986), technological changes result in the appearance of generic technologies and systematic commercialisation of technical competencies (Delapierre & Mytelka, 2002). Though this idea of socioeconomic change was industry-oriented, we suggest that this transformation is due to innovation caused by the inner organisational synthesis of strategy, technology, and management expressed at the various socioeconomic levels (Fig. 6.2).

The Stra.Tech.Man of the internal organisational environment constitutes the root (a generator) wherein innovation bunches and micro-innovation are organically extended to all other corporate departments and units. Successful innovation derives not only from one Stra.Tech. Man factor, but always from their dynamic synthesis. In addition to how the organisation synthesises these domains, innovation may arise from coalescing individual business functions. In this sense, modern firms must draw and assimilate innovation from any spatial or functional context to the others, realising that potential opportunities and threats only spring up when specific evolutionary strengths and weaknesses develop over time. In this context, every socioeconomic organisation must recognise the idiosyncratic and "physiological" strengths-weaknesses based on

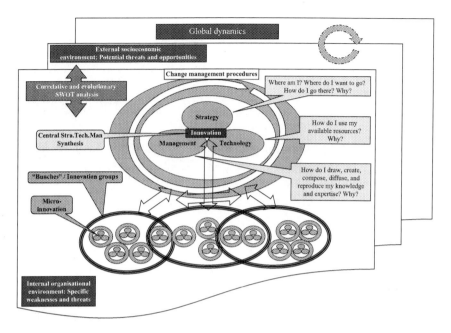

Fig. 6.2 Stra.Tech.Man innovation at the various organisational levels and correlative-evolutionary SWOT analysis

the synthesising Stra.Tech.Man perspective. This realisation opens the path for corresponding specific opportunities and threats derived from today's demanding and labyrinthine global economy and dynamics (Vlados, 2019b). Furthermore, this framework for change becomes increasingly challenging nowadays, considering that globalisation has entered a profound crisis and revolutionary phase (Schwab, 2016; Vlados et al., 2018), especially after the COVID-19 pandemic (Thrassou et al., 2022; Vlados & Chatzinikolaou, 2021).

Therefore, the most profound problems for effectively managing change emerge from the organisation's physiological core. For this reason, the "Stra.Tech.Man" perspective of innovation enlightens the change management effort since it defines the extent of possible paradigmatic mutation and shift (Depoux, 2009). Based on these conceptual bases of business physiology, five change management phases in "Stra.Tech.Man" innovation are suggested (Vlados, 2019c). From this perspective, the steps of managing change determine a continuous cycle (Fig. 6.3).

6 Conceptual Mutations of Change Management...

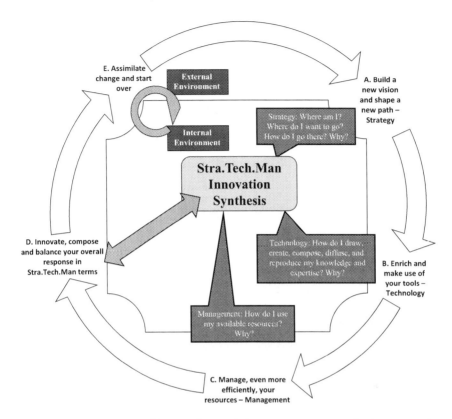

Fig. 6.3 The five steps of innovation and change management in the Stra.Tech.Man approach

This five-step method of understanding change consists of eight points each, setting out a continuous process for transformative business action:

I. Successful strategic development:

   (a) Make clear and deepen the vision and mission—unify the firm's mindset.
   (b) Challenge the organisation's strategic certainties and warn for threats—come closer to its allies and partners.
   (c) Build mechanisms to keep track of changes occurring in the firm's external environment—come closer to the customers, suppliers, and competitors.

(d) Develop an understanding of the firm's internal environment—come closer to its employees and make them part of the strategic process.

(e) Build a correlative and evolutionary SWOT analysis to realise the firm's specific strengths and weaknesses that unlock potential respective opportunities and threats.

(f) Carefully build the firm's alternatives and openly evaluate them—ask those around the firm and realise that there is no one best way.

(g) Choose the strategy that better suits the firm—with ambition but also realism.

(h) Comprehensively and coherently analyse the firm's tactics and policies.

II. Successful technological development:

(a) Understand the firm's technology background.

(b) Get a complete comparative picture of the firm's technological skills.

(c) Develop mechanisms for scouting the environment and collecting new technical information.

(d) Cultivate the internal potential for creating new technical abilities.

(e) Stimulate the firm's mechanisms for modern technology diffusion.

(f) Reinforce the company's tools for technological information assimilation.

(g) Practically support the integrated application of modern technology—do not be afraid of experimentation since mistakes are allowed if they offer meaningful lessons.

(h) Reward the productive application of modern technology.

III. Successful management development:

(a) Experiment with new planning methods.

(b) Make the organisation chart flatter.

(c) Build a meritocratic way of putting the right person in the right place at the right time.

6 Conceptual Mutations of Change Management... 127

(d) Give the firm's people specific leaders they want and inspire them.
(e) Make the firm a learning organisation.
(f) Motivate and specialise the structure of incentives.
(g) Measure and evaluate from a comparative and fair perspective.
(h) Open new communication channels and build new ways to coordinate action.

IV. Successful innovation synthesis:

(a) Clear up the accomplished strategy, technology, and management transformations by carefully preparing the new Stra.Tech. Man synthesis.
(b) Balance and multilaterally adjust this innovational Stra.Tech. Man synthesis.
(c) Spread the revolutionary message and build a dynamic guiding coalition.
(d) Remove obstacles, commission roles, and lead.
(e) Maintain balance during the intervention's implementation.
(f) Generate short-term wins and not over-celebrate them.
(g) Set up checkpoints and evaluate the firm's overall change management and innovation effort.
(h) Do not forget to reward the warriors who fought on this battlefield of innovation.

V. Successful assimilation of change and continuous transformation:

(a) Preserve the acts that brought results and unify them.
(b) Deepen and develop the firm's physiology.
(c) Do not punish those who honestly experimented and failed, but those who abandoned their duties during the battle.
(d) Refresh the hierarchy.
(e) Make yesterday's success a goal to overcome rather than a monument of conservatism.
(f) Put foreigners and "devil's advocates" in the firm and withstand their critique.
(g) Build a firm that can be "loved" by internal and external stakeholders.
(h) Do not rest on laurels. Always start all over again.

In the past, we have used various elements of this Stra.Tech.Man change management and innovation approach by experimentally implementing it with a specific sectoral–industrial focus to offer consulting and advice in diverse organisations. Within this advising direction, this method has prospects to be further systematised, enriched, and used in the field for diagnostic organisational research and surveys. Our team is currently working on a related project that integrates this concept into the "Scorecard" perspective by considering an additional level of fundamental "corporate finance indicators" beyond the five main ones (Vlados, 2021). This complete qualitative and quantitative system of evaluating and self-evaluating an organisation's performance could be implemented in the future for managerial, technological, and strategic control, possibly for smaller organisations besides the bigger ones that most Scorecard methodologies seem to be focusing on (Hoque, 2014; Van Looy & Shafagatova, 2016). This "Stra.Tech.Man" scorecard could be a prolific application in the field of change management because most scorecard-type and performance measurement methodologies do not have an explicit change management framework that can function complementarily and become quickly accessible by all types and physiologies of socio-economic organisations.

References

Andrikopoulos, A. (2009). Irreversible Investment, Managerial Discretion and Optimal Capital Structure. *Journal of Banking & Finance, 33*(4), 709–718. https://doi.org/10.1016/j.jbankfin.2008.11.002

Augsburg, T. (2010). *Becoming Interdisciplinary: An Introduction to Interdisciplinary Studies.* Kendall/Hunt Pub.

Burnes, B. (2009). *Managing Change: A Strategic Approach to Organisational Dynamics.* Prentice Hall/Financial Times.

Burns, T., & Stalker, G. M. (2011). Mechanistic and Organic Systems of Management. In I. M. Godwyn & J. H. Gittell (Eds.), *Sociology of Organizations: Structures and Relationships* (pp. 14–18). SAGE Publications.

Coch, L., & French, J. R., Jr. (1948). Overcoming Resistance to Change. *Human Relations, 1*(4), 512–532. https://doi.org/10.1177/001872674800100408

Covey, S. R. (1989a). *Principle-centered Leadership: Teaching People How to Fish*. Executive Excellence.

Covey, S. R. (1989b). *The 7 Habits of Highly Effective People*. Simon & Schuster.

Covey, S. R. (2004). *The 8th Habit: From Effectiveness to Greatness*. Free Press.

de Geus, A. (2002). *The Living Company*. Harvard Business School Press.

Delapierre, M., & Mytelka, L. K. (2002). Blurring Boundaries: New Inter-firm Relationships and the Emergence of Networked, Knowledge-based Oligopolies. In *The Changing Boundaries of the Firm: Explaining Evolving Inter-firm Relations* (pp. 73–94). Routledge. https://doi.org/10.432 4/9780203443408-10

Depoux, D. (2009). New Paradigms in Organizational Design. In A. Bausch & B. Schwenker (Eds.), *Handbook Utility Management* (pp. 105–133). Springer. https://doi.org/10.1007/978-3-540-79349-6_7

Di Stefano, G., Gambardella, A., & Verona, G. (2012). Technology Push and Demand Pull Perspectives in Innovation Studies: Current Findings and Future Research Directions. *Research Policy, 41*(8), 1283–1295. https://doi. org/10.1016/j.respol.2012.03.021

Duck, J. D. (1993). Managing Change: The Art of Balancing. *Harvard Business Review, 71*(6), 109–118.

Englehardt, C. S., & Simmons, P. R. (2002). Organizational Flexibility for a Changing World. *Leadership & Organization Development Journal, 23*(3), 113–121. https://doi.org/10.1108/01437730210424057

Friedman, T. L. (1999). *The Lexus and the Olive Tree: Understanding Globalization*. Simon and Schuster.

Frodeman, R., Klein, J. T., & Pacheco, R. C. S. (2019). *The Oxford Handbook of Interdisciplinarity*. Oxford University Press.

Georgalis, J., Samaratunge, R., Kimberley, N., & Lu, Y. (2015). Change Process Characteristics and Resistance to Organisational Change: The Role of Employee Perceptions of Justice. *Australian Journal of Management, 40*(1), 89–113. https://doi.org/10.1177/0312896214526212

GEST. (1986). *Grappes Technologiques: Les nouvelles stratégies d'entreprise [Technological Grapes: The Newest Entrepreneurial Strategies]*. McGraw-Hill.

Ghannay, J. C., & Mamlouk, Z. B. A. (2012). Synergy between Competitive Intelligence and Knowledge Management—A Key for Competitive Advantage. *Journal of Intelligence Studies in Business, 2*(2), 23–34. https://doi. org/10.37380/jisib.v2i2.38

Gibson, R. (Ed.). (1998). Rethinking the Future: Rethinking Business Principles, Competition, Control & Complexity, Leadership, Markets and the World. Nicholas Brealey.

Gill, R. (2002). Change Management–or Change Leadership? *Journal of Change Management, 3*(4), 307–318. https://doi.org/10.1080/714023845

Goss, T., Pascale, R., & Athos, A. (1993). The Reinvention Roller Coaster: Risking the Present for a Powerful Future. *Harvard Business Review, 71*(6), 97–106.

Grant, M. J., & Booth, A. (2009). A Typology of Reviews: An Analysis of 14 Review Types and Associated Methodologies. *Health Information & Libraries Journal, 26*(2), 91–108. https://doi.org/10.1111/j.1471-1842.2009.00848.x

Grote, G., & Künzler, C. (2000). Change Management as Risk Factor? *Proceedings of the Human Factors and Ergonomics Society Annual Meeting, 44*(27), 337–340. https://doi.org/10.1177/154193120004402715

Hacklin, F., & Wallin, M. W. (2013). Convergence and Interdisciplinarity in Innovation Management: A Review, Critique, and Future Directions. *The Service Industries Journal, 33*(7–8), 774–788. https://doi.org/10.108 0/02642069.2013.740471

Hoque, Z. (2014). 20 Years of Studies on the Balanced Scorecard: Trends, Accomplishments, Gaps and Opportunities for Future Research. *The British Accounting Review, 46*(1), 33–59. https://doi.org/10.1016/j.bar.2013.10.003

Ismail, N. A., & Kuivalainen, O. (2015). The Effect of Internal Capabilities and External Environment on Small- and Medium-sized Enterprises' International Performance and the Role of the Foreign Market Scope: The Case of the Malaysian Halal Food Industry. *Journal of International Entrepreneurship, 13*(4), 418–451. https://doi.org/10.1007/s10843-015-0160-x

Jacques, E. (2006). *Requisite Organization: A Total System for Effective Managerial Organization and Managerial Leadership for the 21st Century*. Cason Hall.

Jones, D. J., & Recardo, R. J. (2013). *Leading and Implementing Business Change Management: Making Chance Stick in the Contemporary Organization*. Routledge. https://doi.org/10.4324/9780203073957

Kantabutra, S., & Avery, G. C. (2010). The Power of Vision: Statements that Resonate. *Journal of Business Strategy, 31*(1), 37–45. https://doi.org/10.1108/02756661011012769

Kelly, K. (1994). *Out of Control: The New Biology Of Machines, Social Systems and the Economic World*. Basic Books.

Kirkpatrick, S. (2016). *Build a Better Vision Statement: Extending Research with Practical Advice*. Lexington Books.

Kotler, P., & Caslione, J. A. (2009). *Chaotics: The Business of Managing and Marketing in the Age of Turbulence*. American Management Association.

Kotter, J. P. (1995). Leading Change: Why Transformation Efforts Fail. *Harvard Business Review, 73*(2).

6 Conceptual Mutations of Change Management... 131

Kotter, J. P. (1996). *Leading Change*. Harvard Business School Press.

Laudicina, P. A., & Peterson, E. R. (2016). *From Globalization to Islandization* (Global Business Policy Council (GBPC)/Research Report). AT Kearney.

Leavy, B. (2014). Strategy, Organization and Leadership in a New "Transient-Advantage" World. *Strategy & Leadership, 42*(4), 3–13. https://doi.org/10.1108/SL-05-2014-0038

Levitt, T. (1983). The Globalization of Markets. *Harvard Business Review, 61*(3), 92–102.

Martin, R. (1993). Changing the Mind of the Corporation. *Harvard Business Review, 71*(6), 81–89.

McKenzie, J., & Aitken, P. (2012). Learning to Lead the Knowledgeable Organization: Developing Leadership Agility. *Strategic HR Review, 11*(6), 329–334. https://doi.org/10.1108/14754391211264794

McNamara, D. E. (2009). From Fayol's Mechanistic to Today's Organic Functions of Management. *American Journal of Business Education, 2*(1), 63–78. https://doi.org/10.19030/ajbe.v2i1.4023

Meyer, C., & Davis, S. M. (2003). *It's Alive: The Coming Convergence of Information, Biology, and Business*. Crown Business.

Mohajan, H. K. (2018). Qualitative Research Methodology in Social Sciences and Related Subjects. *Journal of Economic Development, Environment and People, 7*(1), 23–48. https://doi.org/10.26458/jedep.v7i1.571

Morabito, J., Sack, I., & Bhate, A. (2018). The Basics of Design in the Knowledge Era: Dialectic and Synthesis. In I. J. Morabito, I. Sack, & A. Bhate (Eds.), *Designing Knowledge Organizations: A Pathway to Innovation Leadership* (pp. 74–77). Wiley.

Nordin, N. (2012). The Influence of Leadership Behavior and Organizational Commitment on Organizational Readiness for Change in a Higher Learning Institution. *Asia Pacific Education Review, 13*(2), 239–249. https://doi.org/10.1007/s12564-011-9200-y

O'Donovan, G. (2008). *The Corporate Culture Handbook: How to Plan, Implement and Measure a Successful Culture Change Programme*. Liffey Press. https://doi.org/10.1108/dlo.2008.08122aae.001

Oreg, S. (2003). Resistance to Change: Developing an Individual Differences Measure. *Journal of Applied Psychology, 88*(4), 680. https://doi.org/10.1037/0021-9010.88.4.680

Peters, M., Schneider, M., Griesshaber, T., & Hoffmann, V. H. (2012). The Impact of Technology-push and Demand-pull Policies on Technical Change – Does the Locus of Policies Matter? *Research Policy, 41*(8), 1296–1308. https://doi.org/10.1016/j.respol.2012.02.004

Raja, A. S., & Palanichamy, P. (2011). Leadership Styles and its Impact on Organizational Commitment. *Asia Pacific Business Review, 7*(3), 167–175. https://doi.org/10.1177/097324701100700315

Schaffer, R. H., & Thomson, H. A. (1992). Successful Change Programs Begin with Results. *Harvard Business Review, 70*(1), 80–89.

Schwab, K. (2016). *The Fourth Industrial Revolution.* Crown Business.

Senge, P. M. (1990). *The Fifth Discipline: The Art and Practice of the Learning Organization.* Doubleday/Currency.

Senge, P. M. (1999). *The Dance of Change: The Challenges of Sustaining Momentum in Learning Organizations: A Fifth Discipline Resource.* Currency/Doubleday.

Senge, P. M. (2008). *Presence: Human Purpose and the Field of the Future.* Crown Business: Currency Books.

Snyder, H. (2019). Literature Review as a Research Methodology: An Overview and Guidelines. *Journal of Business Research, 104*, 333–339. https://doi.org/10.1016/j.jbusres.2019.07.039

Thakkar, B. S. (2021). *Paradigm Shift in Management Philosophy: Future Challenges in Global Organizations.* Palgrave Macmillan. https://doi.org/10.1007/978-3-030-29710-7

Thrassou, A., Orfanos, D., & Tsoukatos, E. (2018). Linking Motivational Leadership with Creativity. In D. Vrontis, Y. Weber, A. Thrassou, S. M. R. Shams, & E. Tsoukatos (Eds.), *Innovation and Capacity Building: Cross-disciplinary Management Theories for Practical Applications* (pp. 77–108). Springer International Publishing. https://doi.org/10.1007/978-3-319-90945-5_5

Thrassou, A., Uzunboylu, N., Efthymiou, L., Vrontis, D., Weber, Y., Shams, S. M. R., & Tsoukatos, E. (2022). Editorial Introduction: Business Under Crises: Organizational Adaptations. In D. Vrontis, A. Thrassou, Y. Weber, S. M. R. Shams, E. Tsoukatos, & L. Efthymiou (Eds.), *Business Under Crisis, Volume II: Organisational Adaptations* (pp. 1–17). Springer International Publishing. https://doi.org/10.1007/978-3-030-76575-0_1

Van Looy, A., & Shafagatova, A. (2016). Business Process Performance Measurement: A Structured Literature Review of Indicators, Measures and Metrics. *Springerplus, 5*(1), 1797. https://doi.org/10.1186/s40064-016-3498-1

Vlados, C. (2019a). *Stra.Tech.Man (Strategy-Technology-Management): Theory and Concepts.* KSP Books. http://books.ksplibrary.org/978-605-7602-83-1/

Vlados, C. (2019b). On a Correlative and Evolutionary SWOT Analysis. *Journal of Strategy and Management, 12*(3), 347–363. https://doi.org/10.1108/JSMA-02-2019-0026

Vlados, C. (2019c). Change Management and Innovation in the "Living Organization": The Stra.Tech.Man Approach. *Management Dynamics in the Knowledge Economy, 7*(2), 229–256. https://doi.org/10.25019/MDKE/7.2.06

Vlados, C. (2021). The Stra.Tech.Man Scorecard. *International Journal of Business Administration, 12*(2), 36–63. https://doi.org/10.5430/ijba.v12n2p36

Vlados, C., & Chatzinikolaou, D. (2019). Business Ecosystems Policy in Stra.Tech.Man Terms: The Case of the Eastern Macedonia and Thrace Region. *Journal of Entrepreneurship, Management and Innovation, 15*(3), 163–197. https://doi.org/10.7341/20191536

Vlados, C., & Chatzinikolaou, D. (2021). Impact of COVID-19 Crisis, Global Transformation Approaches and Emerging Organisational Adaptations: Towards a Restructured Evolutionary Perspective. In D. Vrontis, A. Thrassou, Y. Weber, S. M. R. Shams, E. Tsoukatos, & L. Efthymiou (Eds.), *Business Under Crisis, Volume II: Contextual Transformations and Organisational Adaptations* (pp. 65–90). Palgrave Macmillan. https://doi.org/10.1007/978-3-030-76575-0_4

Vlados, C., Deniozos, N., Chatzinikolaou, D., & Demertzis, M. (2018). Towards an Evolutionary Understanding of the Current Global Socio-Economic Crisis and Restructuring: From a Conjunctural to a Structural and Evolutionary Perspective. *Research in World Economy, 9*(1), 15–33. https://doi.org/10.5430/rwe.v9n1p15

Vrontis, D., El Nemar, S., Al Osta, B., & Azizi, J. R. (2018). Impact of Innovation and Change Management on Employees' Performance. In D. Vrontis, Y. Weber, A. Thrassou, S. M. R. Shams, & E. Tsoukatos (Eds.), *Innovation and Capacity Building: Cross-disciplinary Management Theories for Practical Applications* (pp. 131–150). Springer International Publishing. https://doi.org/10.1007/978-3-319-90945-5_7

7

The Spread of Artificial Intelligence and Its Impact on Employment: Evidence from the Banking and Accounting Sectors

Bernardo Batiz-Lazo, Leonidas Efthymiou, and Kyra Davies

7.1 Introduction

The current chapter explores the impact of Artificial Intelligence (AI) on employment in two different sectors, namely accounting and banking. AI is relatively new to accounting (ICAEW, 2018). Currently, only a handful of big firms make considerable use of it. However, the growing AI investment by accounting firms cannot go unnoticed. Therefore, the first study looks at the potential impact of AI on the supply of labour while

---

B. Batiz-Lazo
Northumbria University, Newcastle, UK

L. Efthymiou (✉)
School of Business, Department of Management, University of Nicosia, Nicosia, Cyprus
e-mail: efthymiou.l@unic.ac.cy

K. Davies
Delfryn, Eton Park, Rhuddlan, Denbighshire, UK

© The Author(s), under exclusive license to Springer Nature Switzerland AG 2022
A. Thrassou et al. (eds.), *Business Advancement through Technology Volume II*, Palgrave Studies in Cross-disciplinary Business Research, In Association with EuroMed Academy of Business, https://doi.org/10.1007/978-3-031-07765-4_7

answering questions like: are the accountants vulnerable to losing their jobs as AI takes over data analysis and other accounting functions? How do employability prospects, skills and learning change with AI? What is expected of accountants to remain competitive in the labour market? Addressing these questions will enhance our understanding of how accountants could mitigate risks and accommodate the emergence of AI.

Unlike the accounting sector, the use of AI in banks has been increasing for years, varying from clients' experience and support to trading and data management. The second study queries the actual use of AI in banks' recruitment and selection processes within this context. The main questions this second part of the fieldwork sought to answer were: do Cypriot banks use AI in their Human Resource processes? If yes, how is AI utilized in recruitment and selection? And, what are the alleged implications, either positive or negative? The analysis draws on data collected through online interviews. The sample consists of five senior Human Resource managers, each sitting at a different financial institution. It is worth noting that, together, these five entities had a combined market share exceeding 70% of retail deposits (Central Bank of Cyprus, 2021). These interviews were conducted online due to ethical and health and safety guidelines during the pandemic, which required researchers to avoid face to face interation and the need to maintain social distancing.

The two sectors, of course, are not examined as homogenous recipients of technological change. However, their disparity allows comparing and contrasting the narrative of AI (accounting) with its actual impact (banking). The remainder of this chapter is structured as follows: in the next section, the literature review is divided into two distinct parts. The first reviews literature concerning AI in the field of accounting. The second sub-section looks at the application of AI for recruitment and selection in the banking sector. The third section presents the data collection and analysis methods used during fieldwork. The final two sections present fieldwork findings and advance a tentative conclusion.

7.2 Technological Change and the Labor Market

7.2.1 Challenges of AI for the Future Accountant

The practice of accounting is multifaceted. Although these practices have co-existed with applications of computer and information technologies since at least the 1950s, there still remain several time-consuming and labour-intensive processes that need to be undertaken by qualified accountants. Hence, the different forms of AI may impact practice in a number of ways. For instance, the complexity characterizing the tasks of accountants and auditors, alongside the ever-changing environment, could benefit from expert systems (O'Leary, 1986).

One such expert system is so-called machine learning (ML), which is a subset of AI. ML is seen as useful to accountants due to its ability to collect and learn from data. A machine is able to use algorithms to break down data, learn from data and continues to learn (Shalev-Shwartz & Ben-David, 2014). Also, ML can be used to classify a transaction and forecasting (Shimamoto, 2018). For instance, in the United States, 48 million people completed their own tax returns online in 2014 using automatic tax-return software powered by ML applications (Susskind & Susskind, 2017, p. 85).

AI's expert systems can be helpful for both small and large enterprises. For instance, the cash-flows, invoices, receipts and other tasks which are typically assigned by small businesses to accountants, are now undertaken online (Susskind & Susskind, 2017, p. 86). Also, for larger companies, tax systems are available which are capable of collecting data, calculating tax returns, annual accounts and other reports. In 2009, 70% of the FTSE-100 companies prepared and submitted their corporate tax returns through an expert system designed by accounting consultants Deloitte (ibid.). 'Deloitte Revatic Smart' allows companies to recover foreign VAT payments using optical character recognition software with little human interference.

Li and Zheng (2018) suggest that AI improves usage of time, efficiency, reduces errors, and improves the industry's competitiveness. For example, 'robot accountants' can offer business solutions to clients, while accountants concentrate on decision making (Shimamoto, 2018). It is a hybrid process where AI works along with humans rather than separately (Shimamoto, 2018; Susskind & Susskind, 2017); a good example here is when tax returns are completed and submitted online, whereas tax-experts serve as advisors. Besides, some authors argue that AI is just not good enough to undertake an accountant's full role (Marr, 2018; Taylor, 2018).

More recently, it seems that accounting companies have been experimenting with AI for a broader range of purposes. According to Zhou (2017), three of the 'big four' accounting firms are testing different approaches. Ernst and Young (EY) focuses on AI's Return on Investment (ROI). PriceWaterhouseCoopers (PwC) have been using 'sprints' by offering clients a demonstration of a working system and then improving it. Deloitte has a team dedicated to innovation, which focuses almost 80% of its work solely on applications of AI to improve the accounting and auditing functions. Also, while attempting to facilitate and enhance an understanding of AI, the Institute of Chartered Accountants in England and Wales (ICAEW) offers guidance and training to stakeholders, including regulators, governments and policymakers.

But despite the innovations mentioned above, it remains the case that AI is still relatively new to the accounting profession. For some, the application of AI solutions in auditing and accounting remains in its infancy when compared to other industries and sectors (ICAEW, 2018). However, the increasing use of AI applications and the growing investment by big accounting firms beg the question, 'what would be the impact of AI on the accounting profession?'. As discussed in the next section, some worries and uncertainties have been recorded through fears that the increase of AI may threaten job prospects as the skill set of auditors and accountants, in general, is disrupted (Li & Zheng, 2018).

7.2.2 The Possible Impact of AI on Employment

McGaughey (2018) questioned whether the advent of the Internet, robotics and AI would bring a 'jobless future'. This question is not entirely new. There has been an ongoing concern about the effects of digitisation on employment; and whether people will become unemployed. Some evidence suggests a negative effect on employment and wages for low and middle educated industrial workers (Mann & Püttmann, 2017). The employment to population ratio increases within the commuting distance of a new automation technology innovation. Similarly, Acemoglu and Restrepo (2018) contend that the effects on wages and employment with one robot to a thousand workers would decrease employment to population ratio and wages, but only slightly. However, if the ratio of robots to humans is set to quadruple by 2025, then the effects would be much more serious.

Evidence from a study in 17 countries between 1993 and 2007 by Graetz and Michaels (2017, 2018), claimed that the increase of robots increases total productivity and wages. Also, robots may be reducing low-educated employment and the number of hours worked. In the same vein, Kemeny and Osman (2018) find that in metropolitan areas of the United States, growth in tech employment offers benefits to non-tradable (areas of work where the product cannot be produced in one country and sold in another) workers real wages.

Moreover, based on a study of 702 occupations in the United States, out of which 42% were on the verge of digitisation, Frey and Osborne (2017) confirmed that the introduction of machine learning and big data change certain types of tasks. Cognitive and non-routine tasks are becoming more obtainable, which in turn changes the structure of the workforce. This finding is consonant with Graetz and Michaels (2018), who claim that low-educated jobs are non-susceptible to computerization, whereas vacancies may relocate to more creative and social intelligence occupations. Following these findings, Study 1 will further explore the use and impact of AI on employment in the accounting sector.

7.2.3 AI for Recruitment and Selection in the Banking Sector

Digital systems become increasingly necessary across a wide range of industries around the world. The examples include educational platforms (Efthymiou & Zarifis, 2021; Doukanari et al., 2021; Efthymiou et al.,

2021), platform-based supply-chains in the cruise industry (Sdoukopoulos et al., 2020; Efthymiou et al., 2022, the digital economy (Batiz-Lazo & Efthymiou, 2016a, b, c; Efthymiou & Michael, 2016), big data and analytics in tourism (Efthymiou, 2018; Efthymiou et al., 2020), blockchain and robots in hotels (Efthymiou et al., 2019), to mention a few. However, Artificial Intelligence (AI) is characterised by some distinguishing aspects. AI is a computerized system that is programmed by humans to work and respond in human-like manners. It is an artificial mimicry of tasks and capacities that would otherwise require human knowledge (Ryan, 2020). But most importantly, it seems that AI has the ability to redefine what can be digitised.

Currently, all AI is 'narrow', meaning it can only do what it is designed to do through specific algorithms. Yet, narrow AIs are mostly much better than humans at the task they were made for (van Duin & Bakhshi, 2017). Therefore, AI systems can be programmed to specialize in certain tasks, such as the function of recruitment and selection in banks. At the same time, conventional sourcing methods, such as handing-in job applications, are increasingly falling out of favour. Their place is taken over by e-recruitment and other internet-based processes.

AI appears as a solution to problems occurring in the ever-changing business landscape (Javed & Kabir Brishti, 2020). For example, the banking sector can utilize AI to automate pre-screening in the hiring process. The platform can support employers in locating candidates, examining their CVs, gathering reactions to pre-screening questions and leading psychometric tests. Candidates can be granted, and remain in continuous communication with the platform, on a 24/7 basis (Flinders, 2018). Using AI in the recruitment process saves time to recruiters, and enables them to step in later in the recruitment process. In other words, recruiting managers do not need to invest time overseeing huge pools of candidates. Rather, they can just focus on interviews and closing offers.

Another innovation in AI is the use of chatbots to communicate with candidates. Chatbots facilitate individualized commitment with candidates. Similar to virtual personal assistants like Siri, and Google Now, chatbots utilize regular language to understand messages and react to them. What is more, AI may use algorithmic computations, and comparative processes, to recognize if a candidate is dishonest. That can be achieved through repetitive questions with different sequence and meaning (Wilfred, 2018). Email, SMS, social media, and messaging apps are correspondence channels that can utilize chatbot applications to ease correspondence among candidates and organizations without time and area constraints (Ibrahim & Hassan, 2019).

Moreover, another AI function for recruitment and selection, which has become increasingly popular, is the so called 'Video Interviews'. Video interviews can take place remotely, save time, and help overcome certain challenges, such as the need for social-distancing requirements during the coronavirus pandemic. AI has its own role to play in this process. It can be used to break down non-verbal communication patterns and facial expression during video interviews. Additionally, human bias during interviews is reduced, whereas, the interviewer is able to examine the recordings at a later stage, and take more precise decisions (Ibrahim & Hassan, 2019). AI works without the inadequacies innate to people, like exhaustion, feelings, predispositions, and restricted time. Also, the increasing intelligence of these machines makes them able to distinguish irregularities and recognize different particulars among large bases of data (Wilfred, 2018).

What is more, AI reduces the need for external organizations specializing in sourcing talent, along with their costs (Wilfred, 2018). In addition, AI can help organizations discover passive talents. This is because it utilizes bots to scan the web for potential candidates, including websites, virtual gatherings and tech chat-rooms, as well as traditional social media sites (Oswal et al., 2020). The bots aim at discovering a great match for the work, based on the set qualifications and standards of the position. They also explore if a certain individual is potentially ready for a job change, making it possible for organizations to poach talents which are uncommon to discover (Iqbal, 2018).

Furthermore, AI-supported technology makes the recruitment process faster. Unlike the conventional HR methods, where it is hard to screen numerous candidates simultaneously, organizations can set up an AI-enabled digital recruitment system. An AI recruiting assistant can converse with thousands of candidates at the same time. It answers applicants' inquiries, positions them depending on pre-characterized factors, and alerts them when a position has been filled (Iqbal, 2018; Tambe et al., 2019).

Nonetheless, while AI can enhance the procedure of recruitment and selection, it also comes with certain challenges. While AI systems are incredible when dealing with repeated assignments, their creativity and imagination are limited. The affectability or innovation that comes from having the sense of seeing, hearing and feeling, cannot be imitated in the most intricate of machines. The natural sensibilities that people have during interviews can never be reproduced in machines (Wilfred, 2018). While human knowledge can be expressed through algorithms, human feelings and virtues can never be incorporated into them (Wilfred, 2018; Ibrahim & Hassan, 2019).

Departing from this review, the analysis sets out to explore phenomena through two different studies. The first study, which is conceptual, focuses on accounting firms, to explore the impact of AI on employment. The second study, which is empirical, examines the potential application of AI for recruitment and selection in the banking sector. The next section presents the study's research design.

7.3   Research Design

The current research draws on mixed methods (empirical and conceptual), within the research philosophy of 'pragmatism' (Menand, 1997; Rescher, 2000; Rorty, 2000). Pragmatism 'offers a method for selecting methodological mixes that can help researchers better answer many of their research questions' (Johnson & Onwuegbuzie, 2004, p. 17). While 'mixed methods' research usually combines quantitative and qualitative research techniques into a single study, 'pragmatism' is open to additional typologies, dimensions and considerations. As explained below, the current chapter constructs a mixed model, by comprising conceptual (Study 1) as well as empirical (Study 2) studies.

Study 1: To examine the possible impact of AI on the accounting professions, the study has reviewed literature published by experts in the field of AI. The review looks at the intersection of AI, employment and accounting, published within the last 10 years. The search located 15 articles through the University's online library, 59 articles on ProQuest, 53 articles on SAGE, and several practitioner reports through random searches on the Internet.

The literature was examined, coded, categorized and analyzed using the NVIVO software. Use of the 'word frequency' and 'matrix' have been made throughout the research. For the 'word frequency' creation, there were 'stop-words' in place to avoid irrelevant words. There was also a restriction of 50 words, and words with three letters and over. Through coding and breaking down each code, an analysis of the data collection was able to take place. NVIVO facilitated a systematic review through 'case classification'; the creation of a visualisation of various trends; and the creation of big paragraphs of analysis.

Study 2: To explore the use of AI for recruitment and selection in the Cypriot Banking sector, along with its possible benefits and challenges, online interviews have been conducted with banks officials. The interviews took place in Spring, 2021. The interviews were meant to take place physically, through face-to-face meetings. However, the coronavirus outbreak (SARS-Cov-2) resulted in several postponements, and eventually, the collection of findings through online interviews. The method of in-depth interviews has been selected to secure a good level of responses.

Gaining access and consent proved to be a very difficult process, due to the data-security protocols applied in banks. Indicatively, only 50% of the predetermined sample accepted the invitation. However, after the first interview, the responder was kind enough to introduce us to colleagues in additional banks. At the end, five individuals accepted invitations to participate in the study. Although the sample size may seem to be small, the participants work in five main Cypriot commercial banks, with a combined market share of deposits of over 70% (Central Bank of Cyprus, 2021). They are also experts in their field, as they hold managerial positions in Human Resource departments. Therefore, the sample is representative of the Cypriot banking sector. The fieldwork was conducted in line with international Research Ethics standards. Informed consent, confidentiality and anonymity were applied to all interviews.

7.4 Findings

7.4.1 Study 1: Views About the Impact of AI on the Accounting Profession

The first visualisation from NVIVO shows that the papers based on accounting had both optimistic and pessimistic views. In nine papers, AI and its effects on the accounting profession are seen as positive. In one paper, AI's impact is seen as negative. The four papers under the optimistic node believe that AI is likely to have a positive effect on accounting. They also rule out any possibility of AI taking over the profession and marginalizing human employees. When the nodes were further analysed it was found that a significant amount of views suggest that the accounting profession is not at risk by AI diffusion, now or in the short term. In five out of 13 papers, optimism concerns the short-term. This included statements like 'Don't press the panic button yet' (Nagarajah, 2016, p. 35) and 'widespread adoption in business and accounting is still in early stages' (ICAEW, 2018, p. 8).

7.4.2 Accountants' Attitudes

Another theme from the accounting papers was the need for change of accountants' attitudes. Under the 'accountants' attitudes' node, there were 10 papers with 30 references. All papers support the notion that accountants should have the ability to change when it comes to AI. The 'accountants' attitudes' node was then sub-coded into the 'need to embrace AI' and 'types of personality'. The results suggest a clear instruction for change in the accountants' attitudes, which cannot be ignored. 'Need' was one of the most used words for this node. Moreover, the percentages produced by NVIVO about individual nodes, reconfirmed the lack of articles exploring AI and its impact on the accounting profession.

7.4.3 Skills, Robots, Data, Future and Investment Nodes

The node 'skill' included discussions based around the need for humans to be creative to stay relevant as AI cannot be creative yet. While there are accountants' routine jobs being taken over by AI, other skills work hand in hand with AI. Another node concerns 'robots'. It was found that robots are discussed along with their possible impact on all professions. Since robots are only getting cheaper and safer to use, reports state that jobs will be susceptible to this technology, as well as AI, sooner than we think. The node 'data' included 10 papers with 26 references making it a popular topic amongst the papers. It is clear from the node that data is beneficial to professions and there is an increasing amount of data which can be utilized. Unlike AI, 'big data' was discussed in a positive way in regards to its use. The node 'future' for both the accounting and non-accounting was split into two categories, optimists and pessimists. A common theme from the pessimist nodes was that AI will have effects on humans lives but not knowing exactly how or when. For the optimists, for as long as humans adjust their skill set, AI will not have massive effects. The node 'investment' showed the lack of investment in AI in the accounting industry. Whilst larger companies have begun research on AI, the slow return on the investment seems to have reduced the intentions to spend further in the accounting profession.

7.4.4 Study 2: The Digital Realm

Initial discussions with participants were centred around the ongoing digitization and algorithmic diffusion in the banking sector. For instance, one participant explained the importance of encouraging customers towards digital means and electronic banking. She mentioned: '*[e]lectronic banking uses different algorithms. One example is the chat box, where customers ask for clarifications or additional help. These days, the majority of customers prefer to make their transactions electronically*'. In another example, a participant explained how algorithms offer to customers a statistical analysis for the amount spent per week, month and year. The overwhelming impression was that bank officials support fully the digital turn, and expect customers to do the same.

Then, discussions focused on AI. Participants seemed to be aware of this technology, as well as the way it works for hiring purposes in the banking sector. As one participant mentioned, AI can be applied for recruitment purposes in several ways: '*It can create accurate job descriptions. By analyzing current employee's characteristics, abilities and skills, AI can define what the actual needs of the company are. Such job descriptions are likely to attract candidates, who fit the job description*'. In another bank, a participant explained how AI can be used to find not only active, but also passive candidates. With AI, the attempt to find the perfect match for specific positions is increasing. All these findings resemble previous studies, as discussed earlier in the second section where extant literature was reviewed (e.g. Iqbal, 2018).

Another participant suggested that AI can be used for screening: '*All applications are examined [whereas], applications that do not meet the required criteria are rejected. Instead of interviewing hundreds of candidates, AI simplifies the process*'. These findings are consonant with previous studies, supporting that AI is indeed capable of saving labour time and related costs. The same participant explained the use of AI through the chatbot before the interview. Candidates '*can answer a set of questions, created by AI, so that the number of interviews are reduced*'. At the same time, she added, the chatbot remains available on a 24/7 basis, for uninterrupted communication with candidates.

Also, a participant explained that AI can be used for minimizing human involvement. '*It evaluates candidates through automated questionnaires, prior to the interview, and produces objective results. For example, if the interview is online, through a camera, AI can recognize if a candidate is lying about something by understanding the body language.* This is also relevant to previous studies, and adds extra objectivity to the recruitment and selection process.

However, while participants are well informed about the benefits of AI, none of the five banks is currently using it for recruitment and selection. As presented below, the reasons for not using AI vary.

7.4.5 Reasons for Not Utilizing AI in the Cypriot Banking Sector

One of the reasons for not using AI in Cypriot banks concerns the downsizing and restructuring of the sector. *'Unlike 20 years ago, the bank now hires a considerably lower percentage. Fifteen years ago, we were hiring three-to four-hundred employees per year. Now, we only hire thirty to forty employees. The recruitment and screening department consists by specialists in the HR field, who now have to deal with fewer applications'*, a participant mentioned. Another participant added, *'[t]hey have the desired abilities, skills, knowledge and experience to deal with day to day operations'*. In the same vein, a participant emphasized the team of experts that is currently in charge of recruitment and selection. *'Our hiring needs have been reduced. There is a team consisting of well-trained and experienced employees. They evaluate candidates based on their skills, qualifications and behaviour. If an appropriate candidate cannot be located, they reach out to recruitment agencies'*. Therefore, in all five banks, HR employees perform the hiring tasks without utilizing AI.

These findings are indicative of the intense downsizing and restructuring of the banking sector, which took place in Cyprus in the last decade. Cypriot banks with hundreds of branches around Cyprus and abroad downsized severely after the collapse of the economy in 2013 (e.g. Efthymiou & Michael, 2016). Of course, one of the questions arising from such findings is, what is better at times of downsizing and long-term cost efficiency, teams of human experts, or automation and Artificial Intelligence? As a participant admitted, *'...more time and employees are needed to study, analyse the CVs, and continue with all remaining hiring stages, including rejection to short-listing, first interview, further shortlisting, additional interviews and more'*.

Moreover, the findings reveal that the banks are interested in a very specific type of employee. A participant explained that since the hiring percentage has decreased dramatically, the bank seeks candidates who are already specialists on their fields. For example, they screen Cypriot bank employees who worked in London, where the banking system is similar. Also, the bank's existing employees are asked to approach people they may know, with required skills and characteristics for specific positions and vacancies. According to the participants, these methods consume far less resource, and work in a targeted manner. Similarly, a participant mentioned: '*we do not announce vacant positions publicly*', but later admitted that '*AI could help as obtain a variety of CVs, for both active and passive candidates*'.

Three of the participants referred to the lack of necessary infrastructure to support AI operations. They also referred to the high cost for implementing and running AI, along with the required knowhow. In addition, two of the participants revealed their discomfort with using advanced technology. They also revealed that their uncertainty concerning the use of an unknown technology, and the possibility of it being implemented inadequately, could affect their performance negatively.

But overall, most participants admitted that AI could help in some ways. As a participant mentioned, '…*if AI was used for creating job description and processing applications, biases would be eliminated and selection criteria would be applied more accurately. Also, the use of AI during the interviews would prevent possible biases and add sustainability to the process*'. In another bank, the HR coordinator mentioned that '*[t]he use of AI would minimise possible discrimination, and evaluate each candidate with the same criteria. AI reviews are more objective than human reports; therefore, the final decisions are likely to be more objective*', another participant added.

In another bank, the participant added: '*[h]umans' choices are subjective, their decisions are based on their beliefs, values and perception. For example, to me, a high school certificate is a key factor for selecting the best possible candidate. For another recruiter, the high school certificate could be useless. But I believe that less time will be needed in recruitment as AI will complete a major part of the hard work. So, recruiters will focus more on details and other important tasks. Currently, no other competitors use it in Cyprus and Greece*'.

Such findings reveal the contradictory nature of participants' expressions. On the one hand, participants argue for AI's potential benefits, especially in terms of objective evaluations, cost reduction and efficient hiring. On the other hand, the same participants negate previous arguments. Equally important are the findings concerning ethical consideration in the next section.

7.4.6 Challenges and Ethical Concerns for Using AI in Recruitment

The use of AI raises some ethical concerns. According to a participant, some candidates may belong to an older generation and be unfamiliar with the use of advanced technology. The obligatory use of AI during an online interview could cause stress and anxiety. Therefore, their performance as well as their 'equal opportunity' are likely to be affected negatively. Similarly, a participant, added, *'we would like to see clear guidelines by the European Union and the Cyprus Government concerning bias prevention and towards ensuring equal opportunities and fair processes'*.

Another participant expressed a concern on whether AI is intelligent and credible enough to produce objective evaluations. *'If we cannot establish trust, the impact on our mission will be negative rather than positive'*. Another participant added, *'we often trust our guts and feelings of intuition, regarding a candidate's potential fit into the team, or, we rely on references submitted to us by our network. By using AI in recruitment, the human factor will be eliminated and other implications could occur'*. In the same vein, a participant questioned whether AI is really capable of understanding body language, tone of voice and different dialects. For example, *'[i]n Cyprus we have a different dialect from Greece. Is AI capable of recognizing Cypriot language expressions?'*

7.5 Discussion and Conclusions

While examining the use of AI in accounting and banking, along with its potential implications on employment, it seems that our findings have generated more questions than answers. In Study 1, we identified a number of interesting points. Although the use of AI in the accounting industry is currently limited, bigger firms have already started to invest in its utilization. AI has great potential and may become prominent as it becomes cheaper and smarter. Among the different types of AI, Machine Learning (ML) and Artificial Neural Networks (ANN) seem to be the most likely to spread in the sector. ML is currently being used in accounting firms, but not in smaller firms. ANN is deemed a complicated form of AI, which is yet to be used in the accounting industry. However, sooner or later, AI will become part of the profession. Therefore, accountants will have no choice but to embrace it. In order to remain employable, humans should first learn how to work along with AI. Then, they have to focus on skills that AI cannot replicate, such as creativity. This is potentially an area of future research in the field of HRM, especially in terms of new skills, new job specifications and arising needs.

Furthermore, in Study 2, the participants agreed on the benefits of using AI for hiring. They emphasized the weaknesses of current hiring methods, prior to suggesting that AI is likely to enhance the objectivity of the hiring process. Such findings raise some interesting questions. For instance, what are the implications on employment for sectors that are yet to adopt AI? What is the impact on the practice itself? Moreover, while the participants argue AI's potential benefits, especially in term of objective evaluations, eliminating discrimination and biases, cost reduction and efficient hiring, the same participants expressed contradictory views. They actually voided previous statements by supporting the idea that AI lacks intuition.

Also, another paradox has to do with the feasibility of Cypriot banks in the long term. According to the officials participating in the study, AI is unnecessary due to the ongoing downsizing and reorganisation of the sector. However, would not AI be helpful for a sector trying to reduce costs? Would it not be beneficial to have digital expert systems (along with human experts) at times of downsizing and cost reengineering? Moreover, the Cypriot banks are interested in a very specific type of employee, with existing skills and experience. Fundamentally, such findings position the organizations against the principles of proper recruitment and selection. Certain benefits, such as developing a diversified and inclusive workforce, are reduced. Overall, such contradictory expressions have blurred our understanding even further. Equally important are the findings about ethical considerations. However, the concerns were expressed by officials who have no direct engagement with AI, in a sector that lacks the necessary infrastructure and knowhow to operate such expert systems. Therefore, it seems that the concerns were expressed on a rather hypothetical basis.

Overall, the comparison between the narrative of AI in accounting, and its actual impact in banking, provide evidence that the use of AI is not as widespread as its narrative would lead us to believe. However, stemming from both studies are some potentially problematic implications for current employees and future job applicants. It seems that bank employees, even at managerial levels, are uncertain and ambiguous about the actual use and benefit of AI. At the same time, accountants are muddled concerning AI's impact on their jobs. In closing, it seems that for certain sectors and tasks, AI remains a foggy shadowland.

References

Acemoglu, D., & Restrepo, P. (2018). *Artificial Intelligence, Automation and Work*. American Economic Review Papers and Proceedings [online] NBER Working Papers 24196. Accessed December 9, 2018, from https://economics.mit.edu/files/14641

Batiz-Lazo, B., & Efthymiou, L. (2016a). *The Book of Payments: Historical and Contemporary Views on the Cashless Economy*. Palgrave Macmillan.

Batiz-Lazo, B., & Efthymiou, L. (2016b). Introduction: The 360 Degrees of Cashlessness. In B. Batiz-Lazo & L. Efthymiou (Eds.), *The Book of Payments: Historical and Contemporary Views on the Cashless Economy* (pp. 1–10). Palgrave Macmillan.

Batiz-Lazo, B., & Efthymiou, L. (2016c). Preface: News from the Cashless Front. In B. Batiz-Lazo & L. Efthymiou (Eds.), *The Book of Payments: Historical and Contemporary Views on the Cashless Economy* (pp. ix–xi). Palgrave Macmillan.

Central Bank of Cyprus. (2021). *Register of Credit Institutions Operating in Cyprus* [online] www.centralbank.cy. Accessed July 23, 2021, from https://www.centralbank.cy/en/licensing-supervision/banks/register-of-credit-institutions-operating-in-cyprus

Doukanari, E., Ktoridou, D., Efthymiou, L., & Epaminonda, E. (2021). The Quest for Sustainable Teaching Praxis: Opportunities and Challenges of Multidisciplinary and Multicultural Teamwork. *Sustainability, 13*, 7210. https://doi.org/10.3390/su13137210

Efthymiou, L. (2018). Worker Body-Art in Upper-Market Hotels: Neither Accepted, Nor Prohibited. *International Journal of Hospitality Management, 74*, 99–108. https://doi.org/10.1016/j.ijhm.2018.02.012

Efthymiou, L., & Michael, S. (2016). The Cyprus Cash Crash: A Case of Collective Punishment. In B. Batiz-Lazo & L. Efthymiou (Eds.), *The Book of Payments: Historical and Contemporary Views on the Cashless Economy* (pp. 131–140). Palgrave Macmillan.

Efthymiou, L., & Zarifis, A. (2021). Modeling Students' Voice for Enhanced Quality in Online Management Education. *The International Journal of Management Education, 19*(2), 1–16. https://doi.org/10.1016/j.ijme.2021.100464

Efthymiou, L., Orphanidou, Y., & Panayiotou, G. (2019). The Latest from the Tourism Front: Technology, Innovation and Disruption. *The European Financial Review, 4*(5), 39–43.

Efthymiou, L., Orphanidou, Y., & Panayiotou, G. (2020). Delineating the Changing Frontstage and Backstage Segregation in High-End and Luxury Hotels. *Hospitality & Society, 10*(3), 287–312. https://doi.org/10.1386/hosp_00025_1

Efthymiou, L., Ktoridou, D., & Epaminonda, E. (2021, April 21–23) A Model for Experiential Learning by Replicating a Workplace Environment in Virtual Classes. In *IEEE Xplore Proceedings of EDUCON 2021, IEEE Global Engineering Education Conference, SS03B: Special Session Experiential Learning Practices, Vienna, Austria.*

Efthymiou, L., Dekoulou, E., Orphanidou, Y., Sdoukopoulos, E., Perra, V. M., Boile, M., & Bras, I. (2022). Crisis, Adaptation and Sustainability: Digital System Interoperability in the Cruise Industry. In A. Thrassou, D. Vrontis, Y. Weber, R. Shams, E. Tsoukatos, & L. Efthymiou (Eds.), *Business Under Crisis: Avenues for Innovation, Entrepreneurship and Sustainability* (Palgrave Studies in Cross-Disciplinary Business Research in Association with EuroMed Academy of Business). Palgrave Macmillan (Springer).

Flinders, K. (2018) *Bank Uses AI to Select Job Candidates* [online] ComputerWeekly.com. Accessed April 4, 2021, from https://www.computerweekly.com/news/252443238/Bank-uses-AI-to-select-job-candidates

Frey, C., & Osborne, M. (2017). The Future of Employment: How Susceptible Are Jobs to Computerisation? *Technological Forecasting and Social Change, 114*(C), 254–280. Accessed December 11, 2018, from https://doi.org/10.1016/j.techfore.2016.08.019

Graetz, G., & Michaels, G. (2017). Is Modern Technology Responsible for Jobless Recoveries? *American Economic Review, 107*(5), 168–173.

Graetz, G., & Michaels, G. (2018). *Robots at Work* [online] Accessed December 11, 2018, from http://personal.lse.ac.uk/michaels/Graetz_Michaels_Robots.pdf

7 The Spread of Artificial Intelligence and Its Impact...   153

Ibrahim, W. M., & Hassan, R. (2019). Recruitment Trends in the Era of Industry 4.0 Using Artificial Intelligence: Pro and Cons. *Asian Journal of Research in Business and Management, 1*(1), 16–21.

ICAEW or Institute of Chartered Accountants in England and Wales. (2018). *Artificial Intelligence and the Future of Accountancy* [online] ICAEW. Accessed March 24, 2019, from https://www.icaew.com/media/corporate/files/technical/information-technology/technology/artificial-intelligence-report.ashx?la=en

Iqbal, F. M. (2018). Can Artificial Intelligence Change the Way in Which Companies Recruit, Train, Develop and Manage Human Resources in Workplace? *Asian Journal of Social Sciences and Management Studies, 5*(3), 102–104.

Javed, A., & Kabir Brishti, J. (2020). *The Viability of AI-Based Recruitment Process.* Diva-portal.org. Accessed April 4, 2021, from https://www.diva-portal.org/smash/get/diva2:1442986/FULLTEXT01.pdf

Johnson, R. B., & Onwuegbuzie, A. J. (2004). Mixed Methods Research: A Research Paradigm Whose Time Has Come. *Educational Researcher, 33*(7), 14–26.

Kemeny, T., & Osman, T. (2018). The Wider Impacts of High-Technology Employment: Evidence from U.S. Cities. *Research Policy, 47*(9), 1729–1740.

Li, Z., & Zheng, L. (2018). The Impact of Artificial Intelligence on Accounting. *Advances in Social Science, Education and Humanities Research (ASSEHR), 181*, 181.

Mann, K., & Püttmann, L. (2017). *Benign Effects of Automation: New Evidence from Patent Texts* [online]. Accessed December 9, 2018, from https://www.aeaweb.org/conference/2018/preliminary/paper/2BAErzhG

Marr, B. (2018). *The Digital Transformation of Accounting And Finance - Artificial Intelligence, Robots and Chatbots* [online]. Forbes.com. Accessed December 1, 2018, from https://www.forbes.com/sites/bernardmarr/2018/06/01/the-digital-transformation-of-accounting-and-finance-artificial-intelligence-robots-and-chatbots/#98b803b4ad89

McGaughey, E. (2018, January 10). *Will Robots Automate Your Job Away? Full Employment, Basic Income, and Economic Democracy.* Centre for Business Research, University of Cambridge, Working Paper no. 496, Accessed from SSRN https://ssrn.com/abstract=3044448 or https://doi.org/10.2139/ssrn.3044448

Menand, L. (1997). *Pragmatism: A Reader.* Vintage.

Nagarajah, E. (2016). *PWC* [online]. Engagement. Accessed July 23, 2021, from https://www.pwc.com/my/en/assets/press/1608-accountants-today-automation-impact-on-accounting-profession.pdf

O'Leary, D. (1986). Expert Systems in a Personal Computer Environment. *Georgia Journal of Accounting, 7*, 107–118.

Oswal, N., Khaleeli, M., & Alarmoti, A. (2020). Recruitment in the Era of Industry 4.0: Use of Artificial Intelligence in Recruitment and Its Impact. *PalArch's Journal of Archaeology of Egypt/Egyptology, 17*(8), 39–47.

Rescher, N. (2000). *Realistic Pragmatism: An Introduction to Pragmatic Philosophy.* State University of New York.

Rorty, R. (2000). Pragmatism. *International Journal of Psychoanalysis, 81*, 819–823.

Ryan, M. (2020). In AI We Trust: Ethics, Artificial Intelligence, and Reliability. *Science & Engineering Ethics, 26*(5), 2749–2767. https://doi.org/10.1007/s11948-020-00228-y

Sdoukopoulos, E., Perra, V. M., Boile, M., Efthymiou, L., Dekoulou, E., & Orphanidou, Y. (2020). Connecting Cruise Lines with Local Supply Chains for Enhancing Customer Experience: A Platform Application in Greece. In E. G. Nathanail, G. Adamos, & I. Karakikes (Eds.), *Advances in Mobility-as-a-Service Systems, CSUM2020* (Part of the Advances in Intelligent Systems and Computing Book Series) (Vol. 1278, pp. 1086–1096). Springer. https://doi.org/10.1007/978-3-030-61075-3_104

Shalev-Shwartz, S., & Ben-David, S. (2014). *Understanding Machine Learning: From Theory to Algorithms.* Cambridge University Press.

Shimamoto, D. (2018). *Why Accountants Must Embrace Machine Learning | IFAC* [online] Ifac.org. Accessed December 1, 2018, from https://www.ifac.org/knowledge-gateway/preparing-future-ready-professionals/discussion/why-accountants-must-embrace-machine-learning

Susskind, R., & Susskind, D. (2017). *The Future of the Professions - How Technology Will Transform the Work of Human Experts* (1st ed.). Oxford University Press.

Tambe, P., Cappelli, P., & Yakubovich, V. (2019). Artificial Intelligence in Human Resources Management: Challenges and a Path Forward. *California Management Review, 61*(4), 15–42.

Taylor, A. (2018). The Automation Charade [online]. *Logic Magazine.* Accessed December 1, 2018, from https://logicmag.io/05-the-automation-charade/

7 The Spread of Artificial Intelligence and Its Impact... 155

van Duin, S., & Bakhshi, N. (2017). *Part 1: Artificial Intelligence Defined | Deloitte | Technology Services*. [online]. Deloitte Sweden. Accessed July 23, 2021, from https://www2.deloitte.com/se/sv/pages/technology/articles/part1-artificial-intelligence-defined.html

Wilfred, D. (2018). AI in Recruitment. *NHRD Network Journal, 11*(2), 15–18. https://doi.org/10.1177/0974173920180204

Zhou, A. (2017). *EY, Deloitte and PwC Embrace Artificial Intelligence for Tax and Accounting* [online]. Forbes.com. Accessed March 24, 2019, from https://www.ou/2017/11/14/ey-deloitte-and-pwc-embrace-artificial-intelligence-for-tax-and-accounting/#504d49e83498

8

Machine Learning, Artificial Intelligence and the Future of Work: Impact on HR, Learning and Development Professionals

Niki Kyriakidou, Karen Trem, Joy Ogbemudia, and Nehal Mahtab

8.1 Introduction

Artificial intelligence (AI) is often seen as the simulation of human intelligence. It is the process of making intelligent machines, especially intelligent computer programs, perform practical tasks related to human intelligence (McCarthy, 2007). However, today's workplaces evolve too rapidly and are too complex to offer nothing more than how-to learning experiences. Therefore, it focuses on human behaviour rather than directly aiming at the notion of intelligence and has broadened the scope and horizon of "intelligence" to include human-like behaviour. AI is the

---

N. Kyriakidou (✉) • K. Trem • J. Ogbemudia
Leeds Business School, Leeds Beckett University, Leeds, UK
e-mail: n.kyriakidou@leedsbeckett.ac.uk

N. Mahtab
Nottingham Business School, Nottingham Trent University, Nottingham, UK

© The Author(s), under exclusive license to Springer Nature Switzerland AG 2022
A. Thrassou et al. (eds.), *Business Advancement through Technology Volume II*, Palgrave Studies in Cross-disciplinary Business Research, In Association with EuroMed Academy of Business, https://doi.org/10.1007/978-3-031-07765-4_8

development of technologies that can perform complex human-like tasks such as understanding human language, performing mechanical tasks, and solving computer-based complex problems quickly. AI is further defined by Bhave et al. (2020), cited in Vrontis et al. (2021, p. 12) as "computing technologies that simulate or imitate intelligent behaviours relevant to the ones of humans despite that they act differently from them". In Human Resource Management (HRM), AI is most relevant in job replacement, the collaboration between AI and humans, recruitment, decision-making, and training. In the context of this study, AI can be defined as algorithms or systems with learning purposes and cognitive abilities which can execute tasks that would usually require human intelligence (Guenole & Feinzig, 2018; Oh et al., 2017), and references to HRM include Learning and Development (L&D).

Considered a subset of AI, Machine Learning (ML) focuses not only on the experiential "learning" associated with human intelligence and interaction (Bini, 2018) but also on the ability for continuous learning and improving its analyses through the use of computational algorithms in order to train the machine to make autonomous recommendations or decisions (Helm et al., 2020).

AI&ML are not new, though they have only become buzzwords in recent times (Splunk, 2020). They are seen as the "most transformative and disruptive technology of our age" (Finlay, 2021) as they rise in popularity and adoption. However, many companies and enterprises are slow in the implementation process due primarily to the need for proper training, people-friendly models, and the need to debunk the myth that AI&ML will replace people at work. Nevertheless, innovative developments in contemporary organisations are providing the technological infrastructure and the financial resources towards alternative solutions to HR in functions and work roles traditionally requiring human interaction and communication, causing a dramatic swift both in the organisational structures and the nature of work (Malik et al., 2020; Colbert et al., 2016).

The arrangement of this chapter is as follows. It first provides a background of ML and AI's evolution and how it has been applied in different functions of HR. Next, it provides cases from a qualitative study with

8 Machine Learning, Artificial Intelligence and the Future... 159

HR and Learning and Development Professionals to assess the impact ML, and AI has on HR roles; Finally, the chapter concludes with a discussion of future research and contributions in this field.

8.2 The Impact of AI and ML on Human Resources

Since the industrial revolution, technology has evolved and altered the services delivered by Human Resource Management (HRM). Contemporary technology, including humanoid robots and AI bots, are creating opportunities to improve the efficiency of existing systems and services, and changing the nature of work and organisational structures, even creating some job-specific obsolescence (Malik et al., 2020; Fjellström et al. 2020; Luo et al., 2019, Colbert et al., 2016, Araujo, 2018; Go & Sundar, 2019; Lariviere et al., 2017; Thomaz et al., 2020).

The most common HRM systems to be impacted by the advancement of AI and technology in greater efficiency are e-learning, e-recruitment, and e-competence. Technological change, innovation, and digitalisation within the business itself also impact HRM, since new ways of working are reflected in all aspects of the employment journey, from recruitment and onboarding to training and talent development, work design, succession planning offboarding, including redundancy or redeployment. Employee engagement can be more accurately measured, and technology greatly enhances employee retention. AI also enables greater efficiency in management and some tedious routine human tasks, such as documenting, scheduling, inspecting equipment, collecting data, and conducting preliminary analyses (Jaiswal et al., 2021). Tools such as logic-based programming, robotic process automation, expert systems, descriptive and predictive analytics are used to enhance practices and transform the workplace (Vrontis et al., 2021). HR is an enabler of organisational change and work reorganisation (Seeck & Diehl, 2017; Zanko et al., 2008).

AI and other breakthrough technologies dynamically reinvent traditional HRM practices on a global scale regarding usage, potential and business contribution (Ancarani et al., 2019; Florkowski & Olivas-Luján, 2006). Research conducted by Lariviere et al. (2017) demonstrated a radical change in the interconnection between organisations and customers and in the automation of HRM activities and tasks.

Although AI as a concept in academic literature is still in the early stages of theoreticalisation, development, and practical implementation (Bughin et al., 2018; Rao & Verweij, 2017), emerging research demonstrates that AI can provide great benefits to companies by improving their HRM performance (Faliagka et al., 2014). Indeed, leading industry reports (McKinsey, PWC) expect a dramatic increase in AI usage within the coming decade, contributing to a 14% increase in global GDP by 2030, with a projected 26% boost in AI which has shown great potential in changing HRM landscapes (Vrontis et al., 2021).

8.2.1 How AI & ML Affects HR Practices

The initial application of AI in organisations was task-oriented and a threat to lower-skilled jobs (Huang et al., 2019; Huang & Rust, 2018). The rapid advancement of technologies such as virtual assistants threatens customer service jobs and allows organisations to provide a 24-hour question-and-answer service (Glavas et al., 2019). Technology also reduces distance, meaning that one centre may serve a global business, particularly when the system has language translation abilities. On the other hand, there are great opportunities for human-AI collaboration and integration, enabling the development of more bespoke and valuable services (Marinova et al., 2017; Singh et al., 2017). AI also enables faster and more focussed data mining and analysis so that the human professionals can be better informed and more accurate in their work and decision making (Jung et al., 2017); thus, AI and technology may, but do not necessarily lead to job losses.

Recruitment will possibly be the most impacted, from the way applicants are sourced to online application systems and the selection of candidates for interviews. The procedures become faster, better, and a more cordial relationship between applicant and employer is developed. However, Mujtaba and Mahapatra (2019) argue that there is the

8 Machine Learning, Artificial Intelligence and the Future... 161

possibility of AI carrying over biases from humans and creating machine learning bias, which re-invents the old problem. Despite the shortcomings that may be associated with AI&ML, Wright and Atkinson (2019) posits that AI is a game-changer, as it enables HR to deliver cost-effective, high-quality recruitment processes, and commenting on the machine-human recruitment process in IBM, Guenole and Feinzig (2018) said, "Deploying AI in recruitment allows faster and more accurate hiring."

8.2.2 The Role of HR Information Systems (HRIS)

Key research demonstrated that the development and implementation of electronic HR information systems (HRIS) and other innovative technologies provide more opportunities for work advancement and cost reduction of HRM functions through enabling improved speed and efficiency, and reducing cost in shortlisting job applicants, evaluating employee performance appraisals, and improving communication and collaboration (Abraham et al., 2019; Bondarouk et al., 2017a, b; Cooke et al., 2019a, b; Parry & Tyson, 2011).

Employee self-service (ESS) technology enables employees to access and update their personal data, reducing HR workload and costs, and removing a data input stage that risks error. In addition, electronic forms are increasingly used, and electronic monitoring of such things as phone and internet usage provides accurate work monitoring and provides information in performance review and discipline meetings.

8.2.3 How AI & ML Impacts the Future of Work

Arguably larger organisations will benefit more from a move to e-HRM than smaller ones in process and cost improvements (Bondarouk et al., 2017a, b). AI and technology will also impact jobs, potentially leading to more contingent and less standard full-time jobs; there is also likely to be a refocusing of job content, with humans doing more of the communication and problem solving that is done less well by computers. There is a danger of over-reliance on computers and automation, and technology should be used as a support tool rather than an HR professional's replacement (Vrontis et al., 2021). Even when jobs are not immediately threatened and performance is improved using technology, people can perceive a threat to their autonomy, status, and job security, since computers can deal with more options and address more complex situations (Lawler & Elliot, 1996). Procedural justice is important in decision making, whether AI systems or people do it since it positively impacts employee attitudes and behaviours (Otting & Maier, 2018).

Robotics, the development of machines that can mimic human behaviour and perform human tasks, are related to AI&ML and are relevant to HR as they impact the nature of work within organisations. Robots are used in manufacturing and have replaced traditional jobs and created new opportunities for jobs in their design, maintenance, and repair (though some of that is done by robots too). Humanoid robots such as virtual assistants and those that serve in restaurants may also pose a threat to jobs, though they also provide opportunities to remove repetitive tasks and for collaboration and improved service. It is likely that "more skilled and educated employees are needed in the era of human and robots' symbiosis and collaboration" (Ma & Sun, 2020; Aleksander, 2017).

AI, robotics, and other technologies impact HR in terms of activities including recruitment, work performance and training, and in a strategic dimension in relation to HR and succession planning, including job replacement, collaboration between humans and AI, and new learning opportunities and decision making. AI and technology are changing how HR professionals do their work and the work they do within their organisations. It is suggested by Vrontis et al. (2021) that "HR researchers could be benefited from collaborating with IM researchers or computer scientists to analyse the ethical challenges of AI technologies in decision-making processes as well as the factors that affect the way that human employees can accept these technologies."

Priorities for management lie in recognising the potential benefits of AI and technology in individual and organisational performance and embracing it in supporting human activity such as problem-solving, decision making, learning and development and communication (Behrend & Thompson, 2011; Singh et al., 2017); organisations should be places where people and technology coexist comfortably. For this to happen, people need sufficient knowledge, skills, and training to work with technology; learning can be enhanced through collaboration with external experts (Ferraris et al., 2019). Whilst AI enables the minimisation of distance in communication and business transactions, relationships benefit from human input, and there is a careful balance to maintain to ensure that AI and technology support and enable human performance rather than replacing it.

Looking at the impact of AI & ML on current employees skillsets and future work requirements, a McKinsey report states that by 2030 as many as 375 million workers or 14% of the global workforce may need to switch occupational categories as AI&ML disrupts work routines (Illanes et al., 2018). However, it is becoming clearer that although some jobs will be eliminated, AI&ML will create more jobs and enhance collaboration intelligence within any type of organisations organisations (Wilson & Daugherty, 2018; Daugherty et al., 2019; Clifton et al., 2020; Kokuytseva & Ovchinnikova, 2020).

Virtualisation technologies developed from the gaming industry provide opportunities to enhance communication and individual and organisational training (Arik, 2021; Vrontis et al., 2021). Simulation and animated characters in training situations are more effective and engaging than a traditional computer or video-based learning.

The impact of AI&ML on HR will account for the creation of new jobs and require different skills; therefore, reskilling and upskilling will be top on HR agenda (Barnes et al., 2021; Blumenfeld et al., 2017; Reilly, 2018); however, Martin (2019) suggests that the lack of AI&ML talent in all sectors and industries has left employers struggling and more than four in ten businesses are worried that they will not be able to find the talent they require.

8.2.4 Ethics and Other Considerations

When used in recruitment, AI&ML can speed up the process, make it more systematic, and reduce human bias as well as applicant attempts to influence the process, if bias is not inadvertently built into the system (Sajjadiani et al., 2019). There are, however, questions relating to access to and use of personal data and ethics, not least in relation to the data that is captured during psychometric tests, recorded interviews, and assessments, which may be used to create psychological profiles and predict potential fit (Suen et al., 2019; Bhave et al., 2020). Whilst there are many benefits to be gained with AI, there are ethical considerations, data usage concerns and a potential need for further regulation in this context (Vrontis et al., 2021).

8.2.5 The ML and AI Research Project and Its Impact on HR Professionals

Existing research reviewed in the previous sections suggests that AI&ML impacts the HR profession in terms of its own systems and how it supports organisational operations. However, there is a general inability to work alongside Data Analysis and IT professionals in the design and development of applications. In agreement with Vrontis et al. (2021), this study advocates that HR professionals with sufficient Data Analytics and ML knowledge and understanding can work confidently in a design and development team with data specialists as hybrid professionals. Our overall project research aims to gain an oversight of perceptions of the future use of technology from HR professionals at different stages in their careers. Reflecting on the work of Jaiswal et al. (2021) and Vrontis et al. (2021), the theoretical framework of this study is based on the use of dynamic skills, AI job replacement and neo-human capital-NHCT theories to contribute to the understanding of HR development in the context of AI. These theories help conceptualise and advance our knowledge around the role of skill demand due to technological change.

Dynamic skills theory (Fischer et al., 2003) is related to the cognitive development process that considers human activities and skills development as an outcome of interrelated, organisational, and country-specific human interactions (Kunnen & Bosma, 2003); the first objective of the research was to **identify current levels of skills, knowledge, and awareness of the use of AI&ML with the HR profession.**

We also reflect on the theory of AI job replacement (Huang & Rust, 2018) to critically discuss how AI is increasingly reshaping service by performing various tasks, constituting a major source of innovation, yet threatening human jobs (p.155). Even though key research was conducted in this area by Huang and Rust (2018), Vrontis et al. (2021) demonstrated that while AI experts are developing and training machine-learning algorithms to mimic human capabilities and reduce human interactions (Jaiswal et al., 2021), interpersonal skills are extremely difficult to rival using AI (Huang & Rust, 2018). Therefore, the second objective of our study was **to understand key developments in AI&ML and their impact on the work of key professionals.**

As Jaiswal et al. (2021) argued in their research, with the extensive use and proliferation of AI technologies across different countries and industries, there will be increasing demand for new skillsets and higher levels of human capital concentration. Neo-Human Capital theory (NHCT) deals with the development of human capital due to technology-driven transformations in the workplace and the increasing demand for digital literacy skills (Karjaluoto, 2020; Zucchetti et al., 2020; Pereira & Malik, 2015). The purpose of our study is to consider the hybrid professional as a key role for the future in HR to participate in the reshaping of work and required skills, including their jobs (Tschang & Mezquita, 2020). Therefore, the **final objective of the study is to conceptualise possibilities for the use of AI&ML within the HR profession.**

8.3 Research Methodology

A qualitative approach provided greater insight into the perceptions of AI&ML of a group of professionals. The participants in the research were selected to include those with experience as HRM students within the business school of a HE institution and as practitioners working in different sectors and organisations, all operating in the UK. Reflecting on the research objectives, there were two phases of research proposed within this study:

In Phase I, the researchers conducted individual semi-structured interviews in MS Teams fully recorded and transcribed, with 15 HR Professionals as follows:

- Three undergraduates with some understanding of AI & ML and who were interested in the use of technology in their future practice as HRM professionals
- Six HR practitioners currently working in middle management with some experience of using AI&ML within their role but not in a position to influence current organisational strategy
- Six HR practitioners currently working at the senior management level within organisations and able to influence organisational strategy

All interviews were conducted in English and lasted for 45–80 mins. An interview schedule using open questions guided the semi-structured interviews with the HR professionals reflecting on their experiences with digital transformation in the workplace in the last two years, the use of AI&ML in their current roles and the range of skills yet to be developed. The interviews also helped identify enablers and barriers to the digital transformation of the workplace and the need to gain new skillsets in the near future. More specifically, the themes for the interviews were the following:

- Role analysis—current responsibilities and stage of career/level of influence within the organisation
- Knowledge awareness of what AI&ML is, and the current use of it in (their) organisations
- Skills and competencies required to engage fully in the design and implementation of AI&ML
- Personal skills gaps
- Perception of possible future uses and benefits of use within organisations

8.4   Evaluation of the Impact of AI and ML: Cases from HR and L&D Professionals

The Second Phase of the research study, presented in this chapter, focused on developing case studies derived from interviews carried out with three of the senior HR and L & D professionals in our sample from different

8 Machine Learning, Artificial Intelligence and the Future...

sectors within the UK. The purpose of the case studies is to share managers' experiences, gain insight into the current use and application of AI & ML in the management of people in organisations, and identify skills and competence required to fully engage in the use and application of AI&ML in the workplace. The semi-structured interviews were recorded and transcribed then participant responses were analysed, paraphrased, and summarised to create the following case studies:

8.4.1 Case Study 1: The UK Retail Sector

This large retailer has a central head office, retail stores throughout the UK and an online presence catering for home delivery and click-and-collect purchases. A third-party specialist manages logistics and warehousing.

From an HR perspective, AI&ML is developed by individuals, and the constructed algorithms incorporate their pre-conceived ideas and thoughts; the computer builds on what is input, generating potentially infinite possibilities. In addition, technology is used to improve efficiency; for example, horizon scanning uses basic systems to search databases of articles identifying relevant sources of information.

Absence reporting systems have been adapted for covid restrictions, tracking the nature and frequency of absences, demographics, levels of vulnerability, covid status, and the likelihood to close workplace contacts; areas of risk are identified to anticipate cover needs for business continuity. AI&ML is used in recruitment shortlisting and to review documents checking right to work and age compliance where that is important in selling licenced goods or for driving. Hiring for attitude and training to upskill, scanning for personality, and removing bias in shortlisting algorithms are necessary and difficult, so systems must continuously evolve, and person-to-person stages are integrated into the recruitment system.

Having current licenses for tobacco and alcohol sales outlets is critical; to minimise the risk of missing expiry dates, practitioners work with IT to develop systems that scan licencing documentation and give advance warning of renewals.

The demographic of counter staff most likely to sell age-restricted products to underage customers is already known; additional training for these groups could improve compliance levels. Till cameras could also be used to establish a customer's age when buying restricted goods, reducing the possibility of abuse to staff. The retailer is currently working with a third party IT provider and central/local government on trialling this technology.

Training is important and could be delivered more efficiently if training plans were tailored to individual and organisational needs. For example, bespoke reports per business unit could identify accident risk locations, tasks, roles, time and frequency, enabling targeted mitigations. Camera technology could capture accidents, identify danger spots, and record risk-related behaviours, leading to tailored staff training. It is illegal in the UK to sell products past their use-by date. Currently, dates are checked, and outdated products are removed from the shelves manually. Detailed sales patterns are known and help staff to locate outdated products. Greater efficiency could be achieved if that data were used for staff training and further computerised the process.

There are insufficient skills in the business; some key people do read, learn, and encourage others into new ways of working. Credible external trainers are required to emphasise the benefits of new approaches. People need to learn and reassurance that technology will enable improved performance rather than steal jobs. As technology evolves, new jobs and opportunities are being created.

Becoming too reliant on smart technology is a danger, particularly if any vulnerability in the systems enables hackers to access or steal personal or business critical data. In addition, as more data is collected to help the business, more employee personal data is held, and people need to know that this will be used ethically. Most importantly, digital transformation is more effective when technology and systems are designed for the future rather than merely computerising existing systems.

8.4.2 Case Study 2: The British Armed Forces

AI & ML uses algorithms, systems, and platforms to deliver information more quickly and support decision making. Some systems interrogate data lakes or sit over legacy digital platforms that will not be updated,

8 Machine Learning, Artificial Intelligence and the Future... 169

extracting management information, creating dashboards, and improving organisational efficiency. Organisations must continuously advance their use of technology because peers and adversaries do.

Senior leaders read and learn extensively; as they learn more about the potential of AI&ML, their desire to change increases, and they are more able to adapt and accept its use. Leaders are responsible for meeting organisational strategic goals and can do so more effectively with more timely, accurate and extensive information. When managers and individuals interact with personal data and communicate effectively in real-time through electronic devices, decision making is quicker and better informed. The army is very task and team-focused; through the advancement of technology, it is becoming more agile and flexible, and ways of working are changing with implications for recruitment and training. Therefore, people need to be more adaptable and willing to learn and change.

A digital team at Army headquarters supports the deluge of new technologies; civilian contractors are engaged for installation and basic maintenance of technologies and development of staff skills. In a high performing ethos, consistency of approach is valued, diversity of thinking and access to specialised skill sets comes from bringing in these externals.

For example, more complex technology in tanks means that operators need more extensive training to operate, maintain, and carry out repairs in the field. In addition, the technical and cyber skills required in the workforce are changing, technically qualified graduates are increasingly required, and either recruited externally or trained internally. There are other recruitment and retention implications, as not all those with technical and cyber skills want to be part of the uniformed, disciplined service, and civilian salaries are higher. More lateral entry and flexible contracts may be required to attract and retain vital skills.

Virtual Reality (VR) has the potential to radically change training, using AI-generated, realistic environments to enable training in for example, situational problem solving or repairing equipment in battlefield conditions.

Currently, information is captured from sources including tanks, drones, and aircraft on a battlefield to improve environmental and operational understanding, allowing Commanders to make quicker decisions.

There are automated drones in development, using AI&ML to speed up the process of scanning and risk assessing buildings and terrain assimilating and making sense of information for better and safer decision making. Drones can assimilate data and share it with computerised armoured vehicles (CAV) in the field, creating exceptional situational awareness and creating the possibility of removing the platoon commander who traditionally sits in the CAV. A weaponised, fully autonomous CAV would dominate the environment and be very destructive. Ethically though, it may not be able to distinguish between an aggressor CAV and a bus full of school children. The human operator in the 'kill decision' is critical. Over-reliance on technology can have ethical implications.

Breaching army values and standards is taken seriously, and all personnel have annual, mandatory values training. However, this will need continuous adaptation to allow for the impact of technology, as people are still responsible for the outcomes of fully autonomous technology.

8.4.3 Case Study 3: The UK Health Sector

A business that employs specialist clinicians and technicians who work in partnership with Health Service clinicians and individual patients to provide equipment and support. The demographic profile of the business is ageing; many staff have 20–40 years' service, creating implications for organisational culture, knowledge transfer, recruitment, and training. In the technical side of the business, there is sophisticated assistive technology. However, this knowledge is not applied internally to HR and management systems and many of these are manual. From an HR perspective, AI is seen as enabling gathering information and data in different ways, including surveys and focus groups, and analysing it for application in strategic decision-making and change.

Headcount, absence, and turnover data is used to support managers in identifying and resolving issues; for example, high turnover within the first year of employment might point to induction and integration issues. Most recruitment, onboarding and offboarding are manual, as is the process of getting approvals within the business. The pandemic has enabled

8 Machine Learning, Artificial Intelligence and the Future... 171

some changes in communication, moving from post to email and the use of text messages.

While the HR team has basic data analysis skills and works with the IT department, who develop the reports required, stronger analytical skills and an understanding of the systems to enable developing reports themselves would be beneficial. Faster systems would create more time to gather and consider more meaningful data.

An e-training portal records attendance as well as reminds people when training is due; there is also significant use of traditional training methods. Technology in the future will enable the capture of individual learning needs and give individuals an insight into how they are doing against their objectives and how these align with business objectives. Although there will always be a need for the personal touch, business and HR systems cannot become fully automated.

Staff can access linked benefits and wellbeing platforms though it is hard to get people to engage with it. The platform enables managers and other employees to access guidance, policies, and links to other systems and information they need, including absence reporting and booking holidays. Background data from the platform can be used by HR to identify what wellbeing support people are interested in, and communications can then be tailored. More of this could be introduced in future, relating to training and development and managing time and attendance. Since the pandemic necessitated remote working, the business is becoming more flexible in its approach to measuring time, attendance and work-related performance and outputs. Some work in the business is easier to measure than others.

It is possible that 3D printing could be introduced into manufacturing in the future, and links are being developed with local colleges to consider ways of introducing apprenticeships and younger generations into the business. With a younger workforce, technology may also be easier to introduce. In addition, access to real-time and integrated HR data would enable more effective and responsive succession and resource planning, recruitment, onboarding, engagement and offboarding, and the HR department is beginning to appreciate just how useful technology could be to them in improving and streamlining systems, and in more focussed and frequent staff surveys to support engagement strategies.

8.5 Conclusion

An analysis of the three case studies revealed some common themes, summarised in Table 8.1.

In all three case studies, and line with the findings of Jaiswal et al. (2021), AI & ML plays as an important role in the improvement of operational efficiency, including the digitalisation of existing systems (what they refer to as tedious routine human tasks), and the opportunity to evaluate and improve systems before digitalisation. This efficiency improvement is more evident in the operational side of the organisations than in the HR and management systems, which is interesting since the

Table 8.1 Common themes in the case studies

Theme	Case study 1	Case study 2	Case study 3
Efficiency improvement	X	X	X
Predictive analytics	X	X	X
Recruitment processes	X	X	X
Tailored training and development	X	X	X
Bespoke reporting	X	X	X
Digitalisation of systems	X	X	X
Improved access to data and data analysis	X	X	X
Improved decision making	X	X	X
Lack of current skills	X	X	X
Need for Human input as well as technology	X	X	X
Creation of new jobs	X	X	X
Danger of over reliance on technology	X	X	
Ethical issues relating to application of technology	X	X	
Staff safety	X	X	
Improved Communication		X	X
Need for external trainers and expertise	X	X	
Absence reporting	X		X
Potential for bias	X		
Need for reassurance that jobs won't be 'stolen'	X		
Staff resistance			X
Changes in ways people are employed		X	
Need to keep up with adversaries and competition		X	

literature review focused mostly on the uses of AI & ML within the HR function. However, both literature and the case study examples agree that the increasing use of technology requires changes in job design and the introduction of new jobs, impacting recruitment, selection, engagement, training and development of the employees who use it, therefore impacting HR activity.

In applying AI&ML in HR systems and processes, the most common usage is in recruitment and selection, whether that is in scanning documents as part of the process or using technology in the attraction, engagement, and communication with prospective applicants. However, a review of literature also found that the use of good HRIS enables HR to improve speed and efficiency and reduce cost in systematic tasks, including shortlisting job applicants (Abraham et al., 2019; Bondarouk et al., 2017a, b; Cooke et al., 2019a, b; Parry & Tyson, 2011).

Unanimously, technology enables better access to and analysis of data, and therefore, as also stated by Seeck and Diehl (2017) and Zanko et al. (2008), better management and strategic decision making. For example, access to detailed real-time data in the military is significant in improving decisions relating to the deployment of people and resources. In all cases, quality data also enables predictions to be made, and in the HR context, this can be applied in HR planning, succession planning, and training and development, both to meet strategic objectives and ensure that mandatory training are completed before there is time expiration.

More specifically in training and development, practitioners see the possibility and benefits of tailored training plans for each employee, based on individual and organisational need, learning style, frequency of use of the subject of the training, and performance relating to the individual, organisational objectives. Interestingly, bespoke training plans was not a feature of the literature reviewed. Bespoke reporting throughout the organisation on health and safety, accidents, and compliance with regulations enables hot-spots to be identified and tailored responses, including training, to be introduced.

It is common to bring in contractors, at least in the early days of digitalisation, to install and maintain new equipment and systems, and to support internal staff in developing new skill sets. However, all organisations interviewed reported a lack of knowledge and skills in house, this is in common with the findings of Reilly (2018) and Martin (2019) who report a general lack of talent in all sectors, leaving employers unable to recruit the talent they require. The case study participants suggested that though over time, these skills and the confidence and willingness to use technologies do increase. Perhaps the most important is for organisations to become more adaptable and open to change.

Significantly, in these three very different organisations, a common focus was on the ethical and legal dimensions of integrating AI&ML, leading to new training and development needs in this area. As in Vrontis et al. (2021), there was also an emphasis on the need to introduce technologies to support people in their jobs, rather than to replace them. Human input is and will still be required; however, with appropriate use of technology, organisations can become more efficient, and access and use more accurate, timely and relevant data in their strategy development and decision making, and as stated by (Seeck & Diehl, 2017; Zanko et al., 2008), this impacts HR who are an enabler of organisational change and work reorganisation.

8.6 Implications

AI is technology that can perform complex human-like tasks, including problem-solving, more quickly than a human can. ML is where a computer program can learn to produce results and behaviours from the data and feedback it accesses, which the human author has not explicitly created.

AI&ML enable organisations to perform an increasing range of operational, management and HRM tasks with accuracy, efficiency, speed and cost-effectiveness. According to both our research and literature review, the most common usage in HRM is e-recruitment and the digitalisation of HRM systems.

Research suggested that the application of technology is generally more advanced in the operational rather than management and HRM systems aspects of organisations. There is scope to learn from this and collaborate with more complex uses of AI&ML in the delivery of HRM support within businesses. For this, HR professionals should develop sufficient knowledge, skills, and confidence to confidently collaborate with data analytics and technology specialists in designing and developing systems and solutions.

In delivering and monitoring learning and development, organisations use e-learning applications and VR. Research showed a strong desire for developing tailored development plans, using data collected through such things performance management systems and data collected through e-monitoring of work tasks. Learning and development and recruitment are enabled through the use of AI&ML. However, they are also impacted by its growing usage, as technology changes the nature of work within organisations. Technology inevitably affects jobs; however, whilst some jobs become obsolete, new jobs are being created. In addition, there is generally a shortage of appropriate skills across all sectors, leading to recruitment challenges and a need to re-train and upskill existing employees.

Research and literature review both identified the need to consider ethics in the use of technology and the potential vulnerabilities relating to security of personal and other confidential data. Therefore, there is a need for further training of employees in ethics and data security and the development of more regulation in these areas.

This research study contributes to the necessary groundwork as reviewed in its literature. In addition, it expands our understanding and expertise to identify HR and T &D literature gaps by critically considering how the role of key People Management professionals can be adapted to ensure sustainability and benefit to others in an age of machine learning, artificial intelligence and associated processes. Consequently, the chapter focused more deeply on the skills and competencies required by the hybrid professional in the future workplace. AI & ML are here to stay; HR professionals should embrace the possibilities it brings and become comfortable collaborating with technology and those who design and develop it with us.

References

Abraham, M., Niessen, C., Schnabel, C., Lorek, K., Grimm, V., Moslein, K., & Wrede, M. (2019). Electronic Monitoring at Work: The Role of Attitudes, Functions, and Perceived Control for the Acceptance of Tracking Technologies. *Human Resource Management Journal, 29*(4), 657–675. https://doi.org/10.1111/1748-8583.12250

Aleksander, I. (2017). Partners of Humans: A Realistic Assessment of the Role of Robots in the Foreseeable Future. *Journal of Information Technology, 32*(1), 1–9. https://doi.org/10.1057/s41265-016-0032-4

Ancarani, A., Di Mauro, C., & Mascali, F. (2019). Backshoring Strategy and the Adoption of Industry 4.0: Evidence from Europe. *Journal of World Business, 54*(4), 360–371. https://doi.org/10.1016/j.jwb.2019.04.003

Araujo, T. (2018). Living up to the Chatbot Hype: The Influence of Anthropomorphic Design Cues and Communicative Agency Framing on Conversational Agent and Company Perceptions. *Computers in Human Behavior, 85*, 183–189. https://doi.org/10.1016/j.chb.2018.03.051

Arik, K. (2021). While Machine Learning and AI Are Extremely Exciting Technologies, Human Creativity Is the True Differentiator. *The Estates Gazette, 5*, 23.

Barnes, S., Rutter, R. N., Paz, A. I. L., & Scornavacca, E. (2021). Empirical Identification of Skills Gaps Between Chief Information Officer Supply and Demand: A Resource Based View Using Machine Learning. *Industrial Management and Data Systems, 21*(8), 1749–1766. Accessed from https://www.emerald.com/insight/0263-5577.htm

Behrend, T. S., & Thompson, L. F. (2011). Similarity Effects in Online Training: Effects with Computerised Trainer Agents. *Computers in Human Behavior, 27*(3), 1201–1206. https://doi.org/10.1016/j.chb.2010.12.016

Bhave, D. P., Teo, L. H., & Dalal, R. S. (2020). Privacy at Work: A Review and a Research Agenda for a Contested Terrain. *Journal of Management, 46*(1), 127–164. https://doi.org/10.1177/0149206319878254

Bini, S. (2018). Artificial Intelligence, Machine Learning and Cognitive Computing: What Do These Terms Mean and How Will They Impact Health Care? *The Journal of Arthoplasty, 33*(8), 2358–2361. https://doi.org/10.1016/j.arth.2018.02.067

Blumenfeld, S., & Ashish Malik, A. (2017). Human Capital Formation Under Neo-liberalism: The Legacy of Vocational Education Training in Australasia and Implications for the Asia-Pacific Region. *Asia Pacific Business Review, 23*(2), 290–298. https://doi.org/10.1080/13602381.2017.1306358

Bondarouk, T., Harms, R., & Lepak, D. (2017a). Does e-HRM Lead to Better HRM Service? *The International Journal of Human Resource Management, 28*(9), 1332–1362. https://doi.org/10.1080/09585192.2015.1118139

Bondarouk, T., Parry, E., & Furtmueller, E. (2017b). Electronic HRM: Four Decades of Research on Adoption and Consequences. *The International Journal of Human Resource Management, 28*(1), 98–131. https://doi.org/1 0.1080/09585192.2016.1245672

Bughin, J., Hazan, E., Lund, S., Dahlström, P., Wiesinger, A., & Subramaniam, A. (2018). *Skill Shift: Automation and the Future of the Workforce*. McKinsey & Company/ McKinsey Global Institute.

Clifton, J., Glasmeier, A., & Gray, M. (2020). When machines think for us: The consequences for work and place. *Cambridge Journal of Regions, Economy and Society, 13*(1), 3–23. https://doi.org/10.1093/cjres/rsaa004

Colbert, A., Yee, N., & George, G. (2016). The Digital Workforce and the Workplace of the Future. *Academy of Management Journal, 59*(3), 731–739. https://doi.org/10.5465/amj.2016.4003

Cooke, F. L., Liu, M., Liu, L. A., & Chen, C. C. (2019a). Human Resource Management and Industrial Relations in Multinational Corporations in and from China: Challenges and New Insights. *Human Resource Management, 58*(5), 455–471. https://doi.org/10.1002/hrm.21986

Cooke, F. L., Wood, G., Wang, M., & Veen, A. (2019b). How Far Has International HRM Travelled? A Systematic Review of Literature on Multinational Corporations (2000–2014). *Human Resource Management Review, 29*(1), 59–75. https://doi.org/10.1016/j.hrmr.2018.05.001

Daniella Fjellström, D., Osarenkhoe, A., Pettersson, T., & Tadesse, D. (2020). The Role of Digitalization in SMEs' Strategy Development: The Case of Sweden. In A. Thrassou et al. (Eds.), *The Changing Role of SMEs in Global Business* (Vol. 1, pp. 65–88). dokumen.pub.

Daugherty, P. R., Wilson, H. J., & Michelman, P. (2019). Revisiting the Jobs Artificial Intelligence Will Create. *MIT Sloan Management Review, 60*(4), 1–8.

Faliagka, E., Iliadis, L., Karydis, I., Rigou, M., Sioutas, S., Tsakalidis, A., & Tzimas, G. (2014). Online Consistent Ranking on E-recruitment: Seeking the Truth Behind a Well-Formed CV. *Artificial Intelligence Review, 42*(3), 515–528. https://doi.org/10.1007/s10462-013-9414-y

Ferraris, A., Erhardt, N., & Bresciani, S. (2019). Ambidextrous Work in Smart City Project Alliances: Unpacking the Role of Human Resource Management

Systems. *The International Journal of Human Resource Management, 30*(4), 680–701. https://doi.org/10.1080/09585192.2017.1291530

Finlay, S. (2021). *Artificial Intelligence and Machine Learning for Business: A No-Nonsense Guide to Data Driven Technologies* (4th ed.). Relativistic Books.

Fischer, K., Yan, Z., & Stewart, J. (2003). Adult Cognitive Development: Dynamics in the Developmental Web. In J. Valsiner & K. J. Connolly (Eds.), *Handbook of Developmental Psychology* (pp. 491–516). Sage.

Florkowski, G. W., & Olivas-Luján, M. R. (2006). The Diffusion of Human-Resource Information-Technology Innovations in US and Non-US Companies. *Personnel Review, 35*(6), 684–710. https://doi.org/10.1108/00483480610702737

Glavas, C., Mathews, S., & Russell-Bennett, R. (2019). Knowledge Acquisition Via Internet-Enabled Platforms: Examining Incrementally and Non-incrementally Internationalising SMEs. *International Marketing Review, 36*(1), 74–107. https://doi.org/10.1108/IMR-02-2017-0041/full/html

Go, E., & Sundar, S. S. (2019). Humanising Chatbots: The Effects of Visual, Identity and Conversational Cues on Humanness Perceptions. *Computers in Human Behavior, 97*, 304–316. https://doi.org/10.1016/j.chb.2019.01.020

Guenole, N., & Feinzig, S. (2018). *The Business Case for AI in HR with Insights and Tips on Getting Started*. IBM. Accessed April 10, 2020, from https://www.ibm.com/downloads/cas/AGKXJX6M

Helm, J. M., Swiergosz, A. M., Haeberle, H. S., Karnuta, J. M., Schaffer, J. L., Krebs, V. E., Spitzer, A. I., & Ramkumar, P. N. (2020). Machine Learning and Artificial Intelligence: Definitions, Applications, and Future Directions. *Current Reviews in Musculoskeletal Medicine, 13*(1), 69–76. https://doi.org/10.1007/s12178-020-09600-8

Huang, M. H., & Rust, R. T. (2018). Artificial Intelligence in Service. *Journal of Service Research, 21*(2), 155–172. https://doi.org/10.1177/1094670517752459

Huang, M.-H., Rust, R., & Maksimovic, V. (2019). The Feeling Economy: Managing in the Next Generation of Artificial Intelligence (AI). *California Management Review, 61*(4), 43–65. https://doi.org/10.1177/0008125619863436

Illanes, P., Lund, S., Mourshed, M., Rutherford, S., & Tyreman, M. (2018). *Retraining and Reskilling Workers in the Age of Automation*. McKinsey Global Institute.

Jaiswal, A., Arun, C. J., & Varma, A. (2021). Rebooting Employees: Upskilling for Artificial Intelligence in Multinational Corporations. *The International Journal of Human Resource Management, 1–30*. https://doi.org/10.108 0/09585192.2021.1891114

Jung, J., Song, H., Kim, Y., Im, H., & Oh, S. (2017). Intrusion of Software Robots into Journalism: The Public's and Journalists' Perceptions of News Written by Algorithms and Human Journalists. *Computers in Human Behavior, 71*, 291–298. https://doi.org/10.1016/j.chb.2017.02.022

Karjaluoto, A. (2020). Bridging the AI Skills Gap for Machine Manufacturers: More Knowledge Is Needed for Use of Artificial Intelligence (AI) for Machine Learning (ML) Applications. See Four Ways to Improve Artificial Intelligence, Machine Learning Education. *Control Engineering, 67*(8). Accessed from https://www.controleng.com/articles/bridging-the-artificial-intelligence-skills-gap-for-machine-manufacturers/

Kokuytseva, T., & Ovchinnikova, O. (2020). Digital Transformation as a Source of Innovative Growth for Small and Medium Enterprises in Russia. In A. Thrassou et al. (Eds.), *The Changing Role of SMEs in Global Business* (Vol. 1, pp. 131–154). Springer.

Kunnen, E. S., & Bosma, H. A. (2003). Fischer's Skill Theory Applied to Identity Development: A Response to Kroger. *Identity, 3*(3), 247–270. https://doi.org/10.1207/S1532706XID0303_05

Lariviere, B., Bowen, D., Andreassen, T. W., Kunz, W., Sirianni, N. J., Voss, C., Wunderlich, N. V., & De Keyser, A. (2017). "Service Encounter 2.0": An Investigation into the Roles of Technology, Employees and Customers. *Journal of Business Research, 79*, 238–246. https://doi.org/10.1016/j.jbusres.2017.03.008

Lawler, J., & Elliot, R. (1996). Artificial intelligence in HRM: An experimental study of an expert system. *Journal of Management, 22*(1), 85–111.

Luo, X., Tong, S., Fang, Z., & Qu, Z. (2019). Frontiers: Machines vs. Humans: The Impact of Artificial Intelligence Chatbot Disclosure on Customer Purchases. *Marketing Science, 38*(6), 937–947. https://doi.org/10.1287/mksc.2019.1192

Ma, L., & Sun, B. (2020). Machine Learning and AI in Marketing – Connecting Computing Power to Human Insights. *International Journal of Research in Marketing, 37*, 481–504. https://doi.org/10.1016/j.ijresmar.2020.04.005

Malik, A., Budhwar, P., Patel, C., & Srikanth, N. R. (2020). May the Bots Be with You! Delivering HR Cost-Effectiveness and Individualised Employee Experiences in an MNE. *The International Journal of Human Resource Management, 2020*, 1–3. https://doi.org/10.1080/09585192.2020.1859582

Marinova, D., de Ruyter, K., Huang, M. H., Meuter, M. L., & Challagalla, G. (2017). Getting Smart: Learning from Technology-Empowered Frontline Interactions. *Journal of Service Research, 20*(1), 29–42. https://doi.org/10.1177/1094670516679273

Martin, E. J. (2019). The AI Skills Gap. *International Journal of Speech Technology*.

McCarthy, J. (2007). *From Here to Human-Level AI*. Computer Science Department, Stanford University. [Online]. Accessed December 2, 2021, from https://reader.elsevier.com/reader/sd/pii/S0004370207001476?token =E20430C88B8D5501A7C0F4EC660BB5A1AF0836936038DB43A3B F07FA2D9CFF310967F4175703E99344EF5710F8D5760D&originRegi on=eu-west-1&originCreation=20211215141700

Mujtaba, D. F. & Mahapatra, N. R. (2019). Ethical Considerations in AI-Based Recruitment. In *2019 IEEE International Symposium on Technology and Society (ISTAS)*. IEEE, p. 1.

Oh, J., Singh, S., & Lee, H. (2017). *Value Prediction Network*. arXiv:1707.03497v2 [cs.AI] 6 Nov. Accessed from: https://arxiv.org/pdf/1707.03497.pdf

Otting, S. K., & Maier, G. W. (2018). The Importance of Procedural Justice in Human–Machine Interactions: Intelligent Systems as New Decision Agents in Organisations. *Computers in Human Behavior, 89*, 27–39. https://doi. org/10.1016/j.chb.2018.07.022

Parry, E., & Tyson, S. (2011). Desired Goals and Actual Outcomes of e-HRM. *Human Resource Management Journal, 21*(3), 335–354. https://doi. org/10.1111/j.1748-8583.2010.00149

Pereira, V., & Malik, A. (2015). *Human Capital in the Indian IT/BPO Industry* (1st ed.). Palgrave Macmillan.

Rao, A. S., & Verweij, G. (2017). *Sizing the prize: What's the real value of AI for your business and how can you capitalise?* PWC Report. Accessed from: http:// preview.thenewsmarket.com/Previews/PWC/DocumentAssets/476830.pdf

Reilly, P. (2018, November). *The Impact of Artificial Intelligence on HR Function, IES Perspectives on HR*. Member Paper 142.

Sajjadiani, S., Sojourner, A. J., Kammeyer-Mueller, J. D., & Mykerezi, E. (2019). Using Machine Learning to Translate Applicant Work History into Predictors of Performance and Turnover. *Journal of Applied Psychology, 104*(10), 1207–1225. https://doi.org/10.1037/apl0000405

Seeck, H., & Diehl, M. R. (2017). A Literature Review on HRM and Innovation–Taking Stock and Future Directions. *The International Journal of Human Resource Management, 28*(6), 913–944. https://doi.org/10.108 0/09585192.2016.1143862

Singh, J., Brady, M., Arnold, T., & Brown, T. (2017). The Emergent Field of Organisational Frontlines. *Journal of Service Research, 20*(1), 3–11. https:// doi.org/10.1177/1094670516681513

8 Machine Learning, Artificial Intelligence and the Future... 181

Splunk Inc. (2020). *5 Big Myth of AI and Machine Learning Debunked* [Online]. Accessed from https://www.splunk.com/pdfs/ebooks/5-big-myths-of-ai-and-machine-learning-debunked.pdf

Suen, H. Y., Chen, M. Y. C., & Lu, S. H. (2019). Does the Use of Synchrony and Artificial Intelligence in Video Interviews Affect Interview Ratings and Applicant Attitudes? *Computers in Human Behavior, 98*, 93–101. https://doi.org/10.1016/j.chb.2019.04.012

Thomaz, F., Salge, C., Karahanna, E., & Hulland, J. (2020). Learning from the Dark Web: Leveraging Conversational Agents in the Era of Hyper-Privacy to Enhance Marketing. *Journal of the Academy of Marketing Science, 48*(1), 43–63. https://doi.org/10.1007/s11747-019-00704-3

Tschang, F. T., & Mezquita, E. A. (2020). Artificial Intelligence as Augmenting Automation: Implications for Employment. *Academy of Management Perspectives, 35*(4). https://doi.org/10.5465/amp.2019.0062

Vrontis, D., Christofi, M., Pereira, V., Tarba, S., Makrides, A., & Trichina, E. (2021). Artificial Intelligence, Robotics, Advanced Technologies and Human Resource Management: A Systematic Review. *The International Journal of Human Resource Management.* https://doi.org/10.1080/0958519 2.2020.1871398

Wilson, H. J. & Daugherty, P. R. (2018). Collaborative Intelligence: Humans and AI Are Joining Forces. *Harvard Business Review, 96*(4), 114–123. [Online]. Accessed December 12, 2021, from https://www.accenture.com/t20180828t222720z__w__/us-en/_acnmedia/pdf-84/accenture-collaborative-intelligence-2018.pdf

Wright, J., & Atkinson, D. (2019). The Impact of Artificial Intelligence Within the Recruitment Industry: Defining a New Way of Recruiting. *Carmichael Fisher,* 1–39. [Online]. Accessed December 6, 2021, from https://www.coursehero.com/file/104827091/James-Wright-The-impact-of-artificial-intelligence-within-the-recruitment-industry-Defining-a-new-wa/

Zanko, M., Badham, R., Couchman, P., & Schubert, M. (2008). Innovation and HRM: Absences and Politics. *The International Journal of Human Resource Management, 19*(4), 562–581. https://doi.org/10.1080/09585190801953616

Zucchetti, A., Cobo, C., Kass-Hanna, J., & Lyons, A. C. (2020). *Leaving No One Behind: Measuring the Multidimensionality of Digital Literacy in the Age of AI and other Transformative Technologies, G20 Insights* [Online]. Accessed December 14, 2021, from https://www.g20-insights.org/policy_briefs/leaving-no-one-behind-measuring-the-multidimensionality-of-digital-literacy-in-the-age-of-ai-and-other-transformative-technologies/

9

Technological Innovation and Performance Measurement in the Sport Sector

Mario Nicoliello

9.1 Introduction

Technological innovation is playing an increasingly important role in the field of sports performance measurement. The new technologies have in fact made it possible to refine the timing and measurement systems, as well as have allowed the collection of numerous data on the athlete's performance, which in the past was not possible to have.

This chapter intends to analyse the impact of technology in measuring the sports performance of athletes, presenting the concrete case of Omega, the Swiss company that offers timing and measurement services at the Olympic Games, as well as the main world sports championships.

Worldwide Olympic Partner Omega, the Official Timekeeper of Tokyo 2020+1 Olympic Games, has given fans a totally new understanding of each athlete's performance during the last summer Olympics.

M. Nicoliello (✉)
Researcher in Business Administration, University of Genoa, Genoa, Italy
e-mail: mario.nicoliello@unige.it

© The Author(s), under exclusive license to Springer Nature Switzerland AG 2022
A. Thrassou et al. (eds.), *Business Advancement through Technology Volume II*, Palgrave Studies in Cross-disciplinary Business Research, In Association with EuroMed Academy of Business, https://doi.org/10.1007/978-3-031-07765-4_9

Building on the company's long legacy of Olympic timekeeping innovations dating back to the 1932 Los Angeles Olympic Games, Omega's latest technologies have collected a full range of real-time data during events, providing athletes, coaches and fans with a broader vision than ever (IOC, 2021). Regarding the experience of Tokyo 2020+1, in athletics, for example, athletes have been equipped with motion sensor tags on their starting numbers, which would interact with receivers around the track. Omega was therefore able to provide real-time information, such as real-time positions during races, real-time speed, acceleration, deceleration and total distance (IOC, 2021). Meanwhile, in swimming, image-tracking cameras around the pool were used to track each swimmer's exact movements and provide similar data, including the number of strokes and distances between swimmers (IOC, 2021). Image-tracking cameras have also been used in beach volleyball, providing detailed information on how each point was scored, including ball speed and how high players jumped for each shot (IOC, 2021). In gymnastics, a slightly different technology has been used, known as pose detection. This incredibly advanced system recorded each athlete's complete movements and was also used as a judgment tool for judges (IOC, 2021).

Omega's latest innovations have also been seen in equestrian events, with special action-tracking image tracking technology and laser sensing used to pinpoint the horses' movements. This provided data such as flight time and trajectory on jumps and the cyclist's exact path along the route (IOC, 2021).

Using the framework of the Innovation Theory, the chapter will illustrate the consequences of the new technological systems both on the technical gesture of the athletes and on the communication language of the sporting event. The research aims to demonstrate how technology can be a driving force both in improving the performance of athletes and in disseminating the sporting event to an ever-increasing audience of users.

The chapter will continue as follows. Paragraph two will contain the literature review of the previous works on the field. We found articles and books searching in databases about innovation and sports sector. Paragraph three will contain the methodology of the research. The heart of the analysis will be the fourth paragraph, which will first present the history of Omega at the Olympic Games and then the innovations at

Tokyo 2020. Finally, the paragraph five will contain some concluding remarks.

9.2 Literature Review

Innovation is a much debated element in the management literature, therefore different definitions have been provided by the authors in the past. The one considered to be the most comprehensive was provided by Damanpour: innovation involves the successful exploitation of new ideas that can generate value (Damanpour, 1996). Following this path it is possible to link the innovation with different concepts: product, process, service or technology (Oke et al., 2007). Innovation is a feature that characterizes organisations over time, impacting on management behaviours and styles (Smith & Tushman, 2005), therefore according to Damanpour, from one side organisations have a history of innovation due to their ability to develop better effectiveness with implementation of successful innovations (Damanpour et al., 2009) and from the other side, the innovation is important to the growth of resources devoted to creative activity (Damanpour & Schneider, 2006).

Very often innovations bring about a radical change, which requires a new use of resources (Damanpour, 1996). To this end, a real innovation strategy is needed that describes the way in which an organisation positions itself in its competitive environment for the development of new products and markets (Ratten & Ferreira, 2017). The innovation strategy requires management to make specific decisions about innovation goals, deciding how to allocate the resources that lead to innovation (Li & Atuahene-Gima, 2001). According to Saleh and Wang, the relationships between innovation and strategy will have an impact on the actions, behaviours and culture of the organisation (Saleh & Wang, 1993).

The innovation management literature distinguishes between the adoption and appropriation process (Clark et al., 1989). In sports, these topics were developed by Newell and Swan (1995), who discussed how decisions are made to use new ideas in the sport sector and how ideas are translated within an organisation (Newell & Swan, 1995). Obviously these elements can also be considered from a functional and psychological perspective (Antioco & Kleijnen, 2010).

According to Ratten and Ferreira (2017), the main objective of innovation in the sports context concerns sports organisations that innovate to increase the number of members and to add more services (Thibault et al., 1993). This is a result of consumers playing a crucial role in sports organisations by generating new ideas as they have a more emotional attachment (Franke & Shah, 2003).

In fact, within the sports field, innovation is developed by consumers or participants given their high level of involvement (Newell & Swan, 1995). This means that sports innovation is different from other types of innovation, which is usually developed within an organisation through research and development (Franke & Shah, 2003).

In particular, according to Ratten and Ferreira (2017), sports innovation is different from others because very often users innovate equipment on their own instead of waiting for an organisation to do it. This brings innovation in sport to be dynamic as it is refined by members of the sporting community. Sports innovation by users rather than manufacturers is popular due to the performance reward that comes with the change. This user-driven innovation can occur in organisations that wish to keep the innovation secret while benefiting for revenue-sharing reasons (Von Hippel, 2007).

Sports innovation tends to focus on the idea of improving the way sports are played, seen or watched. This research work fits precisely into this area, which aims to investigate the level of innovation introduced in the timekeeping system at the Olympic Games. Inside this last stream we want to follow the previous works by Nicoliello (2022) and Walvadkar and Kaufmann (2022), the first one dedicated to the impact of Covid19 on the organisation of Olympic Games, the second one regarding the role of technology during a crisis (Vrontis et al., 2022).

9.3 Methodology

This research has developed following the method of the case study (Yin, 1984), telling through the experience of Omega, how innovation has been carried out over the years at the Olympic Games.

In particular, the first part of the research was the construction of the historical evolution of the innovations promoted by Omega over the years, while the second focused on the innovations introduced at the Tokyo 2020+1 Olympic Games.

The research was able to benefit from the use of primary sources, since the material was requested directly from the company involved in the case study. In particular, the author contacted Omega's external relations office directly, which provided descriptive material about Omega's commitment to the Olympic Games from 1932 to 2021 and when it was made again for Tokyo 2021.

Other sources that were used in the case study were the press information released by both Omega and the International Olympic Committee during the Tokyo Games.

9.4 Analysis

9.4.1 The History of Omega at Olympic Games

As the Official Timekeeper of the Olympic Games in 29 editions since 1932, Omega has experienced many innovative and memorable moments. In Los Angeles 1932, a single watchmaker is selected as the Official Timekeeper of the Olympic Games. Omega is the winner of the prestigious title, based on the unrivalled reputation earned through records of precision and excellence. It is a decisive year in the history of sports timekeeping. The brand sends a watchmaker directly from Biel to Los Angeles, armed with 30 high-precision chronometers that allow an approximation to the tenth of a second in the measurement.

Omega's first Winter Olympic Games are held in the German municipality of Garmisch-Partenkirchen in 1936. Compared to summer competitions, winter events pose new challenges to the Swiss watch brand, in particular alpine skiing, for which, in the absence of a telephone or radio connection between the start and finish, the brand is forced to indicate on a slip of paper at the exact start time and send it to the judges at the foot of the mountain by inserting it in the pocket of the next skier. But Omega's precision and dedication shine once again. Like the sun and the perfect weather conditions of this edition, setting the stage for another year of historical results and times.

Two of the major revolutions in sports timekeeping appear for the first time in the summer at the 1948 Olympics. It is the beginning of the "electronic age", when technology begins to supplant the capabilities of the human eye by offering better performance. Among the Omega technologies stand out the first photo finish, able to precisely identify the finishing positions in the races, and the first photoelectric cell, which electronically stops the chronometer at the precise moment in which the first athlete crosses the finish line.

As a sign of appreciation for Omega's 20 years at the Olympic Games, in 1952 the brand was awarded the Cross of Merit by the IOC for "exceptional services rendered to the world of sport". A dutiful tribute to the achievements up to that moment, but also to the continuous progress and innovations, such as the Quartz Time Recorder, an extraordinary electronic chronograph equipped with a high-speed printer that allowed competitions to be timed and instantly printed results to the hundredth of a second.

Swimming has always posed a series of specific challenges to timekeepers due to the extreme environment in which the devices, immersed in water, find themselves operating. In 1956, however, Omega took a huge step forward by introducing the Swim Eight-O-Matic Timer, the world's first semi-automatic stopwatch for swimming competitions. Pressing the trigger of the starting gun automatically activates the start time, while the counters at the finish line are stopped by manual electric stopwatches. The system finally manages to distinguish the winner between two swimmers who arrived almost at the same instant, marking the beginning of new discoveries in the sports field.

With the introduction of Omegascope technology, the Olympic viewing experience changes forever thanks to Omega. The new device

9 Technological Innovation and Performance Measurement... 189

introduces the concept of communicating sports results in "real time", thanks to the live superimposition of the athletes' times on the lower part of the screen. From this moment, Omega precision is under the eyes of millions of spectators: the margin of error is getting smaller and smaller. Never had the public had such quick information about an event that took place miles away.

The advent of the contact plates invented by Omega is considered one of the most important moments in the history of timekeeping. The plates, 90 cm high and 240 cm wide, were immersed in water for two thirds of the surface. They reacted to the slightest touch of the athletes who, having reached the finish line, stopped time simply by touching them with their hand. Since then, the accuracy of the results of swimming competitions could no longer be questioned.

In Montreal 1976, the new Omega Video Matrix Scoreboard is capable of displaying times, scores and rankings, as well as offering black and white video recordings. Designed for multiple alphabets, it transmits information to the entire Stade Olympique. The results of sporting events will help lay the foundations for the numerous advances and technical innovations of which the scoreboards will be protagonists in the future.

The 1984 Olympics are famous for the numerous and memorable athletic results achieved, including the four gold medals won by the American Carl Lewis. On the track, Omega takes giant steps in timing, presenting the first false start detector, an extremely sensitive device that works by measuring the pressure exerted by each athlete on the starting blocks. During the forward momentum, the athlete's physical strength triggers the reaction time, allowing Omega to detect every slightest false start.

The 1988 Seoul Summer Olympics are the first to boast computerized timekeeping. Instead of simply measuring, attributing and printing times, Omega is now also able to digitally record information and statistics that are essential for a better understanding of each sport. In addition to ensuring future data security, the brand is also committed to providing real-time information to spectators in the main stadium, thanks to a new video matrix display that broadcasts the first images and video in colour.

For the first time since 1992, Omega returns to the position of Official Timekeeper of all Olympic events in Turin 2006. In speed skating, the brand's brand new technology attracts attention: for the first time at the

Olympics, athletes wear special transponders on the ankles. These are microchips capable of sending and receiving signals via radio, thus allowing Omega to record specific time measurements during each race.

In London 2012, with enhanced resolution of one millionth of a second, Omega's new Quantum Timer marks the beginning of a new generation of timekeeping tools. The resolution is 100 times higher than previous devices and, with a maximum variation of just one second every million seconds, it is five times more accurate.

PyeongChang 2018 represents the beginning of a new and no less daring era for Omega. With the use of unprecedented motion sensors and positioning systems, the Official Timekeeper is able to provide constant performance measurements of each athlete from start to finish. From the real-time speed of a single alpine skier to the formation of an entire ice hockey team, Omega provides specific information for each event as it unfolds. For athletes, the new technology provides the perfect analysis of their performance, while for viewers it ensures a better understanding of the event in progress.

9.4.2 The Innovation at Tokyo 2020 Olympic Games

Tokyo 2020 has been the 29th time that Omega has acted as Official Timekeeper for the Olympic Games, with the company set to measure every second of action across 339 events in 33 sports. This monumental task has required 400 tonnes of equipment, 530 timekeepers and on-site professionals, 900 trained volunteers, 350 sport-specific scoreboards, 85 public scoreboards and approximately 200 km of cables and optical fibre (Omega, 2021).

Each sporting event corresponds to timing systems and specific technologies for the individual disciplines. On this paragraph, firstly we show some of the Omega instruments most used during the Olympic Games. In particular: the electronic starting gun; the starting blocks; the new photo finish; photocell technology; the swimming light show; the contact plates for swimming; the Quantum Timer; the high resolution scoreboards (Omega, 2021).

The Electronic Starting Gun

The problem with traditional guns is that sound travels at a slower speed than light, thus causing a delay in the acoustic perception of the starting signal by athletes in the furthest lanes. Therefore, the closer you get to the starter, the sooner the signal will be heard. The solution is an electronic pistol connected to speakers positioned behind each athlete's shoulders. By pressing the trigger, the device automatically produces a sound, emits a bright flash and activates stopwatches. The fairest system to guarantee equal conditions at the start (Omega, 2021).

The Starting Blocks

In addition to the loudspeakers, sensors that measure the force exerted by the athlete on the platform have been integrated into the starting blocks used in athletics competitions 4000 times per second. The sensing system instantly sends force measurements to an on-site computer so the starter can visually recognize false starts. According to the rules established by World Athletics, the minimum reaction time is 100 milliseconds (one tenth of a second). Any reaction below this limit is considered premature, placing the athlete in a false start situation (Omega, 2021).

The Photo Finish

The Scan'O'Vision MYRIA is the most advanced photo finish in Omega's history. Positioned on the finish line of sprint, obstacle course and other disciplines, it is able to capture up to 10,000 frames per second, generating a composite photo thanks to which the judges will be able to detect the times and draw up the official rankings of each event. The images captured by the photo finish are now emblematic of the Olympic Games, demonstrating how much the gap between athletes in some competitions can really be reduced (Omega, 2021).

Photocell Technology

Since 1948, the traditional ribbon at the finish line of athletics competition, it has been replaced by photocell technology, based on the emission of light rays. The moment the winner crosses the rays, the winning time is recorded instantly. Omega currently uses four photocells positioned on the finish line, all integrated into a single module, thus allowing the detection of multiple bodies. Although the system offers the timekeepers immediate finish times, the official times are nevertheless taken from the photo finish (Omega, 2021).

The Swimming Light Show

The innovative system called Swimming Light Show involves the assembly of lighting devices on the starting blocks at the end of the pool. At the end of the race, the appearance of a single large illuminated dot indicates the winner, two medium-sized dots show the runner-up and three smaller dots confirm third place. The ideal solution to allow athletes and spectators to immediately grasp the outcome of the race (Omega, 2021).

The Contact Plates for Swimming

At the end of a swimming competition, the famous contact plates positioned at both ends of the pool allow swimmers to "stop the clock" by exerting a pressure of 1.5–2.5 kg. Thanks to the contact plates, swimming has long been the only sport in which the competitors themselves stop their race time. The technology, first introduced by Omega at the 1968 Olympic Games, remains to this day the most accurate method for timing the times in such a demanding sport (Omega, 2021).

The Quantum Timer

Mechanical stopwatches are a thing of the past. Today, Omega timekeeping is based on the Quantum Timer, which has an enhanced resolution of one millionth of a second. Powered by a component created from micro crystal and incorporated into the timer, it boasts a resolution 100 times higher than previous devices and, with a maximum variation of just one second every ten million seconds, it is five times more accurate (Omega, 2021).

The High Resolution Scoreboards

In addition to displaying text and information in real time, Omega's high-resolution scoreboards transmit animations, videos and images of the athletes. Thanks to the use of modern effects, they show the names, results and national flags of the winners with great visibility, contributing to the spectacularity and exciting atmosphere of each event (Omega, 2021).

Now, we will focus on the specific sports, presenting the innovation inside the following competitions: athletics; swimming, beach volleyball, gymnastics and equestrian.

Athletics

The athletes on the Tokyo tracks were all equipped with plates with motion sensors applied to the race numbers. The tags interact with numerous receivers positioned around the field and send essential information. Thanks to this technology, we are able to provide the following information in real time: positions in real time (not only intermediate ones); speed in real time; acceleration; deceleration; the distance.

Now it is possible to watch the 400 m knowing exactly the actual position of all the athletes at each lap. It was possible to watch the 100 m knowing who made the best acceleration at the start, or when the winner reached top speed. And it was even possible to look at the 10,000 m knowing the distance between the runners, or who is speeding up and who is slowing down (Omega, 2021).

Swimming

The performance of the swimmers was also subject to complete measurements, in this case thanks to cameras for tracking images positioned around the pool, capable of detecting the movements of each athlete.

The data collected thanks to Computer Vision technology made it possible to provide the following information: the positions in real time (not only at each turn); speed in real time; acceleration; deceleration; the distances between the swimmers; the number of strokes.

Now you can watch the tight 200 m freestyle competitions knowing the real-time positions of all swimmers. It was possible to watch the 100 m butterfly by comparing the number of strokes to understand how the race was won. And it was even possible to witness the hard-fought finals knowing who accelerated the most in the last meters (Omega, 2021).

Beach Volleyball

For this sport, characterized by dynamic races held on the sand, cameras were used to track the images installed around the playing field, capturing every moment of action. The cameras followed the ball and the players, providing detailed information on the game and the scoring of each point.

Among the information that has been provided, we point out: the distances covered by each player; the speed of the players and the ball; the techniques of the individual players, including number of jumps and height; the type of shots (blocks, spikes, etc.)

Thanks to all the data collected, it was possible to carry out a complete tactical analysis of the game, discovering the strengths and strategies of each player and each team (Omega, 2021).

Gymnastics

A slightly different technology was used for gymnastics, known as Pose Detection, an extremely advanced system that represents a huge step forward for sports timing, capable of detecting the complete movements and positions of each athlete.

Pose Detection technology has also been used by match judges as an evaluation tool, at their disposal to examine athletes' technique. For instance: to evaluate the synchrony of gymnasts in the trampoline discipline or to evaluate the horizontal movement in the trampoline (Omega, 2021).

Equestrian

The special image tracking technology followed the action in equestrian disciplines, while the laser detection also made it possible to identify the movements of the horse. In this sport, the difference between gold and silver can depend on only one obstacle, so every second is of great importance.

The information provided concerned: the distances; average and real-time speeds; the flight time during a jump; the accuracy of the path followed by the rider; the trajectory during a jump (Omega, 2021).

9.5   Discussion

Using the framework of the Innovation Theory, this chapter has illustrated the consequences of the new technological systems both on the technical gesture of the athletes and on the communication language of the sporting event, in order to demonstrate how technology can be a driving force both in improving the performance of athletes and in disseminating the sporting event to an ever-increasing audience of users (Table 9.1).

The case of Omega can be of help to understand to corroborate the thesis underlying the study. The continuous innovation that has taken place since 1932 in timekeeping has in fact influenced the athlete's gesture, as athletes have adapted to the new means of measurement. Think of the case of the photo finish in athletics competitions, which has completely changed the preparation and approach in the last meters of the

196   M. Nicoliello

Table 9.1 The innovations of Omega at Tokyo 2020 Olympic Games

Innovations	Results
The electronic starting gun	Equal conditions at the start
The starting blocks	Better recognise false starts
The new photo finish	Gap between athletes in some competitions can really be reduced
Photocell technology	Allowing the detection of multiple bodies
The swimming light show	To allow athletes and spectators to immediately grasp the outcome of the race
The contact plates for swimming	The competitors themselves stop their race time
The Quantum Timer	It boasts a resolution 100 times higher than previous devices
The high resolution scoreboards	Contributing to the spectacularity and exciting atmosphere of each event

Sports	Performance measurements
Athletics	Positions in real time; speed in real time; acceleration; deceleration; the distance between athletes
Swimming	Positions in real time; speed in real time; acceleration; deceleration; the distances between the swimmers; the number of strokes
Beach volleyball	The distances covered by each player; the speed of the players and the ball; the techniques of the individual players; the type of shots
Gymnastics	Detecting the complete movements and positions of each athlete
Equestrian	Average and real-time speeds; the flight time during a jump; the accuracy of the path followed by the rider; the trajectory during a jump

Source: Our elaboration on data derived from Omega (2021)

race, when the sprinter arrives at the finish line with the torso forward. But we can also mention the case of the starting blocks, which have completely revolutionized the first phase of running, with the athletes who now try to exploit the tool to better launch themselves, assuming a particular rhythm of running in the first part of the speed races. Similar examples can also be drawn within the world of swimming, where the electric plate has upset the last phase of the competitions, with swimmers who have specialized in the final strokes and on the correct methods of

9 Technological Innovation and Performance Measurement...

approaching the plate, which requires receive a specific force in order to block the stopwatch.

Innovation in the technological field has then completely upset the communication methods of the sporting event. First of all, the data and information that can be conveyed to the public has increased. Staying in the field of athletics, the reaction time to the shot has become a parameter for measuring the efficiency of the start phase, just as the measurement of the point at which each sprinter achieves the maximum speed has become a way to critically analyse the races. In beach volleyball, on the other hand, the accuracy of the dunk, or the distance travelled by the athletes or the speed reached by the serve are now elements that form the basis of communication regarding the matches. Technological innovation has therefore increased the numbers available to all professionals and allowed the processing of useful statistics for coaches to set up matches, for players to improve in some aspects, for fans to better appreciate some phases of the game, for journalists to fill their reports with numbers, and for statisticians who have found a precious source in the databases full of data to experiment with new elaborations.

On the one hand, the innovation has improved the performance of athletes, on the other hand it has increased the audience of sporting events, since all the innovations described in the previous paragraph have made it possible to enjoy the competition better, to immerse yourself more in the atmosphere of the race, to have fun using a new concept of the event.

Compared to previous works, the case told in this chapter allows us to affirm how technological innovation has changed the way in which sport is not only played, but also observed. Following the conclusions of Ratten and Ferreira (2017), this chapter shows how the technology can create a new type of product in a sport event, because the innovation improves the way in which the performance can be measured and communicated. Carrying on the work by Li and Atuahene-Gima (2001) the case of Omega confirms how the choice of resources' allocation is strategic in order to guarantee the success: focusing on the most important and popular sports Omega has reached a great audience with its innovations. Athletes have played an important role in the process established by Omega, therefore this case confirm also the thesis of Newell and Swan

(1995) about the involvement of people in the innovation process. Finally, the case of Omega confirms what was previously stated in the literature, regarding the ability of technological innovation to completely change the use of a sporting event (Ratten & Ferreira, 2017).

Furthermore, the Omega case is interesting because it allows for a comparison over the years, considering the lasting presence of the Swiss company at the Olympic Games, and to be able to broaden the spectrum of analysis also to the future. The words of the number one of the Olympic family are significant in this regard. According to IOC President, Thomas Bach, "The Olympic Games is about sports, and sports is about results. We are always excited about how Omega is driving timekeeping forward and adapting it to the new world we are living in. We have the same interests: to serve the athletes, to enrich their experience and enrich the experience of fans all over the world".

In 2017, Omega extended its Worldwide Olympic Partnership with the IOC through to 2032, when the company will mark 100 years since it started its relationship with the Olympic Games.

We therefore expect that the history of innovation will continue and that other innovations will be introduced in the field of timekeeping so as to confirm what emerged from the case presented in this chapter. This new story could be the potential future developments of this research.

References

Antioco, M., & Kleijnen, M. (2010). Consumer Adoption of Technological Innovations: Effects of Psychological and Functional Barriers in a Lack of Content Versus a Presence of Content Situation. *European Journal of Marketing, 44*(11/12), 1700–1774.

Clark, P. A., Staunton, N., & Rogers, E. M. (1989). *Innovation in Technology and Organisation.* Routledge.

Damanpour, F. (1996). Organisational Complexity and Innovation: Developing and Testing Multiple Contingency Models. *Management Science, 42*(5), 693–716.

Damanpour, F., & Schneider, M. (2006). Phases of the Adoption of Innovation in Organisations: Effects of Environment, Organisation and Top Managers. *British Journal of Management, 17*(3), 215–211.

Damanpour, F., Walker, R. M., & Avellaneda, C. N. (2009). Combinative Effects of Innovation Types and Organisational Performance: A Longitudinal Study of Service Organisations. *Journal of Management Studies, 46*(4), 650–675.

Franke, N., & Shah, S. (2003). How Communities Support Innovative Activities: An Exploration of Assistance and Sharing Among End-Users. *Research Policy, 32*(1), 157–178.

IOC. (2021). *Omega's Tradition of Olympic Timekeeping Innovations Continues at Tokyo 2020*. Accessed July 22, 2021, from https://olympics.com/ioc/news/omega-s-tradition-of-olympic-timekeeping-innovations-continues-at-tokyo-2020

Li, H., & Atuahene-Gima, K. (2001). Product Innovation Strategy and the Performance of New Technology Ventures in China. *Academy of Management Journal, 44*(6), 1123–1134.

Newell, S., & Swan, J. (1995). Professional Associations as Important Mediators of the Innovation Process. *Science Communication, 16*(4), 371–387.

Nicoliello, M. (2022). The Impact of Covid-19 on the Mega Sport Events: The Case of the Postponement of Olympic Games "Tokyo 2020". In D. Vrontis, A. Thrassou, S. M. Yaakov Weber, R. Shams, E. Tsoukatos, & L. Efthymiou (Eds.), *Business Under Crisis* (Vol. I). Springer.

Oke, A., Burke, G., & Myers, A. (2007). Innovation Types and Performance in Growing UK SMEs. *International Journal of Operations & Production Management, 27*(7), 735–753.

Omega. (2021). *Press Information Olympic Games Tokyo 2020*, Bienne.

Ratten, V., & Ferreira, J. J. (Eds.). (2017). *Sport Entrepreneurship and Innovation*. Routledge.

Saleh, S. D., & Wang, C. K. (1993). The Management of Innovation: Strategy, Structure, and Organisational Climate. *IEEE Transactions on Engineering Management, 40*(1), 14–21.

Smith, W. K., & Tushman, M. L. (2005). Managing Strategic Contradictions: A Top Management Model for Managing Innovation Streams. *Organisation Science, 16*(5), 522–536.

Thibault, L., Slack, T. B., & Hinings, B. (1993). A Framework for the Analysis of Strategy in Nonprofit Sport Organisations. *Journal of Sport Management, 7*, 25–43.

Von Hippel, E. (2007). *The Sources of Innovation*. Springer.

Vrontis, D., Thrassou, A., Weber, Y., Shams, S. M. R., Tsoukatos, E., & Efthymiou, L. (2022). Business Under Crisis: Organisational Adaptations (Vol. II), Palgrave Studies in Cross-Disciplinary Business Research. In *Association with EuroMed Academy of Business*. Palgrave Macmillan.

Walvadkar, J. R., & Kaufmann, H. R. (2022). Business Under Crisis: Digital Transformation of Learning & Development. In D. Vrontis, A. Thrassou, S. M. Yaakov Weber, R. Shams, E. Tsoukatos, & L. Efthymiou (Eds.), *Business Under Crisis* (Vol. I). Springer.

Yin, R. K. (1984). *Case Study Research: Design and Methods*. Sage.

10

Opening up the Black Box on Digitalisation and Agility: Key Drivers and Main Outcomes

Salim Chouaibi, Matteo Rossi, Jamel Chouaibi, and Alkis Thrassou

10.1 Introduction

Nowadays, digitalisation or more specifically digital transformation is on the lips of all executives in all sectors thanks to its magical effect on business performance. Indeed, digital technologies are important because

---

S. Chouaibi • J. Chouaibi
Faculty of Economics and Management of Sfax, University of Sfax, Sfax, Tunisia

M. Rossi (✉)
Department of Law, Economics, Management and Quantitative Methods (DEMM), University of Sannio, Benevento, Italy
e-mail: mrossi@unisannio.it

A. Thrassou
School of Business, Department of Management, University of Nicosia, Nicosia, Cyprus
e-mail: thrassou.a@unic.ac.cy

© The Author(s), under exclusive license to Springer Nature Switzerland AG 2022
A. Thrassou et al. (eds.), *Business Advancement through Technology Volume II*, Palgrave Studies in Cross-disciplinary Business Research, In Association with EuroMed Academy of Business, https://doi.org/10.1007/978-3-031-07765-4_10

they can be used to coordinate resources more efficiently. In addition, the integration of digital technologies affects large parts of companies and even exceeds their capacities and borders. They impact products, business processes, sales and even supply chains. Thus, it should be noted that digitalisation has many advantages. First, it optimizes business performance by increasing productivity, based on better communication between the various stakeholders (Downes & Nunes, 2013). Nevertheless, the use of digital technologies also has drawbacks such as security problems, the risk of loss of information and the problem of dispersion. Thus, since we have new technologies and new tools, we have new technical problems.

On the one hand, digital technologies have a remarkable impact on the competitive advantage of companies and on their organisational performance and on the other hand it affects the strategy of sustainability. According to Strange and Zucchella (2017), they allow the organisation to face new competitive threats and they create a strong competitor of the company that does not dare to contribute to the new digitalized markets without any concern to be more flexible to changes. As a result, a company can use different types of digital technologies, such as the Big Data, to improve their competitive advantages (Pagani & Pardo, 2017; Strange & Zucchella, 2017). Similarly, digitalisation also influences the sustainable development of the firm. According to Pagani and Pardo (2017), digitalisation has become a necessity in the sustainable development strategy of most companies. In fact, it ensures the creation and use of new, more socially responsible products and services while also helping to promote them. Digitisation facilitates the integration of stakeholders into the eco-responsible strategy of their companies.

Our paper attempts to solve the problems of digital transformation on the firm's organisational performance and sustainable development. Also, given the scarcity of works on the role of digital technologies in competitive advantage and sustainable development, we found that a study on this field can be useful as it can help Tunisian companies enormously to carry out their business of a more efficient way. Based on what has been advanced, we can ask the following question:

Q1: What is the impact of technological and digital transformation within the company on their organisational performance?

Q2: To what extent does the adoption of a digital and innovative strategy affect the firm's sustainable development?

It follows that the objective of this work is to examine the effect of digital technologies on organisational performance and sustainable development.

On the theoretical level, we seek to present the theoretical foundations of the relationship between digital transformations and organisational performance on the one hand and sustainable development on the other one. On a practical level, this work presents some managerial contributions for decision-makers in the Tunisian context. Indeed, our results may be useful to business managers facing from problems regarding the implementation of digital technologies within companies and how to exploit them effectively. Our study enables the company to better assess the digital transformation as well as the investments in innovation technologies and its future growth opportunities in a context where the digitalisation and innovation occupy a central position in business valuation.

The remainder of this document is organized as follows: Sect. 10.2 reviews the literature and outlines the hypotheses development. Section 10.3 describes the sample selection and its characteristics, the data sources, and the model specification. The main empirical results and the contributions as well as the implications of our study are presented and discussed in Sect. 10.4. Finally, concluding remarks are given in Sect. 10.5.

10.2 Literature Review and Hypotheses Development

In general, the venture undertaking act is a complex concept that can be studied via different approaches and perspectives. Relying on the innovation-based approach, transformation and digital technologies are usually recognized as the innovative creation of new organisational performance and sustainable development.

10.2.1 Digital Technologies and Organisational Performance

The relationships binding digital technologies, various resources and capabilities, likely to boost corporate organisational performance, seems worth investigating for an effective enhancement of business growth, expansion and internationalisation to take place (Coviello et al., 2017; Neubert, 2018; Wittkop et al., 2018).

The term digitisation refers to the implementation of digital technologies and relevant infrastructures in the business, economic and social realms (Autio, 2017). In effect, companies usually apply different types of digital technologies, such as e-commerce, for the sake of setting up and boosting organisational performance (Autio, 2018; Nambisan, 2017). These companies could therefore deploy new technologies to enhance their competitive advantages and organisational performance (Pagani & Pardo, 2017; Strange & Zucchella, 2017).

Indeed, following the rapid evolution of technology, companies are compelled to reconsider the idea of implementing innovative technical solutions to achieve productivity gains and win competitive advantages. Moreover, several countries are thinking about their future competitive advantages, highly dependent on good and service based industries entailing a high degree of knowledge and heavily reliant on new technologies. These goods and services are characterized with a high added-value on the world market, which influences organisational performance, likely to generate considerable wealth (Anderson, 1997).

However, there are clear examples where new technologies are already having a revolutionary impact. These technologies drive innovation in manufacturing, defense and aerospace, medicine, transportation, financial services, entertainment and education. But even in traditionally low-tech market sectors, new technologies are transforming the rules of competition.

To remain competitive in today's business world and continue to grow and evolve, firms must embrace digital technologies in a mainstream and incremental manner. Indeed, engaging in digital transformation can allow companies to overcome the various difficulties and maintain an increasing rate of performance and therefore increase operational efficiency (Rybacki & Kowalski, 2018). It can be concluded from the above that there is a strong positive correlation between the use of digital technologies and improved organisational performance.

A company can use different types of digital technologies to improve their organisational performance and ensure their competitive advantages (Pagani & Pardo, 2017; Strange & Zucchella, 2017). Thus, the use of digital technologies can bring new business opportunities to the company, and improve the roles of operators in the value chain, which automatically increases the organisational performance of the firm.

Thus, the use of digital technologies provides a competitive advantage over other market players (Delahaye et al., 2019). Similarly, according to Barlatier and Burger-Helmchen (2019) "organisations are becoming 'digital'; they increasingly rely on complex information technologies to reduce their transaction costs and increase their competitive advantages (Strandhagen et al., 2019). To conclude, "While competition has always been fierce, the novelty generated by digital is that we no longer know where the threat will come from. Hence the need for very active monitoring. Digitisation is an important phenomenon these days and represents a real danger for companies, which are seeing their number of competitors double or even triple. ».

H1: Digital transformation is positively associated with organisational performance.

10.2.2 Innovation Intensity and Organisational Performance

The world has experienced extreme environmental degradation in recent decades. Indeed, the extensive growth mode has resulted in severe environmental pollution and ecological devastation, which has deeply affected people's normal life. Companies are generally considered to be the main cause of environmental problems and therefore they are subject to enormous pressure for environmental legitimacy from various stakeholders (Bansal & Clelland, 2004).

In addition, pressure from the media, consumers and other stakeholders has prompted companies to adopt innovative measures to improve their environmental performance. For this, we seek to know to what extent the responsible innovation strategy influences the organisational performance of the company and its competitive advantage in the market. At this stage, a lot of research has shown that innovation has always played an important role in the life of firms (Li et al., 2017). In fact, it represents a determining factor in their strategy to ensure their competitiveness and profitability (Michelino et al., 2014; Delgado-Ceballos et al., 2012; Murillo-Luna et al., 2011).

There are also several innovation strategies chosen by the company to ensure its sustainability, such as responsible innovation or green innovation. From different points of view, the innovation strategy is not only to develop the environmental performance of the company, but also to provide a competitive advantage (Phillips & Gully, 2015). Thus, a positive synergy occurs between the objectives of the firm and those of its environment in order to have a sustainable and productive research objective and a good policy of innovation in order to improve organisational performance (Horváthová, 2012; Amores-Salvadó et al., 2014; Lee & Min, 2015). As a result, a new innovation strategy based on the concept of corporate social responsibility appears to set the objectives of the company and its environment. Consequently, all companies are increasingly called upon to be socially responsible in terms of innovation to better manage their environmental impact and ensure organisational performance (Bi et al., 2016).

Several have examined the effect of business innovation on their organisational performance, even at times of crisis (Vrontis et al., 2022a, b, c). In fact, most theoretical and empirical studies recognize that knowledge and innovation are essential to creating organisational performance. For example, Thornhill (2006) showed that the interaction between innovation and knowledge significantly improves business performance. Similarly, Chang (2011) claim that a company's innovation performance has a positive effect on organisational performance. For their part, Conding et al. (2012) claim that innovation which has a positive relationship with ecological performance and environmental performance of the company is an important dimension of organisational performance.

Likewise, in the light of a study carried out by Dangelico and Pujari (2010), innovation has a direct link with the productivity of the company, such as the reduction of toxic components in products, the reduction of emissions and energy consumption which positively influences its organisational performance. In particular, innovation explains well the major changes concerning the environmental performance and the competitive advantage of the company.

Gueguen and Isckia (2011) notes that in some cases, innovation can lead the company to a monopoly situation and therefore an improvement in its organisational performance. Thus, on the basis of these developments, we can see that the degree of innovation intensity of companies positively and significantly influences organisational performance. Therefore, and in the light of this theoretical and empirical literature, it is possible to formulate the following hypothesis:

H2. The degree of innovation intensity of companies has a positive impact on their organisational performance

10.2.3 Digital Technology and Sustainable Development

Nowadays, corporate social responsibility and digital transformation are one of the most important factors of competitiveness. Indeed, the modern business and social environment is constantly changing. These changes are strongly influenced by technological advances. Additionally, sustainable development is a relatively new concept generally influenced by two main factors; the first factor is the second manages the world as for the second, it manifests itself in digitalisation. The Internet, as a digital technology, has become a tool for CSR discussion and analysis in the era of digitalisation. Moreover, digital transformation has largely contributed to the reduction of pollutant emissions and therefore better environmental protection.

As one of the well-known examples of digital technologies, the internet remains a tool for improving the sustainable development of organisations in the era of digitalisation. Indeed, the digital transformation has largely contributed to the reduction of pollution and the effective protection of the environment. Also, this transformation allows people to solve their traditional problems in a modern and especially digital way. Moreover, it is not just a series of activities based on digital tools but also a stimulus for cultural and social change (Orbik & Zozuľaková, 2019).

In recent years, we have seen the emergence of a new concept which is the embryo of the encounter between the term CSR and digitalisation which is corporate digital responsibility. In fact, the latter is the new corporate direction that merges its ethical considerations, trying to ensure socially responsible transitions for an increasingly digitized workforce. In addition, the use of digital technologies and sustainable development remain strategic imperatives that converge by triggering major transformations within the company as well as society (Kiron & Unruh, 2018; Osburg, T., & Lohrmann, 2017). This convergence is seen as a winning combination, not exempt from challenges that offers plenty of opportunities within and beyond organisational boundaries by overcoming the information vacuum. On the other hand, some experts consider that digital technology and sustainable development are two contradictory concepts that lead to changes in social and ecological systems (Gebhardt, 2017). However, the link between the two domains remains poorly explored, there is a lack of experience regarding this relationship and the following questions must be asked: If and to what extent the era of digitalisation could contribute or compromise the situation of sustainable development (Seele & Lock, 2017)? What is the role of digital technologies in the pursuit of social prosperity and how can corporate social responsibility be improved by using digital technologies?

Thus, it can be said that digitalisation is a cultural change that does not only require the use of digital technologies in the management of companies, but involves the awareness of people working in the field of business which influences sustainable development.

Digitisation has given rise to a large number of new services in the public and private sectors. Indeed, it helps people find a common platform to voice their issues, concerns and connect with the rest of the world that not only transforms the way businesses work, but also enables citizens around the world to access the best services in many sectors. Thus, the use of digital technologies makes possible the idea of a "shared economy". This brings potential environmental benefits due to the efficient use of resources (Osburg & Lohrmann, 2017). Therefore, and in the light of this theoretical and empirical literature, it is possible to formulate the following hypothesis:

H3: Technology and Digital transformation is positively associated with sustainable development.

10.2.4 Innovation Intensity and Sustainable Development

Innovation is an important approach to adopt to achieve sustainable development. In this sense, Miozzo et al. (2016) find that an innovative firm is one that chooses to develop a strategy based on its productive resources in order to have a sustainable development situation. Indeed, innovation refers to the generation of new ideas, products, services, processes or management systems that can be used to address environmental issues (Rennings, 2000; Asensio & Delmas, 2015). In addition, it can effectively reduce environmental pollution and negative impacts of resource and energy use processes, thereby creating sustainable development (Kemp & Pearson, 2007; Cormier & Magnan, 2015). According to Bi et al. (2016), low-carbon technological innovation as a responsible innovation activity not only improves the energy efficiency of the company and reduces the intensity of carbon emissions, but also increases its performance.

Thus, innovation also means the development of products that have positive or less negative effects on the environment during their life cycle, which has a sustainable competitive advantage and therefore an improvement in sustainability (Durif et al., 2010). The interaction between innovation and sustainable development is mainly concerned with energy saving, pollution prevention, environmental protection, waste recycling and sustainability, which positively influences and significantly the company's sustainable development (Chen et al., 2006; Cormier & Magnan, 2015). All these examples show the trend of innovative companies in

210   S. Chouaibi et al.

protecting the environment in order to ensure sustainable financial performance.

Due to the interplay between sustainability and innovation, Dangelico and Pujari (2010) state that innovation is nowadays a strategic priority which consists in improving the organisational performance of the company. In the same line, Li et al. (2017) state that innovation is not only an important means for firms to gain competitive advantage in the future, but also a fundamental requirement for gaining legitimacy.

H4. The degree of innovation intensity has a positive impact on sustainable development

10.3   Research Design and Methodology

10.3.1   Sample Selection and Data Collection

The main objective of our paper is to empirically examine the effect of the integration of digital technologies into business practices on organisational performance and sustainable development. As a result, our population is made up of Tunisian companies that belong to different sectors. The nature of the research problem allowed us to retain a quantitative methodology. A survey questionnaire was developed and submitted to a validation process. In order to characterize technological developments and their impact on economic sectors in Tunisia, we used a specific database developed by the Institute of Arab Business Managers (IACE). This database brings together data collected from more than 300 companies from all sectors in Tunisia. The representativeness of the sample is accepted. The survey was carried out during the 2020. The data collection phase allowed us to collect 270 questionnaires. These results reinforce the reliability of our sample because the respondents have the experience required to respond appropriately to our questionnaire. We find that the majority of respondents belong to the banking sector or have a technological activity (Table 10.1).

Table 10.1 Sample selection

Sample	Firms
Overall list	300
Less companies with lack of total data	(6)
Less firms with missing data	(24)
Final sample	270

10.3.2 Data Collection and Variables Measurement

The Data Collection

Data collection was done through the administration of a questionnaire to engineers and administrative teams of Tunisian companies, as well as from annual reports. We will use the database of a survey conducted by the services of the Institute of Arab Business Managers (IACE) specifically implemented for the observation of these phenomena in order to characterize the current dynamics in terms of digitisation. The questions concerning sustainable development were taken from a survey carried out by the National Institute of Statistics and Economic Studies of the Ministry of Economy and Finance of the French Republic. In fact, this survey is devoted to corporate strategy in the field of sustainable development, which is directly related to our research work. Our questionnaire includes only closed questions. This choice allows us to ensure rapid data collection and to carry out a quantitative analysis of all the items addressed to the subjects.

Choice of Used Approach

As part of our empirical analysis, we did, first, the exploratory factor analysis using mainly the method of principal component analysis (PCA). Then we used the multiple linear regression method to test the effect of digital transformation, and the intensity of innovation on organisational performance and on the sustainable development of companies. Both analyzes are performed using SPSS software.

Variables

Our methodological approach is realized by a measurement of the variables, which will be followed by a presentation of the model to test the hypotheses of the study.

10.3.3 Dependent Variable

Organisational Performance (ORG_PER)

Many studies on the value of digitalisation and agility adopt the financial performance to explain how organisations gain and sustain competitive advantage and superior organisational performance by utilizing IT (Amit & Schoemaker, 1993). As part of our analysis, it is proposed to measure the organisational performance «ORG_PER» of the companies in our sample by a score developed by Turel and Bart (2014) to ensure comparability between companies.

What is the relative "performance standing" of the organisation in its industry (i.e., compared to competitors)?, and the Board's satisfaction with the organisation's current financial performance (1 = Significantly low, 7 = Significantly high).

Sustainable Development (SUS_DEV)

Sustainable development is the latest novelty of companies thanks to these effects on the organisational and financial performance of companies. In fact, previous studies present a number of principles related to sustainable development. It concludes that there is a need to develop indicators to monitor progress in this term (Stevens, 2006). Indeed, these indicators are necessary for decision-makers and their environments to become aware of the links that unite economic, environmental and social values as well as the trade-offs that take place between them in order to assess the long-term implications of decisions and current behaviors. The concept of CSR is used to take into account the social and environmental impacts of the company's activities to integrate the challenges of sustainable development within the organisation and in their interactions with their stakeholders. Thus, we can use the measurement of CSR to measure sustainable development. This is what we will do in this study. To measure sustainable development, respondents were asked to provide their assessments of the company's commitment to CSR.

10.3.4 Variables of Interest

Digital Transformation Several categories of business-related explanatory variables can be used to test their effects on organisational performance. We focus on a single variable of interest which is the subject of our study. The adoption of digital transformation and communication technology it is a composite score developed by Scuotto et al. (2017) calculated based on a combination of several items reflecting the ICTs information orientation, R & D investment, Partner intensity and Development of incremental innovation of each company. Composite index of the adoption of digital transformation and communication technology, calculated as combination of several elements (see Table 10.2).

Innovation Level (*INN_LEV*) To determine the innovation level, we will adopt the same measure that has been used in several studies such as: Brown et al. (2013), Hsu et al. (2014), Bena and Simintzi (2016), Zhong (2018). In this paper, the level of innovation is measured by the intensity of research and development (R & D) which is calculated as an investment in R & D divided by total assets.

10.3.5 Control Variables

The link between digitalisation, Innovation level and the sustainable development and organisational performance for Tunisian may be influenced by several other variables that need to be controlled. Thus, we included in our model several control variables.

214 S. Chouaibi et al.

Table 10.2 Measures and items

Measure	Items	Questions (extracted from the definition of each item)	References
ICTs	ICTs information	Implementation of ICTs to inform employees and customers and/or to obtain information and data concerning competitors	López-Nicolás and Soto-Acosta (2010), Zhu and Kraemer (2005)
	ICTs communication orientation	Implementation of ICTs to receive and/or debate Suggestions from employees, customers and partners	López-Nicolás and Soto-Acosta (2010), Zhu and Kraemer (2005)
	ICTs workflow orientation	Implementation of ICTs to support the automation of internal and external processes	López-Nicolás and Soto-Acosta (2010), Zhu and Kraemer (2005)
In-house R & D	R & D investment	The importance of investing in internal R & D to aid the innovation process	Cohen and Levinthal (1990)
	Internal knowledge development	The importance of internal R & D in developing new knowledge	Tidd and Trewhella (1997), Camisón and Villar-López (2014)
	Knowledge storage	The ability of retaining and storing knowledge over time	Alavi and Leidner (2001), Camisón and Villar-López (2014)
Open innovation	Partner intensity	The intensity of relationships with each external source of knowledge	Aloini et al. (2015)
	E-collaboration tools	Interaction with external sources of knowledge Facilitated by the use of Internet technologies	Chan et al. (2012)
	Openness variety	External sources of knowledge are involved in the innovation process	Aloini et al. (2015)

(*continued*)

10 Opening up the Black Box on Digitalisation and Agility: Key... 215

Table 10.2 (continued)

Measure	Items	Questions (extracted from the definition of each item)	References
SME's innovation performance	Development of incremental innovation	The ability of the firm to produce improved products and/or services	Soto Acosta et al. (2016)
	Development of radical innovation	The ability of the firm to produce products and/or services that are completely new	Soto Acosta et al. (2016)
	Opening up of new markets	The opportunity to introduce the business to new markets	Aloini et al. (2015), Soto-Acosta et al. (2016)

Source: Scuotto et al. (2017)

- *Firm size (SIZE):* is measured as the natural log of total assets. On prior research firm size has been shown to be an important determinant of organisational performance. We find that larger firms are likely to be more organisational performance than smaller firms.
- *Leverage (LEV):* is measured as total debt divided by total equity, is included as a control variable as firms that have higher debt-to-equity ratios are not efficient at creating value.
- *Women board directors (WOM_BD):* to calculate the female director ratio, we divided the number of women board members by the total number of board members (Nielsen & Huse, 2010; Sun et al., 2015; Post & Byron, 2015; Adams, 2016).

10.3.6 Model Development

First of all, it should be remembered that our objective is to test the impact of the integration of digital technologies and innovation on the organisational performance and on the sustainable development of Tunisian companies.

$$ORG\_PER_i = \beta_0 + \beta_1 DIG\_TRA_i + \beta_2 INN\_LEV + \beta_3 LEV_i +$$
$$\beta_4 SIZE_i + \beta_5 WOM\_BOD_i + \varepsilon_i \tag{10.1}$$

$$SUS\_DEV_i = \beta_0 + \beta_1 DIG\_TRA_i + \beta_2 INN\_LEV + \beta_3 LEV_i +$$
$$\beta_4 SIZE_i + \beta_5 WOM\_BOD_i + \varepsilon_i \tag{10.2}$$

All the variables are well defined previously in a detailed way. ε is the error term and the indices i represent the companies.

10.4 Empirical Results

10.4.1 Multivariate Analysis

To define the role of "digital transformation", the regression of organisational performance and sustainable development as dependent variables are depicted in Table 10.3. Our findings highlight a positive and significant relationship between digital transformation and organisational performance and between digital transformation and sustainable development confirming the research hypotheses. The results show that all control variables are statistically significant in the explanation of the studied phenomenon. The results of the multiple regression in Table 10.3 support several indications, starting from Fisher's statistics (F) measuring the overall significance of the model, which is equal to 11.814 for M1 and 10.26 for M2, confirming the validity and the reliability of the model at a significance level lower than 1%. R^2 for M1 is equal to 0.2836, meaning that the independent variables explain at 28.36% the variation of the organisational performance. R^2 for M2 is equal to 0.3012. In other words, the model demonstrates an explanatory power equal to 30.12%, a quite significant percentage.

Table 10.3 Regression results

Dependent variable	ORG_PER		SUS_DEV	
Variable	Coefficient	t-statistic	Coefficient	t-statistic
Intercept	3.3256***	3.65	0.473***	4.87
DIG_TRA	0.6532***	4.58	0.066**	2.81
INN_LEV	0.3584**	2.53	0.344***	3.47
SIZE	0.3658*	1.98	0.312	1.89
LEV	−0.7256***	−3.51	0.280*	1.69
WOM_BD	2.3674**	2.64	0.145**	2.05
$R^2 =$	0.2836		0.3251	
R^2 *Adjusted* =	0.2793		0.3012	
F- statistic	11.84 (0.000)		10.261 (0.000)	

***: significant at the threshold of 1%; **: significant at the level of 5%; *: significant at the level of 10%

10.4.2 Results Discussion and Potential Scientific and Managerial Implications

It is worth highlighting that the decision to adopt digital technologies is usually enhanced with improvements in innovation (social networks, mobile connections for professional purposes, as well as dynamic and innovative solutions for organizing meetings). As expected, boosting investments in innovation technologies helps firms address and tackle the current globally dynamic environment. In this respect, the first hypothesis (H1) (Model 10.1) is intended to verify whether digital transformation does positively influence organisational performance. As indicated on Table 10.3, digital transformation is positively (0.6532) and significantly connected with organisational performance (whose associated value is 4.58 with p = 0.000), which allows to accept H1. Such a result corroborates well the study findings of Manyika et al. (2015), outlining that mobile connections, as a new concept, requiring greater attention and reporting, for professional reasons to improve organisational performance (Bodwell & Chermack, 2010; Vecchiato et al., 2020). On the other hand, technological applications appear to provide a noticeable contribution to the academic literature, by supplementing the limited body of research, dealing with organisational performance and corporate governance, with an innovative corporate expansion setting.

As regards the second hypothesis (H2) (Model 10.1), it states that company innovation-intensity degree has a positive impact on its organisational performance. As Table 10.3 illustrates, innovation intensity proves to demonstrate a positive (0.3584) and significant (Student's t = 2.53) effect, denoting that this variable displays an effect on organisational performance in this respect. Such a finding confirms well a number of previous studies published results (Wang & Shyu, 2009; Guiral, 2012; Bourdeau et al., 2020), highlighting that extensive implementation of innovation intensity positively affects and enhances operational performance. Indeed, the innovation process stands as an important driver of performance, for both internal efficiency and competitiveness, exhibiting a key role of innovation in boosting and developing the corporate organisational context. In this regard, digitisation is considered as a systemic organisational value and a strategy highly cherished by leadership. Yet, it is likely to face significant risk of repression or limited impact. Thus, organisational performance turns out to be highly affected by the adoption of digital technologies and digital transformation journeys in a global volatility struck business environment.

As regards the third hypothesis (H3) (Model 10.2), it states that technology and digital transformation have an influence on the sustainable development intention, demonstrating a positive effect in this respect. Actually, this variable relating coefficient is discovered to be positive (0.066) and significant (Student's t = 2.81), reflecting well that technology and digital transformation effectiveness turn out to be significant predictors of sustainable development. Initially, research intensity had a significant impact on productivity, and an increase in research intensity could significantly affect the of sustainable development growth (Wang & Shyu, 2009).

Regarding the fourth hypothesis (H4), maintaining that the degree of innovation intensity helps in influencing sustainable development intention. Appears to display a positive (0.344) and significant (Student's t = 3.47) associated variable coefficient. The innovation intensity degree is specific and measurable in terms of productivity and entrepreneurial development spirit, and then, the innovation intensity is quite powerful to stimulate sustainable development decisions. International research indicates that innovation intensity helps in stimulating the processes of

10 Opening up the Black Box on Digitalisation and Agility: Key...

sustainable development, the use of new approaches in the development and adoption of regulations in the financial market affect sustainable development. In fact, growth in corporate digitalisation and innovation is likely to contribute in effectively implementing prudential rules, including those dealing with the need to protect public interests and increase sustainable development.

10.5 Conclusion

This paper attempted to fill the gap in the literature by theoretically investigating the logically plausible association between the digital transformation and organisational performance in emerging context markets. Our results confirm the expectations regarding the impact of the digital transformation on organisational performance in Tunisian companies. The results of the research have revealed that knowledge, digital transformation and technologies have an impact on firms' intention, as a powerful contributor of organisational performance. Furthermore, our findings show that digital transformation positively influences firms' organisational performance while innovation is reaffirmed as having a positive implication on firm performance.

The results show that technology and innovation, which are drivers for companies to work on during a digital transformation, have a significant impact on companies' quest for sustainable development. Thus, Companies that want to succeed in an ever-changing competitive environment must exploit the potential of digital technologies, rethink and transform their business models for the digital age. This situation forces maintaining relevant, efficient, effective and dynamic control. In terms of security, the emergence of digitisation, fintech and the proliferation of cyber threats have led to changes in perceptions and practices of information management and protection. This dematerialisation presents new challenges for Tunisian companies and their cash distribution networks. Especially since criminals are also benefiting from technological advances and adding "dematerialisation" methods to their arsenal.

Finally, agile organisations combine organisational processes and human resources with advanced technology to meet customer demand for customized, high-quality products and services in a relatively short period of time. This can only happen when digitisation is seen as a strategy, supported by organisational values and systemic governance. However, digitisation may be largely crowded out or limited in impact.

References

Adams, R. B. (2016). Women on Boards: The Superheroes of Tomorrow? *The Leadership Quarterly, 27*(3), 371–386.

Alavi, M., & Leidner, D. E. (2001). Knowledge Management and Knowledge Management Systems: Conceptual Foundations and Research Issues. *MIS Quarterly, 2001*, 107–136.

Aloini, D., Dulmin, R., Mininno, V., & Ponticelli, S. (2015). Key Antecedents and Practices for Supply Chain Management Adoption in Project Contexts. *International Journal of Project Management, 33*(6), 1301–1316.

Amit, R., & Schoemaker, P. J. (1993). Strategic Assets and Organisational Rent. *Strategic Management Journal, 14*(1), 33–46.

Amores-Salvadó, J., Martín-de Castro, G., & Navas-López, J. E. (2014). Green Corporate Image: Moderating the Connection Between Environmental Product Innovation and Firm Performance. *Journal of Cleaner Production, 83*, 356–365.

Anderson, I. (1997). *Combinatorial Designs and Tournaments* (Vol. 6). Oxford University Press.

Asensio, O. I., & Delmas, M. A. (2015). Nonprice Incentives and Energy Conservation. *Proceedings of the National Academy of Sciences, 112*(6), E510–E515.

Autio, E. (2017). Strategic Entrepreneurial Internationalization: A Normative Framework. *Strategic Entrepreneurship Journal, 11*(3), 211–227.

Autio, E. (2018). Creative Tension: The Significance of Ben Oviatt's and Patricia McDougall's Article 'Toward a Theory of International New Ventures'. *International Entrepreneurship, 2018*, 59–81.

Bansal, P., & Clelland, I. (2004). Talking Trash: Legitimacy, Impression Management, and Unsystematic Risk in the Context of the Natural Environment. *Academy of Management Journal, 47*(1), 93–103.

Barlatier, P. J., & Burger-Helmchen, T. (2019). The Digital Organization: Opportunities and Risks. *Revue internationale de psychosociologie et de gestion des comportements organisationnels, 25*(61), 5–24.

Bena, J., & Simintzi, E. (2016). *Labor-Induced Technological Change: Evidence from Doing Business in China.* Accessed from SSRN

Bi, K., Huang, P., & Wang, X. (2016). Innovation Performance and Influencing Factors of Low-Carbon Technological Innovation Under the Global Value Chain: A Case of Chinese Manufacturing Industry. *Technological Forecasting and Social Change, 111*, 275–284.

Bodwell, W., & Chermack, T. J. (2010). Organizational Ambidexterity: Integrating Deliberate and Emergent Strategy with Scenario Planning. *Technological Forecasting and Social Change, 77*(2), 193–202.

Bourdeau, S., Aubert, B., & Bareil, C. (2020). The Effects of IT Use Intensity and Innovation Culture on Organizational Performance: The Mediating Role of Innovation Intensity. *Management Research Review.*

Brown, J. R., Martinsson, G., & Petersen, B. C. (2013). Law, Stock Markets, and Innovation. *The Journal of Finance, 68*(4), 1517–1549.

Camisón, C., & Villar-López, A. (2014). Organizational Innovation as an Enabler of Technological Innovation Capabilities and Firm Performance. *Journal of Business Research, 67*(1), 2891–2902.

Chan, K. M., Guerry, A. D., Balvanera, P., Klain, S., Satterfield, T., Basurto, X., & Woodside, U. (2012). Where Are Cultural and Social in Ecosystem Services? A Framework for Constructive Engagement. *Bioscience, 62*(8), 744–756.

Chang, C. H. (2011). The Influence of Corporate Environmental Ethics on Competitive Advantage: The Mediation Role of Green Innovation. *Journal of Business Ethics, 104*(3), 361–370.

Chen, C. T., Lin, C. T., & Huang, S. F. (2006). A Fuzzy Approach for Supplier Evaluation and Selection in Supply Chain Management. *International Journal of Production Economics, 102*(2), 289–301.

Cohen, W. M., & Levinthal, D. A. (1990). Absorptive Capacity: A New Perspective on Learning and Innovation. *Administrative Science Quarterly, 35*, 128–152.

Conding, J., Habidin, N. F., Zubir, A. F. M., Hashim, S., & Jaya, N. A. S. L. (2012). The Structural Analysis of Green Innovation (GI) and Green Performance (GP) in Malaysian Automotive Industry. *Research Journal of Finance and Accounting, 3*(6), 172–178.

Cormier, D., & Magnan, M. (2015). The Economic Relevance of Environmental Disclosure and Its Impact on Corporate Legitimacy: An Empirical Investigation. *Business Strategy and the Environment, 24*(6), 431–450.

Coviello, N., Kano, L., & Liesch, P. W. (2017). Adapting the Uppsala Model to a Modern World: Macro-context and Microfoundations. *Journal of International Business Studies, 48*(9), 1151–1164.

Dangelico, R. M., & Pujari, D. (2010). Mainstreaming Green Product Innovation: Why and How Companies Integrate Environmental Sustainability. *Journal of Business Ethics, 95*(3), 471–486.

Delahaye, M., Degand, P., & Jacquemin, A. (2019). *Quels sont les impacts de la digitalisation sur les mesures d'accompagnement publiques proposées aux entrepreneurs en Wallonie?*

Delgado-Ceballos, J., Aragón-Correa, J. A., Ortiz-de-Mandojana, N., & Rueda-Manzanares, A. (2012). The Effect of Internal Barriers on the Connection Between Stakeholder Integration and Proactive Environmental Strategies. *Journal of Business Ethics, 107*(3), 281–293.

Downes, L., & Nunes, P. (2013). Big Bang Disruption. *Harvard Business Review*, 44–56.

Durif, F., Boivin, C., & Julien, C. (2010). In Search of a Green Product Definition. *Innovative Marketing, 6*(1), 25–33.

Gebhardt, C. (2017). Humans in the Loop: The Clash of Concepts in Digital Sustainability in Smart Cities. In *Sustainability in a Digital World* (pp. 85–93). Springer.

Gueguen, G., & Isckia, T. (2011). The Borders of Mobile Handset Ecosystems: Is Coopetition Inevitable? *Telematics and Informatics, 28*(1), 5–11.

Guiral, A. (2012). Corporate Social Performance, Innovation Intensity, and Financial Performance: Evidence from Lending Decisions. *Behavioral Research in Accounting, 24*(2), 65–85.

Horváthová, E. (2012). The Impact of Environmental Performance on Firm Performance: Short-Term Costs and Long-Term Benefits? *Ecological Economics, 84*, 91–97.

Hsu, P. H., Tian, X., & Xu, Y. (2014). Financial Development and Innovation: Cross-Country Evidence. *Journal of Financial Economics, 112*(1), 116–135.

Kemp, R., & Pearson, P. (2007). Final Report MEI Project About Measuring Eco-Innovation. *UM Merit, Maastricht, 10*(2), 1–120.

Kiron, D., & Unruh, G. (2018). Business Needs a Safety Net. *MIT Sloan Management Review, 59*(3), 1–6.

Lee, K. H., & Min, B. (2015). Green R & D for Eco-innovation and Its Impact on Carbon Emissions and Firm Performance. *Journal of Cleaner Production, 108*, 534–542.

Li, D., Zheng, M., Cao, C., Chen, X., Ren, S., & Huang, M. (2017). The Impact of Legitimacy Pressure and Corporate Profitability on Green Innovation: Evidence from China top 100. *Journal of Cleaner Production, 141*, 41–49.

Lopez-Nicolas, C., & Soto-Acosta, P. (2010). Analyzing ICT Adoption and Use Effects on Knowledge Creation: An Empirical Investigation in SMEs. *International Journal of Information Management, 30*(6), 521–528.

Manyika, J., Chui, M., Bisson, P., Woetzel, J., Dobbs, R., Bughin, J., & Aharon, D. (2015). *Unlocking the Potential of the Internet of Things* (Vol. 1). McKinsey Global Institute.

Michelino, F., Caputo, M., Cammarano, A., & Lamberti, E. (2014). Inbound and Outbound Open Innovation: Organization and Performances. *Journal of Technology Management & Innovation, 9*(3), 65–82.

Miozzo, M., Desyllas, P., Lee, H. F., & Miles, I. (2016). Innovation Collaboration and Appropriability by Knowledge-Intensive Business Services Firms. *Research Policy, 45*(7), 1337–1351.

Murillo-Luna, J. L., Garcés-Ayerbe, C., & Rivera-Torres, P. (2011). Barriers to the Adoption of Proactive Environmental Strategies. *Journal of Cleaner Production, 19*(13), 1417–1425.

Nambisan, S. (2017). Digital Entrepreneurship: Toward a Digital Technology Perspective of Entrepreneurship. *Entrepreneurship Theory and Practice, 41*(6), 1029–1055.

Neubert, M. (2018). The Impact of Digitalization on the Speed of Internationalization of Lean Global Startups. *Technology Innovation Management Review, 8*(5).

Nielsen, S., & Huse, M. (2010). The Contribution of Women on Boards of Directors: Going Beyond the Surface. *Corporate Governance: An International Review, 18*(2), 136–148.

Orbik, Z., & Zozuľaková, V. (2019). Corporate social and digital responsibility. *Management Systems in Production Engineering, 2*(27), 79–83. https://doi.org/10.1515/mspe-2019-0013

Osburg, T., & Lohrmann, C. (Eds.). (2017). Sustainability in a Digital World. *New Opportunities through New Technologies*. Springer, Heidelberg. https://doi.org/10.1007/978-3-319-54603-2

Pagani, M., & Pardo, C. (2017). The Impact of Digital Technology on Relationships in a Business Network. *Industrial Marketing Management, 67*, 185–192.

Phillips, J. M., & Gully, S. M. (2015). Multilevel and Strategic Recruiting: Where Have We Been, Where Can We Go from Here? *Journal of Management, 41*(5), 1416–1445.

Post, C., & Byron, K. (2015). Women on Boards and Firm Financial Performance: A Meta-Analysis. *Academy of Management Journal, 58*(5), 1546–1571.

Rennings, K. (2000). Redefining Innovation—Eco-innovation Research and the Contribution from Ecological Economics. *Ecological Economics, 32*(2), 319–332.

Rybacki, J., & Kowalski, A. M. (2018). *Moderate Innovator Trap – Does Convergence of Innovative Potential Occur?*

Scuotto, V., Santoro, G., Bresciani, S., & Del Giudice, M. (2017). Shifting Intra- and Inter-organizational Innovation Processes Towards Digital Business: An Empirical Analysis of SMEs. *Creativity and Innovation Management, 26*(3), 247–255.

Seele, P., & Lock, I. (2017). The Game-Changing Potential of Digitalization for Sustainability: Possibilities, Perils, and Pathways. *Sustainability Science, 12*(2), 183–185.

Soto-Acosta, P., Popa, S., & Palacios-Marqués, D. (2016). E-business, Organizational Innovation and Firm Performance in Manufacturing SMEs: An Empirical Study in Spain. *Technological and Economic Development of Economy, 22*(6), 885–904.

Stevens, S. M. (2006). Activist Rhetorics and the Struggle for Meaning: The Case of "sustainability" in the Reticulate Public Sphere. *Rhetoric Review, 25*(3), 297–315.

Strandhagen, J. W., Buer, S. V., Semini, M., & Alfnes, E. (2019, September). Digitalized Manufacturing Logistics in Engineer-to-Order Operations. In *IFIP International Conference on Advances in Production Management Systems,* pp. 579–587.

Strange, R., & Zucchella, A. (2017). Industry 4.0, Global Value Chains and International Business. *Multinational Business Review, 25*(3), 174–184.

Sun, Z. Y., Xue, L. R., & Zhang, K. (2015). A New Approach to Finite-Time Adaptive Stabilization of High-Order Uncertain Nonlinear System. *Automatica, 58*, 60–66.

Thornhill, S. (2006). Knowledge, Innovation and Firm Performance in High- and Low-Technology Regimes. *Journal of Business Venturing, 21*(5), 687–703.

Tidd, J., & Trewhella, M. J. (1997). Organizational and Technological Antecedents for Knowledge Acquisition and Learning. *R & D Management, 27*(4), 359–375.

Turel, O., & Bart, C. (2014). Board-Level IT Governance and Organizational Performance. *European Journal of Information Systems, 23*(2), 223–239.

Vecchiato, R., Favato, G., Di Maddaloni, F., & Do, H. (2020). Foresight, Cognition, and Long-Term Performance: Insights from the Automotive Industry and Opportunities for Future Research. *Futures & Foresight Science, 2*(1), e25.

Vrontis, D., Thrassou, A., Weber, Y., Shams, R., Tsoukatos, E., & Efthymiou, L. (2022a). *Business Under Crisis Volume I: Avenues for Innovation, Entrepreneurship and Sustainability* (Palgrave Studies in Cross-Disciplinary Business Research). Association with EuroMed Academy of Business, Palgrave Macmillan (Springer). https://doi.org/10.1007/978-3-030-76567-5

Vrontis, D., Thrassou, A., Weber, Y., Shams, R., Tsoukatos, E., & Efthymiou, L. (2022b). *Business Under Crisis, Volume II: Organisational Adaptations. Palgrave Studies in Cross-Disciplinary Business Research.* Association with EuroMed Academy of Business, Palgrave Macmillan (Springer). https://doi.org/10.1007/978-3-030-76575-0

Vrontis, D., Thrassou, A., Weber, Y., Shams, R., Tsoukatos, E., & Efthymiou, L. (2022c). *Business Under Crisis, Volume III: Avenues for Innovation, Entrepreneurship and Sustainability* (Palgrave Studies in Cross-Disciplinary Business Research). Association with EuroMed Academy of Business, Palgrave Macmillan (Springer). https://doi.org/10.1007/978-3-030-76583-5

Wang, D. S., & Shyu, C. L. (2009). The Longitudinal Effect of HRM Effectiveness and Dynamic Innovation Performance on Organizational Performance in Taiwan. *The International Journal of Human Resource Management, 20*(8), 1790–1809.

Wittkop, A., Zulauf, K., & Wagner, R. (2018). How Digitalization Changes the Internationalization of Entrepreneurial Firms: Theoretical Considerations and Empirical Evidence. *Management Dynamics in the Knowledge Economy, 6*(2), 193–207.

Zhong, R. I. (2018). Transparency and Firm Innovation. *Journal of Accounting and Economics, 66*(1), 67–93.

Zhu, K., & Kraemer, K. L. (2005). Post-adoption Variations in Usage and Value of E-business by Organizations: Cross-Country Evidence from the Retail Industry. *Information Systems Research, 16*(1), 61–84.

11

Ecosystem Innovation as the Stepping into Other People's Shoes

Gianpaolo Basile, Salvatore Esposito De Falco, Sofia Profita, and Rosario Bianco

11.1 Introduction

Our societies face many pressing challenges regarding healthcare and the environment, which include—to name a few—climate change, biodiversity conservation, air and water pollution (Steffen et al., 2018; Tittensor

G. Basile (✉)
Universitas Mercatorum, Rome, Italy
e-mail: gianpaolo.basile@unimercatorum.it

S. E. De Falco
Università la Sapienza, Rome, Italy
e-mail: salvatore.espositodefalco@uniroma1.it

S. Profita
Santander Bank, N.A., Dallas, TX, USA
e-mail: sofia@profita.it

R. Bianco
Università Telematica Pegaso, Naples, Italy
e-mail: info@rosariobianco.it

© The Author(s), under exclusive license to Springer Nature Switzerland AG 2022
A. Thrassou et al. (eds.), *Business Advancement through Technology Volume II*, Palgrave Studies in Cross-disciplinary Business Research, In Association with EuroMed Academy of Business, https://doi.org/10.1007/978-3-031-07765-4_11

et al., 2014; Moreno et al., 2016 https://unhabitat.org/world-cities-report).

These issues are obviously highly complex and often context-related. Also, their analysis is not always straightforward, as their origin and development are affected by many social, economic, political, historical and environmental agents and/or drivers of change often operating within well-established social and ecological systems (Chávez-Ávila & Monzón-Campos, 2005; Sterner et al., 2019; Avelino et al., 2019).

The constant search for new solutions—or simply the improvement of existing plans—to reach ONU 17 Sustainable Development Goals (SDGs), is benefiting innovative small businesses, start-ups and NGOs focusing on social economy at local, regional and national level (Basile & Cavallo, 2020).

In the COVID-19 era the linear model of innovation (from theoretical to applied research) is turning into a non-linear one, in which the need for innovation comes from many social and economic agents and a growing number of institutions—either for-profit or non-profit—are involved in the production of new operating models and solutions. This means that innovation is now the result of highly collaborative relationships, which are often of multidisciplinary nature and not necessarily aimed at creating new products but more and more often at addressing new social and economic needs (Chesbrough & Di Minin, 2014; Howaldt et al., 2015; Smorodinskaya & Katukov, 2015).

In this scenario, the relationships existing among actors can be seen as uncertain or volatile, are often complex and always of a collective nature. Economic and social stakeholders such as companies, scientists, NGOs, etc. are more and more involved in this collective effort. As such, all actors involved in these innovation processes share their responsibilities and are therefore co-responsible for the results achieved (Parmar et al., 2010; Blok & Lemmens, 2015).

The chapter aim is both to contribute to the ecosystem scientific literature advancement and to stimulate to some empirical applications. To reach these objectives, the work, in the first part, will present a theoretical and definitional background, considering the most important literature published in the last 15 years, finalised to highlight the differences

11 Ecosystem Innovation as the Stepping into Other People's... 229

between ecosystem and network and how this difference is weighty in the current moment signed by a pandemic phenomenon.

In the second part of the work, the authors highlight the crowdsourcing approach as the ecosystem application to prove that companies now do not compete with each other only by employing their own resources and know-how according to stand-alone strategies, but rather moving them toward new business models based—among others—on shared resources, network externalities and government.

Finally, the authors track the conclusion and try to individuate some future scientific implications.

11.2 Theoretical Background

In the past few decades, management scholars have studied the structural form of this web of relations—either formal or informal—highlighting how it does not constitute a network but rather an ecosystem. Therefore, the term ecosystem has been used as an alternative to network to refer to interconnected entities or actors that are linked to, or operate around, a focal company or platform (Adner, 2006; Adner & Kapoor, 2010; Iansiti & Levien, 2004; Moore, 1993, 1996; Teece, 2007).

The difference between the ecosystem construct and other network constructs is that in business ecosystems one can find—in either formal or informal negotiations—participants from both ends of the spectrum (production and use) including suppliers, customers, competitors, research institutions, ONGs, communities, standard setters and the judiciary (Iansiti & Levien, 2004; Teece, 2007; Guittard et al., 2015).

Autio and Thomas (2014) argued that an ecosystem is a network of interconnected actors, built around a focal organization or platform and focusing on the co-creation of social and economic solutions by pursuing innovation. This way ecosystems trigger *innovation contexts*, by engaging the stakeholders involved to voice their needs in order to promote the co-creation of innovation in an environment of mutual understanding (Chesbrough, 2003; Tassey, 2008).

According to principles borrowed from biological studies, an ecosystem can be broadly described as a complex interactive system (Thomas &

Autio, 2013) whose components interact by establishing open and non-linear relations (Russell & Smorodinskaya, 2018) aimed at sustaining 'life' in evolving conditions, and developed not according to a hierarchic model but rather to a horizontal one (Scaringella & Radziwon, 2018; Annesi et al., 2020). Powell and Finger (2013) also argued that an ecosystem is indeed a bridge between the social and the economic, and that such result is achieved through top-down processes which were originally less structured. It is therefore possible to say that an ecosystem is based on the co-creation of activities and on the existence of shared strategies, responsibilities and goals. Such traits set the difference with other network models characterized by the exchange of knowledge and information (Camarihna-Matos & Afsarmanesh, 2008). Russell and Smorodinskaya (2018) argued that an ecosystem is a collaborative whole aimed at pursuing innovation and characterized by non-linear relations between heterogeneous stakeholders that are thus able to achieve dynamic sustainability in a non-linear environment.

Ecosystems are distinctive both because of their structure, and because of the way they address coordination issues. The feature distinguishing ecosystems from market-based arrangements is the role of the final user (Vrontis et al., 2020a). For example, an end user of the Linux software can decide which version to buy and what kind of support to provide in order to improve performance by sharing new developments with other companies, programmers and end users.

What sets ecosystems apart from market-based arrangements is that final customers can choose from a set of producers or developers that are somehow bound together through links of all sorts (the adoption of the same standard, for instance). For this reason, Jacobides et al. (2018) argue that the main difference between an ecosystem and a typical buyer-supplier network is that in the former end users can choose the goods and services on offer among those supplied by each participant and can also, in some cases, choose how they are combined. Such *modularity* allows the production of interdependent system components by different suppliers, with only a limited coordination required across the production (or production and consumption) chain. Organisations have therefore a large degree of autonomy in how they design, price and operate their respective modules, as long as they interconnect with others in agreed and

11 Ecosystem Innovation as the Stepping into Other People's... 231

predefined ways (Baldwin, 2008). The ecosystem is created when the interconnection and its modularity are finally reached. In this sense ecosystems differ from networks (Powell, 2003), and represent more or less standardized alliances between participants where, for example, complementors can choose from a menu of predefined options and are treated in roughly the same way. In ecosystems, end users too are supposed to join (Hagiu & Wright, 2015) a group or platform to be able to use its specific complements, as it happens for example with web apps (Jacobides et al., 2018). An important contribution on this topic is that by Adner (2017), who has considered the ecosystem as characterized by the alignment of a multilateral set of partners that need to interact in order to reach a focal value proposition. In this approach, the *alignment* represents a mutual agreement on positions and flows among the actors involved. This is a growing trend also in the tourism industry, in all cases where local communities participate in order to provide an authentic experience in which the cultural exchange established with tourists is the focus of the social and economic phenomenon (Vrontis et al., 2020b). These authors, along with Thomson and Perry (2006), argued that collaboration is a process in which the different participants interact through either formal or informal negotiations, thus creating new relationships to address social, environmental or economic issues, competitive challenges and in general to meet community needs.

These considerations are useful to draw some significant differences—as shown in Table 11.1—between the network and the ecosystem concepts:

11.2.1 Our Elaboration

Entrepreneurship scholars essentially agree on the fact that the durability and performance of any given ecosystem are affected by the different types of resources employed (Garnsey & Leong, 2008), by environmental conditions (Clauss et al., 2018; Sun et al., 2019) and by the entities involved (Pilinkienė & Mačiulis, 2014). This is the reason why there is currently a tendency among policymakers to import practices seen among thriving ecosystems on the assumption that such practices are somehow

232 G. Basile et al.

Table 11.1 Main differences between ecosystems and networks

Ecosystem	Network
Inner and outer processes	Inner processes
Outer and inner beneficials	Inner beneficials
Formal and informal negotiation mutual agreement	Formal negotiation
Social, environmental and economic aims	Economic aims
Profit and no-profit participants	Business actors
Synergistic processes and modularity	Stepwise movements from one phase to another
The final product as the combination of components chosen by the final user	The final product as the result of standardized processes

'best' ones compared to those found in an economy based on the existence of stand-alone entrepreneurs (Harrison & Leitch, 2010; Motoyama & Watkins, 2014; Spigel, 2017).

For example, the Italian Government is currently funding the creation of innovative ecosystems that include local public institutions, research centers, entrepreneur associations and other social and economic agents, in order to promote social innovation through the redevelopment of local areas.

While the structure of different ecosystems may be similar across the academic studies currently available, evidence suggests however that engagement levels within these complex systems can vary according to the actors' perceptions (Scott et al., 2019), roles (Valkokari, 2015) and decision-making approaches (Kapoor & Lee, 2013).

11.3 Method to Reach Innovation in a Pandemic Era

The pandemic and other social crises are showing that the pursue of growth and entrepreneurship depends more and more on the existence and interaction of different players, such as governments, communities, universities, entrepreneurs, and so on (Acs et al., 2016; Ferreira & Teixeira, 2019).

11 Ecosystem Innovation as the Stepping into Other People's... 233

Acs et al. (2017) and Roundy et al. (2017) argued that a high level of competitiveness worldwide has negatively affected the social and environmental condition of our planet over the past few decades. This in turn has been promoting the creation—either planned or spontaneous—of ecosystems that are openly focused on the assessment of the social and economic impact of their activities. The idea behind all this is that the competitiveness model has changed. Therefore, companies now do not compete with each other only by employing their own resources and know-how according to stand-alone strategies in order to achieve a competitive advantage over their rivals, but rather they are more and more moving toward new business models based—among others—on shared resources, network externalities and government support (Audretsch et al., 2019).

In a scenario like this, collaboration within an ecosystem does not prevent the competition among its actors and between them and the rest of the world from taking place. Companies that are part of the ecosystem cooperate in fact on certain business projects, while fiercely competing on others. When there is a project that involves the whole ecosystem, the participants collaborate with each other on the basis of relational contracts and coordinate their activities by following a common strategy. In a pandemic time like this, the aim is to meet the challenges posed by what is now commonly called *the Great Reset*. The stronger the links within the ecosystem, the higher the mutual benefits in terms of co-created added value will be, and vice versa (Porter, 1990). Collaboration implies therefore the establishment of several types of complex relationships, as well as the existence of a specific dynamic balance within the ecosystem.

In the *Future Knowledge Ecosystems* report (2009) Townsend et al. argued that, thanks to the development of ICT, production processes now involve the cooperation of many small groups of actors, bringing together producers, consumers and intermediaries into *ad hoc* temporary networks that will last for the duration of the project. This is why it is no surprise that the authors in question define any knowledge-based economy as a group economy (Townsend et al., 2009), while other scholars (van Winden et al., 2011) prefer the definition of network economy. Such definitions are indeed complementary and highlight the collaborative and systemic nature of the future industrial landscape, one that

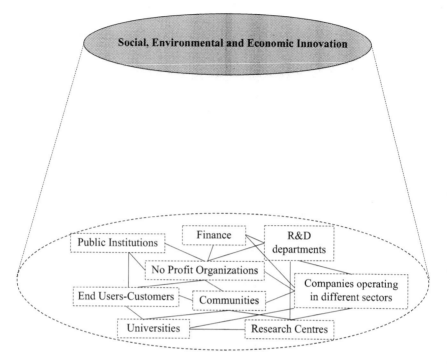

Fig. 11.1 The ecosystem: structure and results

brings together the new production mode with a project-based organisation of mutual activities performed by interconnected players (Bigham et al., 2015).

At this point we can consider the ecosystem *as a combination of social, political, economic, cultural and social agents that supports the development and growth of innovative solutions and encourage entrepreneurs and other actors to meet social, environmental and economic needs* (see Fig. 11.1).

11.3.1 Our Elaboration

During the Covid-19 pandemic, outside-in knowledge-sharing processes have made possible the establishment of crowdsourcing patterns in fields such as the definition of new therapies, of new face mask and hand sanitizer designs, and even of a new ventilator model able to support two patients at once. Such *crowdsourcing* processes show the increasingly relevant role of users in promoting innovation, proving that solutions to complex problems may also come from non-conventional sources, particularly when the users themselves stand to benefit from the solution found (von Hippel, 2017). While studying the issue of leadership within the ecosystem, Moore (1996: 26) argued that although leaders in this kind of context may well change over time, the role of ecosystem leader is always well valued by the community because it allows system members to embrace a shared vision according to which they will coordinate their efforts and operate in mutually supportive roles.

Isenberg (2010) and the World Economic Forum (Blanke & Milligam, 2016, https://www.weforum.org/reports/social-innovation) have argued that the most important factors in order for an ecosystem to reach social and economic goals are the presence of accessible local and international markets, of robust regulatory frameworks, of major universities and advanced digital infrastructures, as well as the availability of both human and financial capital. Recent studies focusing on digital trends have found that entrepreneurship is now more and more often associated—across time and space—with collaborative processes, as showed in Fig. 11.1 (Nambisan et al., 2017). These relationships, supported by either analog or digital tools and processes, provide better solutions to social, economic and environmental needs as a result of agent heterogeneity.

11.4 Findings: Ecosystems, Stakeholder Engagement and Crowdsourcing

In management studies, connections are mainly analyzed according to the stakeholder engagement approach, which focuses on how agents create a series of stable relationships aimed at facilitating knowledge flows among them, thus creating a stronger and more balanced network that is easier to coordinate and where the participants can better satisfy their mutual interests (Dunham et al., 2006; Freeman et al., 2020). This new whole will then create more value than what would have been produced by all the network subgroups had they operated separately (Wasserman & Faust, 1994; Pless & Maak, 2005; Moore, 2006).

Maak and Pless (2006) on the other hand argue that without a stable network of interactions, agents would have neither the resources nor the capabilities to make the most of the relationships established with stakeholders like ONGs or local communities (Chesbrough & Di Minin, 2014; Rayna & Striukova, 2019; Howaldt et al., 2015; Thrassou et al., 2020).

Innovation usually emerges from a complex web of interactions among different stakeholders, including industrial players, investors, entrepreneurs, scholars and governments. In some cases, technological innovations are made possible by the existence of platforms where interactions take place in the form of massive data exchange between devices, like for example in the case of the IoT (internet of things). In this context, a business is not relevant only from a sectoral point of view (Moore, 1993, 1996), but rather should be viewed as an entity belonging to something bigger, more complex and inherently borderless, which has been named *Business Ecosystem* (Daidj et al., 2010, Daidj & Jung, 2011), where social and business communities on the one hand and end users on the other are all part of the same system. The authors argue that this approach can be adopted across all fields of activity. In oncology, for example, some researchers are using blockchain platforms to allow millions of patients to upload their data in order to help Artificial Intelligence-based software in the fight against cancer. Cases like this represent an important transformation in the dynamics of innovation. Until the end of the last century, the company was acknowledged as a place of innovation and—according to the Chandlerian "first mover" model—its internal activities were the object of innovation following a DIY-like approach (Chandler & Jansen, 1992). The new century marks on the other hand the advent of the Ecosystem model, in which know-how sets belonging to third parties have potentially the same role and importance of internal ones, in a new context that promotes the creation of a wide network of relations among the actors involved while at the same time reducing the relevance of hierarchical processes (Santoro et al., 2019).

This kind of stakeholder involvement is the focus of the stakeholder theory (Greenwood, 2007). According to Freeman (1984), the stakeholder approach defines the nature of the relationship with the

11 Ecosystem Innovation as the Stepping into Other People's... 237

stakeholders, and links the management's action to the stakeholders' perception of business activities in order to reduce the level of conflict within the system. An example of this is the creation of Chrome, the browser created by Google and based on an open-source code named Chromium. When it was launched, Internet Explorer and Firefox were the market leaders, both of them created according to a Chandlerian stand-alone strategy. In less than 10 years Chrome, based on a browser-first approach engaging the producer and end users in a collaborative whole, has gained millions of users that now represent a staggering 75% market share. In this sense, Wagner Mainardes et al. (2012) stated that stakeholder engagement is a two-way process in which it is not just the organisation that takes action to influence the behaviour of the relevant stakeholders, but it is also them who agree to interact with the company to try to influence its behavior. Along the same line, other authors (Payne & Calton, 2004; Devin & Lane, 2014) see stakeholder engagement as a two-way relationship in which some stakeholders express their needs and requests not only to the company itself but also to the rest of the stakeholders involved, in order to create a common vision across the web of relations.

Thanks to these bi-directional interactions, stakeholder engagement activities allow the company to increase its social capital (Lin et al., 2017), thus helping organisations in creating a series of stable relations by facilitating knowledge exchanges—either tacit or explicit—between the company and the other agents involved. Such activities also create more stable networks that are easier to coordinate and facilitate the interaction of the actors involved, thus creating an ecosystem community whose actors participate in to satisfy their mutual interests (Freeman & Liedtka, 1997). De Colle (2005) argued that stakeholder engagement activities should be seen as a meta-process, that is a process that on the one hand allows the management to obtain valuable information that can be used to meet stakeholder requests, and on the other hand allows all companies involved to achieve a better economic, social and/or environmental performance. According to Noland and Phillips (2010) on the other hand, one of the main reasons why stakeholder engagement should be the focus of stakeholder theory is the need to go beyond a mere interaction with stakeholders aimed at meeting their needs and leveraging their know-how.

A first advantage of stakeholder engagement practices is getting to know the other actors better. Also, a stable relationship with the other stakeholders will be inevitably based on reciprocity, thus reducing the level of attrition between them (Fassin, 2009). Sharing experiences within the stakeholder network will reduce uncertainty, which helps the know-how exchange by creating a shared platform aimed at mediating between different perspectives (Morsing & Schultz, 2006) and at establishing a climate of trust based on deterrence (Shapiro, 1992).

A second advantage brought by stakeholder engagement is the definition of a set of activities shared with the other stakeholders, who have therefore the opportunity to improve their knowledge of the company and of its activities. According to Burchell and Cook (2006), when the management is able to maintain a large number of relationships with different stakeholders over time and when these are involved in corporate processes, it is possible for the company to obtain greater legitimacy with relation to its activities. In *Free Innovation* (2017) von Hippel further developed the idea of interacting with "large crowds" by highlighting the open and spontaneous nature of innovation-related activities among heterogeneous stakeholders (Gault, 2018).

Howe (2006) described crowdsourcing as the act of a company or institution outsourcing a task or function once performed by internal employees to an undefined (and generally large) network of people through an open call. This can either take the form of peer production (when the job is performed collaboratively), or it can be found as an individual call. Crucial prerequisites are the use of the open call format and the existence of a large network of potential and suitable actors. The crowdsourcing model developed by von Hippel (2017) considers ICT as the tool that allows organisations to harness the efforts, interests and engagement of a virtual crowd in order to perform specific organisational tasks or problem-solving activities (Saxton et al., 2013). This approach is consistent with the ecosystem theory and can contribute toward reducing R&D costs, sharing innovation risks and increasing the speed at which new innovative products and services are put on the market, as it allows the company to have easier access to a wide variety of skills, know-how and expertise.

Crowdsourcing can therefore be defined as a distributed model aimed at problem-solving and pursuing innovation, in which members of online communities contribute to carry out specific tasks. This approach has much potential in the implementation of open innovation strategies and although it has so far mainly found its application in IT or management, it can become a promising tool in global healthcare (Wazny, 2018) and more in general in promoting social and economic innovation (Basile & Mattarella, 2020).

11.5 Conclusion

The present work highlights the existence of a trend moving toward an open and democratic practice for the production of innovation that allows almost anyone to exploit their creative potential in pursuing new solutions taking into account the contribution of different stakeholders, in order to maximize value both at individual and at ecosystemic level. In such processes, being able to correctly guide and manage stakeholder engagement practices can represent a significant advantage not only for the single organisation, but also for the system as a whole (Sciarelli & Tani, 2015).

"Necessity is the mother of invention", as the old-saying goes, so most organisations—either for-profit or non-profit—pursue innovation to find solutions to their needs or to those of the other social and economic stakeholders they are linked to (de Jong & van der Meer, 2017; von Hippel & Suddendorf, 2018). The ecosystem theory supports organisations in creating a steady set of stakeholder engagement practices, and provides tools aimed at facilitating the access to external know-how sources, and identifying those actors that can be more effective in providing new solutions (Porter & Kramer, 2011). This emerging crowdsourcing trend, brought by Covid-19 events, is affecting both business models and strategies and is changing the role and behavior of end users/consumers. This new condition, adequately supported by technological innovation, could represent the scenario in which both for-profit and non-profit organizations, public institutions, consumers and communities will find solutions to their social, environmental and economic needs.

Finally, in the authors opinion one of the most important considerations that emerge from the ecosystem development is that will develop different forms of governance, increasingly, capable to manage social and economic relationships, norms, and trust values, fundamental for the innovative production in the ecosystems, especially when they don't occur in a specific environment.

References

Acs, Z., Åstebro, T., Audretsch, D., & Robinson, D. T. (2016). Public Policy to Promote Entrepreneurship: A Call to Arms. *Small Business Economics, 47*(1), 35–51.

Acs, Z. J., Stam, E., Audretsch, D. B., & O'Connor, A. (2017). The Lineages of the Entrepreneurial Ecosystem Approach. *Small Business Economics, 49*(1), 1–10.

Adner, R. (2006). Match Your Innovation Strategy to Your Innovation Ecosystem. *Harvard Business Review, 84*(4), 98.

Adner, R. (2017). Ecosystem as Structure: An Actionable Construct for Strategy. *Journal of Management, 43*(1), 39–58.

Adner, R., & Kapoor, R. (2010). Value Creation in Innovation Ecosystems: How the Structure of Technological Interdependence Affects Firm Performance in New Technology Generations. *Strategic Management Journal, 31*(3), 306–333.

Annesi, N., Frey, M., Battaglia, M., & Gragnani, P. (2020). *Le cooperative e l'innovazione sostenibile: le nuove sfide dell'Agenda 2030*, pp. 77–110.

Audretsch, D. B., Cunningham, J. A., Kuratko, D. F., Lehmann, E. E., & Menter, M. (2019). Entrepreneurial Ecosystems: Economic, Technological, and Societal Impacts. *The Journal of Technology Transfer, 44*(2), 313–325.

Autio, E., & Thomas, L. (2014). *Innovation Ecosystems. The Oxford Handbook of Innovation Management* (pp. 204–288). Oxford University Press.

Avelino, F., Wittmayer, J. M., Pel, B., Weaver, P., Dumitru, A., Haxeltine, A., & O'Riordan, T. (2019). Transformative Social Innovation and (dis)empowerment. *Technological Forecasting and Social Change, 145*, 195–206.

Baldwin, C. Y. (2008). Where Do Transactions Come From? Modularity, Transactions, and the Boundaries of Firms. *Industrial and Corporate Change, 17*(1), 155–195.

Basile, G., & Cavallo, A. (2020). Rural Identity, Authenticity, and Sustainability in Italian Inner Areas. *Sustainability, 12*(3), 1272.

11 Ecosystem Innovation as the Stepping into Other People's... 241

Basile, G., & Mattarella, B. (2020). La socializzazione dell'impresa profit: dall'open innovation alla social open innovation. *Corporate Governance and Research & Development studies-Open Access, 2*, 33–52.

Bigham, J. P., Bernstein, M. S., & Adar, E. (2015). Human-Computer Interaction and Collective Intelligence. In *Handbook of Collective Intelligence* (Vol. 57). MIT Press.

Blok, V., & Lemmens, P. (2015). The Emerging Concept of Responsible Innovation. Three Reasons Why It Is Questionable and Calls for a Radical Transformation of the Concept of Innovation. In *Responsible Innovation 2* (pp. 19–35). Springer.

Burchell, J., & Cook, J. (2006). It's Good to Talk? Examining Attitudes Towards Corporate Social Responsibility Dialogue and Engagement Processes. *Business Ethics: A European Review, 15*(2), 154–170.

Camarihna-Matos, L. M., & Afsarmanesh, H. (2008). Concept of Collaboration. In *Encyclopedia of Networked and Virtual Organisations* (pp. 311–315). IGI Global.

Chandler, G. N., & Jansen, E. (1992). The Founder's Self-Assessed Competence and Venture Performance. *Journal of Business Venturing, 7*(3), 223–236.

Chávez-Ávila, R., & Monzón-Campos, J. L. (2005). *The Social Economy in the European Union. CIRIEC No. CESE/COMM/05/2005—EESC.*

Chesbrough, H. W. (2003). *Open Innovation: The New Imperative for Creating and Profiting from Technology.* Harvard Business Press.

Chesbrough, H., & Di Minin, A. (2014). Open Social Innovation. *New Frontiers in Open Innovation, 16*, 301–315.

Clauss, T., Breitenecker, R. J., Kraus, S., Brem, A., & Richter, C. (2018). Directing the Wisdom of the Crowd: The Importance of Social Interaction Among Founders and the Crowd During Crowdfunding Campaigns. *Economics of Innovation and New Technology, 27*(8), 709–729.

Daidj, N., & Jung, J. (2011). Strategies in the Media Industry: Towards the Development of Co-opetition Practices? *Journal of Media Business Studies, 8*(4), 37–57.

Daidj, N., Grazia, C., & Hammoudi, A. (2010). Introduction to the Non-cooperative Approach to Coalition Formation: The Case of the Blu-Ray/HD-DVD Standards' War. *Journal of Media Economics, 23*(4), 192–215.

De Colle, S. (2005). A Stakeholder Management Model for Ethical Decision Making. International Journal of Management and Decision Making, 6(3–4), 299–314.

de Jong, M. D., & van der Meer, M. (2017). How Does It Fit? Exploring the Congruence Between Organisations and Their Corporate Social Responsibility (CSR) Activities. *Journal of Business Ethics, 143*(1), 71–83.

Devin, B. L., & Lane, A. B. (2014). Communicating Engagement in Corporate Social Responsibility: A Meta-Level Construal of Engagement. *Journal of Public Relations Research, 26*(5), 436–454.

Dunham, L., Freeman, R. E., & Liedtka, J. (2006). Enhancing Stakeholder Practice: A Particularized Exploration of Community. *Business Ethics Quarterly, 16*(1), 23–42.

Fassin, Y. (2009). The Stakeholder Model Refined. *Journal of Business Ethics, 84*(1), 113–135.

Ferreira, J. J., & Teixeira, A. A. (2019). Open Innovation and Knowledge for Fostering Business Ecosystems. *Journal of Innovation & Knowledge, 4*(4), 253–255.

Freeman, R. E. (1984). *Strategic Management: A Stakeholder Approach*. Pitman Publishing.

Freeman, E., & Liedtka, J. (1997). Stakeholder Capitalism and the Value Chain. *European Management Journal, 15*(3), 286–296.

Freeman, R. E., Phillips, R., & Sisodia, R. (2020). Tensions in Stakeholder Theory. *Business & Society, 59*(2), 213–231.

Garnsey, E., & Leong, Y. Y. (2008). Combining Resource-Based and Evolutionary Theory to Explain the Genesis of Bio-networks. *Industry and Innovation, 15*(6), 669–686.

Gault, F. (2018). Defining and Measuring Innovation in All Sectors of the Economy. *Research Policy, 47*(3), 617–622.

Greenwood, M. (2007). Stakeholder Engagement: Beyond the myth of Corporate Responsibility. *Journal of Business Ethics, 74*(4), 315–327.

Guittard, C., Schenk, E., & Burger-Helmchen, T. (2015). Crowdsourcing and the Evolution of a Business Ecosystem. In *Advances in Crowdsourcing* (pp. 49–62). Springer.

Hagiu, A., & Wright, J. (2015). Multi-Sided Platforms. *International Journal of Industrial Organisation, 43*, 162–174.

Harrison, R. T., & Leitch, C. (2010). Voodoo Institution or Entrepreneurial University? Spin-Off Companies, the Entrepreneurial System and Regional Development in the UK. *Regional Studies, 44*(9), 1241–1262.

Howaldt, J., Kopp, R., & Schwarz, M. (2015). Social Innovations as Drivers of Social Change—Exploring Tarde's Contribution to Social Innovation Theory

Building. In *New Frontiers in Social Innovation Research* (pp. 29–51). Palgrave Macmillan.

Howe, J. (2006). The Rise of Crowdsourcing. *Wired Magazine, 14*(6), 1–4.

Iansiti, M., & Levien, R. (2004). Keystones and Dominators: Framing Operating and Technology Strategy in a Business Ecosystem. *Harvard Business School, 03-061,* 1–82.

Isenberg, D. J. (2010). How to Start an Entrepreneurial Revolution. *Harvard Business Review, 88*(6), 40–50.

Jacobides, M. G., Cennamo, C., & Gawer, A. (2018). Towards a Theory of Ecosystems. *Strategic Management Journal, 39*(8), 2255–2276.

Kapoor, R., & Lee, J. M. (2013). Coordinating and Competing in Ecosystems: How Organisational Forms Shape New Technology Investments. *Strategic Management Journal, 34*(3), 274–296.

Lin, X., Ho, C. M., & Shen, G. Q. (2017). Who Should Take the Responsibility? Stakeholders' Power Over Social Responsibility Issues in Construction Projects. *Journal of Cleaner Production, 154,* 318–329.

Maak, T., & Pless, N. M. (2006). Responsible Leadership in a Stakeholder Society – A Relational Perspective. *Journal of Business Ethics, 66*(1), 99–115.

Moore, J. F. (1993). Predators and Prey: A New Ecology of Competition. *Harvard Business Review, 71*(3), 75–86.

Moore, J. F. (1996). *The Death of Competition: Leadership and Strategy in the Age of Business Ecosystems.* HarperCollins.

Moore, J. F. (2006). Business Ecosystems and the View from the Firm. *The Antitrust Bulletin, 51*(1), 31–75.

Morsing, M., & Schultz, M. (2006). Corporate Social Responsibility Communication: Stakeholder Information, Response and Involvement Strategies. *Business ethics: A European Review, 15*(4), 323–338.

Motoyama, Y., & Watkins, K. (2014). *Examining the Connections Within the Start-Up Ecosystem: A Case Study of St. Louis.* Kauffman Foundation.

Nambisan, S., Lyytinen, K., Majchrzak, A., & Song, M. (2017). Digital Innovation Management: Reinventing Innovation Management Research in a Digital World. *MIS Quarterly, 41*(1), 223–238.

Noland, J., & Phillips, R. (2010). Stakeholder Engagement, Discourse Ethics and Strategic Management. *International Journal of Management Reviews, 12*(1), 39–49.

Parmar, B. L., Freeman, R. E., Harrison, J. S., Wicks, A. C., Purnell, L., & De Colle, S. (2010). Stakeholder Theory: The State of the Art. *Academy of Management Annals, 4*(1), 403–445.

Payne, S. L., & Calton, J. M. (2004). Exploring Research Potentials and Applications for Multi-Stakeholder Learning Dialogues. *Journal of Business Ethics, 55*(1), 71–78.

Pilinkienė, V., & Mačiulis, P. (2014). Comparison of Different Ecosystem Analogies: The Main Economic Determinants and Levels of Impact. *Procedia-Social and Behavioral Sciences, 156,* 365–370.

Pless, N. M., & Maak, T. (2005, August). Relational Intelligence for Leading Responsibly in a Connected World. In *Academy of Management Proceedings* (Vol. 1, pp. I1–I6). Academy of Management.

Porter, M. E. (1990). The Competitive Advantage of Nations. *Competitive Intelligence Review, 1*(1), 14–14.

Porter, M., & Kramer, M. R. (2011). Creare valore condiviso. *Harvard Business Review Italia, 1*(2), 68–84.

Powell, W. (2003). Neither market nor hierarchy: Network forms of organization. *The Sociology of Organizations: Classic, Contemporary, and Critical Readings, 315,* 104–117.

Powell, J. J., & Finger, C. (2013). The Bologna Process's Model of Mobility in Europe: The Relationship of Its Spatial and Social Dimensions. *European Educational Research Journal, 12*(2), 270–285.

Rayna, T., & Striukova, L. (2019). Open Social Innovation Dynamics and Impact: Exploratory Study of a Fab Lab Network. *R&D Management, 49*(3), 383–395.

Roundy, P. T., Brockman, B. K., & Bradshaw, M. (2017). The Resilience of Entrepreneurial Ecosystems. *Journal of Business Venturing Insights, 8,* 99–104.

Russell, M. G., & Smorodinskaya, N. V. (2018). Leveraging Complexity for Ecosystemic Innovation. *Technological Forecasting and Social Change, 136,* 114–131.

Santoro, G., Ferraris, A., & Winteler, D. J. (2019). Open Innovation Practices and Related Internal Dynamics: Case Studies of Italian ICT SMEs. *EuroMed Journal of Business, 14*(1), 47–61.

Saxton, G. D., Oh, O., & Kishore, R. (2013). Rules of Crowdsourcing: Models, Issues, and Systems of Control. *Information Systems Management, 30*(1), 2–20.

Scaringella, L., & Radziwon, A. (2018). Innovation, Entrepreneurial, Knowledge, and Business Ecosystems: Old Wine in New Bottles? *Technological Forecasting and Social Change, 136,* 59–87.

Sciarelli, M., & Tani, M. (2015). Sustainability and Stakeholder Approach in Olivetti from 1943 to 1960: A Lesson from the Past. *Sinergie Italian Journal of Management, 33*(Jan-Apr), 19–36.

Scott, S., Hughes, M., & Kraus, S. (2019). Developing Relationships in Innovation Clusters. *Entrepreneurship & Regional Development, 31*(1–2), 22–45.

Shapiro, M. J. (1992). *Reading the Postmodern Polity: Political Theory as Textual Practice.* U of Minnesota Press.

Smorodinskaya, N. V., & Katukov, D. D. (2015). *The Cluster Approach to Economic Growth: European and Russian Policies. CGES Working Papers, 01.*

Spigel, B. (2017). The Relational Organisation of Entrepreneurial Ecosystems. *Entrepreneurship Theory and Practice, 41*(1), 49–72.

Steffen, W., Rockström, J., Richardson, K., Lenton, T. M., Folke, C., Liverman, D., & Schellnhuber, H. J. (2018). Trajectories of the Earth System in the Anthropocene. *Proceedings of the National Academy of Sciences, 115*(33), 8252–8259.

Sterner, T., Barbier, E. B., Bateman, I., van den Bijgaart, I., Crépin, A. S., Edenhofer, O., & Robinson, A. (2019). Policy Design for the Anthropocene. *Nature Sustainability, 2*(1), 14–21.

Sun, H. P., Tariq, G., Haris, M., & Mohsin, M. (2019). Evaluating the Environmental Effects of Economic Openness: Evidence from SAARC Countries. *Environmental Science and Pollution Research, 26*(24), 24542–24551.

Tassey, G. (2008). Globalization of Technology-Based Growth: The Policy Imperative. *The Journal of Technology Transfer, 33*(6), 560–578.

Teece, D. J. (2007). Explicating Dynamic Capabilities: The Nature and Microfoundations of (Sustainable) Enterprise Performance. *Strategic Management Journal, 28*(13), 1319–1350.

Thomas, L., & Autio, E. (2013, February). Emergent Equifinality: An Empirical Analysis of Ecosystem Creation Processes. In *Proceedings of the 35th DRUID Celebration Conference*, Barcelona, Spain (Vol. 80).

Thomson, A. M., & Perry, J. L. (2006). Collaboration Processes: Inside the Black Box. *Public Administration Review, 66*, 20–32.

Thrassou, A., Vrontis, D., Crescimanno, M., Giacomarra, M., & Galati, A. (2020). The Requisite Match Between Internal Resources and Network Ties to Cope with Knowledge Scarcity. *Journal of Knowledge Management, 24*(4), 861–880.

Tittensor, D. P., Walpole, M., Hill, S. L., Boyce, D. G., Britten, G. L., Burgess, N. D., & Ye, Y. (2014). A Mid-Term Analysis of Progress Toward International Biodiversity Targets. *Science, 346*(6206), 241–244.

Townsend, A., Pang, A., & Weddle, R. (2009). *Future Knowledge Ecosystems. The Next Twenty Years of Technology-Led Economic Development. IFTF Report Number SR-12361.*

Valkokari, K. (2015). Business, Innovation, and Knowledge Ecosystems: How They Differ and How to Survive and Thrive Within Them. *Technology Innovation Management Review, 5*(8), 17–24.

Van Winden, F., Krawczyk, M., & Hopfensitz, A. (2011). Investment, Resolution of Risk, and the Role of Affect. *Journal of Economic Psychology, 32*(6), 918–939.

von Hippel, E. (2017). Free Innovation by Consumers—How Producers Can Benefit: Consumers' Free Innovations Represent a Potentially Valuable Resource for Industrial Innovators. *Research-Technology Management, 60*(1), 39–42.

von Hippel, W., & Suddendorf, T. (2018). Did Humans Evolve to Innovate with a Social Rather than Technical Orientation? *New Ideas in Psychology, 51*, 34–39.

Vrontis, D., Basile, G., Andreano, M. S., Mazzitelli, A., & Papasolomou, I. (2020a). The Profile of Innovation Driven Italian SMEs and the Relationship Between the Firms' Networking Abilities and Dynamic Capabilities. *Journal of Business Research, 114*, 313–324.

Vrontis, D., Basile, G., Tani, M., & Thrassou, A. (2020b). Culinary Attributes and Technological Utilization as Drivers of Place Authenticity and Branding: The Case of Vascitour, Naples. *Journal of Place Management and Development, 14*(1), 5–18.

Wagner Mainardes, E., Alves, H., & Raposo, M. (2012). A Model for Stakeholder Classification and Stakeholder Relationships. *Management Decision, 50*(10), 1861–1879.

Wasserman, S., & Faust, K. (1994). *Social Network Analysis: Methods and Applications.* Cambridge University Press.

Wazny, K. (2018). Applications of Crowdsourcing in Health: An Overview. *Journal of Global Health, 8*(1), 1–20.

Web References

Blanke, J., & Milligam, K. (2016). *Social Innovation A Guide to Achieving Corporate and Societal Value.* Accessed November 12, 2021, from https://www.weforum.org/reports/social-innovation

Moreno, E., Arimah, B., Otieno Otieno, R.; Mbeche-Smith, U., Klen-Amin, A., & Kamiya, M. (2016) *Urbanization and Development: Emerging Futures. World Cities Report 2016.* Accessed November 12, 2021, from https://unhabitat.org/world-cities-report

Index

A

Accounting, 135
Advanced information technology, 91
Agile organisations, 220
Alignment, 231
Artificial intelligence (AI), 27, 70, 135, 157
Athletics, 184
Audience, 184
Augmented reality, 66
Automation, 1, 2, 161
Avatar, 66

B

Banking, 135
Banking and accounting, 11
Big data, 81, 139

Blockchain, 83
Business ecosystem, 236
Business environment, 218
Business Process Management (BPM), 20
Business Process Management (BPM) lifecycle, 21
Business processes, 19

C

Change management, 109
Cloud services, 7
Cognitive RPA, 27
Collaboration, 89, 231
Collaboration tools, 51
Communication, 184
Competitive advantage, 202
Corporate social responsibility, 207

© The Author(s), under exclusive license to Springer Nature Switzerland AG 2022
A. Thrassou et al. (eds.), *Business Advancement through Technology Volume II*, Palgrave Studies in Cross-disciplinary Business Research, In Association with EuroMed Academy of Business, https://doi.org/10.1007/978-3-031-07765-4

248 Index

Cost-saving mechanisms, 3
COVID-19, 228
Crowdsourcing, 235
Cultural change, 208

D

Dematerialisation, 219
Diffusion of information and
communication technology
(ICT), 21
The digital age, 219
Digital divide, 79
Digital HRM, 4–7
Digital security, 80
Digital technologies, 202
Digital transformation, 166, 201
Digitisation, 1, 138
Doing business in the age of
chaos, 111
Dynamic skills theory, 164

E

Ecosystem, 231
E-HRM, 48, 161
Electronic HR information systems
(HRIS), 161
Employees, 88
Employee wellness, 49
Employment, 135
Empower, 88
Empowerment, 91
End-to-end processes, 19
Engagement, 232
Enterprise Resource Planning
(ERP), 57
Environment, 67
Equestrian, 184
E-recruitment, 140

E-selection, 5
Ethics, 163–164
Externalities, 233

F

Financial market, 219
Flat structure, 88
Flatter hierarchy, 95
Formal or informal negotiations, 231
Functional teams, 87
Future of work, 161–163

G

Gaming, 69
Gymnastics, 184

H

High-tech systems, 2
Hiring, 140
Holography, 70
HR leaders, 54
Human-machine collaboration, 3
Human Resource Management
(HRM), 48, 158
Human Resource processes, 136
Human resources, 220
Hybrid reality, 68
Hybrid workplace, 48
Hyper-life, 72
Hyper-reality, 72

I

Idea generation, 88
Incremental innovation, 213
Information technology, 7
Information technology sector, 47

Index   **249**

Innovation, 111, 183
Innovation strategies, 206
Innovation Theory, 184
Integrated electronic ecosystem, 72
The integration of digital
    technologies, 210
Internet-of-Things (IoT), 67
Isolation, 93

J

Job design, 173

K

Knowledge-based economy, 233

L

Labor market, 137–142
Labour-intensive, 137
Leadership, 89
Leadership styles, 91
Leading change, 111
Learning and development
    (L&D), 158
Learning organisation, 110

M

Machine learning (ML), 27,
    137, 158
Maintaining balance, 110–111
Management, 122
Measurement, 183
Metaverse, 65
Mobile devices, 7
Modularity, 230
Multidimensional technology, 4

N

Neo-human capital theory
    (NHCT), 165
Network economy, 233
Neuromarketing, 82
New, 183
New challenges, 219
New work arrangements, 2

O

Olympic Games, 183
Omega, 183
On-life, 72
Online Meeting tools, 47
Open innovation strategies, 239
Organisational performance, 203
Organisation's physiological
    core, 124
Organisation's reinvention, 110

P

Paradigm-shift and change
    in the organisation's
    mind, 110
Participants, 231
Performance, 183
Performance of teams, 91
Post-pandemic work
    environment, 93
Predictors, 218
Principal component analysis
    (PCA), 211
Privacy, 71
Process mining, 24
Process monitoring, 28
Process selection, 25
Project methodology, 23

250   Index

R

Real-time data, 184
Recruitment, 160
Recruitment and selection, 136
Reducing the relevance of
   hierarchical processes, 236
Restructuring, 88
Results-based change management
   maintaining balance, 111
Robot, 139
Robot-human interaction, 27
Robotic Process Automation
   (RPA), 9, 19
Robotics, 2, 162

S

Shared resources, 233
Social capital, 237
Socio-technological, 67
Stakeholder theory, 236
Start-ups, 88
Stra.Tech.Man, 122
Stra.Tech.Man organisational
   generator, 120
Strategy, 122
Strategy–technology–
   management, 11
Sustainable development,
   202, 208
Swimming, 184
SWOT analysis, 124
Synthesis of strategy, technology, and
   management, 111
Systematic literature review, 20
Systems thinking, 110

T

Team integration, 94
Technological, 67
Technological change, 137, 159
Technological diffusion, 90
Technologies, 53, 122, 183
Theory of AI job replacement, 164
3D, 69
Timekeeping, 184
Tokyo 2020+1, 183
Transformative leadership, 90
Tunisia, 210
Tunisian companies, 211

U

User Generated Content (UGC), 70

V

Virtualisation technologies, 163
Virtual reality, 66
Virtual workplace, 90
Virtual world, 89
Vision, 184
Volatility, Uncertainty, Complexity,
   and Ambiguity (VUCA), 92

W

Working conditions, 7
Working from home, 47

Z

Zoom, 58